My Time

Bradley Wiggins grew up in Kilburn in London. He won the
World Junior Pursuit title before going on to win seven
Olympic medals including four gold medals spanning four
games, and seven World Track Championship titles. In
2012 he became the first Briton to win the Tour de France,
a feat that Sir Chris Hoy described as 'the greatest sporting
achievement' by a British athlete. He was awarded the OBE
in the 2005 New Year's honours list, the CBE in 2009 and
a knighthood in 2012. He won the BBC Sports Personality
of the Year Award in 2012. He currently lives in the north-
west of England with his wife, Cath, and their two children,
Ben and Isabella.

Bradley Wiggins
with William Fotheringham

My Time

YELLOW JERSEY PRESS
LONDON

Published by Yellow Jersey Press 2013

8 10 9

Copyright © Bradley Wiggins 2012

Bradley Wiggins has asserted his right under the Copyright, Designs
and Patents Act 1988 to be identified as the author of this work

First published in Great Britain in 2012 by
Yellow Jersey Press
Random House, 20 Vauxhall Bridge Road,
London SW1V 2SA

www.vintage-books.co.uk

Addresses for companies within The Random House Group Limited can be
found at: www.randomhouse.co.uk/offices.htm

The Random House Group Limited Reg. No. 954009

A CIP catalogue record for this book
is available from the British Library

ISBN 9780224092142

Penguin Random House is committed to a sustainable future for
our business, our readers and our planet. This book is made from
Forest Stewardship Council® certified paper.

Printed and bound in Great Britain by Clays Ltd, St Ives plc

For Cath, Ben, Isabella, Mum, Nan, George and Ryan

CONTENTS

FOREWORD by Robert Millar

My first Tour de France was a muddle of feelings and emotions, but I did have one moment of clarity. I was hot, I was tired, and my lower limbs felt as if someone had filled them with lead. I wasn't even certain where I was, all I knew was that it was a village somewhere in south-central France and there were about 60km to the finish that day. My main focus for the last hour had been the mosquito bite that had developed angrily on my heel, just where shoe and foot met. It was driving me crazy and I couldn't work out if it actually hurt more than my legs. I knew it was my own fault as I had a habit of sticking one foot out of bed when I was trying to sleep and some enterprising biting insect had noticed the lack of citronella just where the rough skin starts and given me a souvenir for visiting his airspace. I looked up the road and saw we were temporarily leaving the countryside and entering a small piece of civilisation, slightly uphill on the way in meant slightly downhill on the way out, so for something to do I decided to move up a few places in the bunch. That might help me forget the mosquito bite.

It was a typical French village where you could sense nothing much ever happened, but because the Tour de France was passing through they were having a typical French village fête day to celebrate our arrival. The Tricolore flew from the village hall, there was a bit of bunting, trestle tables with food, there was drinking, merriment and laughter. The whole village had turned out to greet us and they were enjoying themselves just like the mosquito had. I felt annoyed. And then on the right-hand side, just as we left the houses and headed back into the trees, I noticed an old woman sitting on a chair outside her door. Dressed all in black like old women in France tend to be, she must have been eighty if she was a day but she had a youthful twinkle in her eye and the world's biggest smile. Her happiness was that complete happiness you have when you are eight and you are having a great time, but she must have been a grandmother – maybe even a great-grandmother. Through the noise I heard her say, 'Allez les petits' – go my little ones. To her we were her children, and I realised she was beaming with pride that we had come to see her. I knew then it was my duty not to disappoint her: I had to do my best, to be as good a Tour rider as I could be.

There's always a touch of theatre about each Tour de France; it may be a sporting competition but more often than not there's human drama each day. There are hidden clues in the terminology that imply it's as much a show as it is a bike race.

The French call each day *un étape*, which when you translate it as they intended means part of a journey; in English each day is a stage which of course is a word that has little to do with travelling and much to do with the world of acting and performing. The outfits of the main players are appropriate to the entertainment world too. Something bright to distinguish the lead part, so a distinctive yellow jersey for the star of the show ensures everyone knows where to look and who to concentrate on. Then the other parts of the story fall into place: green for the envious one, red spots for the minstrel and white for the innocence of youth. It has all the ingredients to be the perfect sporting play acted out for three weeks in the perfect setting.

To be part of the show you already have to be good – very good. And to play one of the main roles you need every ounce of your talent, every last drop of your passion, to use every piece of your history to your advantage, question every part of your commitment. The journey to Tour stardom is as much about understanding yourself as it is about preparing yourself for the physical and mental battle ahead: every aspect of your character and ability will be tested to the maximum. There'll be times when emotionally you'll be drained by the sacrifices. The selfishness involved will affect those around you and the mental preparations will have you asking questions of yourself that expose faults and nerves you didn't want touching. There'll be plenty of times when you step beyond your physical limit and have to reassess the whole adventure and yet it's a journey you have a duty to travel if you get the opportunity.

Bradley Wiggins's arrival on cycling's greatest stage hasn't been a steady progression up the stairs to stand in the Parisian limelight. It has taken a certain time, considering the talent he possesses. Leaving the comfort of French teams and removing the crutches of his first home, track racing, forced him to change his ways. There have been dazzling highs but there have also been hesitations and desperate moments. As a career plan it has resembled a complex novel with some of the difficult passages as much his own doing as they were misfortune, but like all the best books it's come good in the end.

Over the following pages Bradley Wiggins takes you through the trials and tribulations, through the tears and the training that have seen him transformed from mere contender to stand on the Champs-Elysées as a Tour de France champion.

What it took to be as good as he could be.

Robert Millar
November 2012

OPEN ROAD

Saturday 21 July, 15:33 European Summer Time
Rue de la Résistance, Bonneval
Stage 19, 2012 Tour de France

It is the last hour before the final time trial of the Tour de France, and I am within reach of my open road. In every race, that's what I'm looking for: that sense of having clear space in front of me. That's when I feel truly in control. That open road can be the moment in a summit finish in the mountains where my last teammate peels off the group and it's all down to me; it can be the point where the strongmen in a stage race emerge and the fighting for position stops, or the moment when I have to come out of the jostling pack, and ramp the pace up so that Mark Cavendish can nail a finish sprint. That's where the physical side takes over and all I have to do is turn the taps on full.

The routine for this time trial is the same one I've built and perfected over fifteen years; as I go through it thoughts and images flash through my mind. These moments are ones you live so intensely, and it's surprising what details stick. I can still see the sun coming through the one-way window of the team bus, and the woman standing outside the warm-up area. She'd been waiting for an autograph for a while, and I think she'd been there the day before, so I found a spare race number in my suitcase and asked the mechanic to take it over to her.

I can remember every minute of every time trial in 2012. It is all so precisely timed. In each time trial, screens tick over the minutes in front of the turbo trainers where the team staff set up the fans to cool us down and the bottles of energy drinks. The first thing the staff do as soon as they arrive at the start area in the morning is to sync all the clocks with the start clock on the ramp. There's no point in timing your warm-up using your watch. It might be five minutes fast, in which case you'd arrive at the start with eight minutes to go instead of three and be sitting around for too long; worst of all, if your watch is slow, you'd get there late.

My routine counts back from the warm-up. In my head that's when my race starts: the moment when I leave the bus and get on the turbo at precisely the right second. The warm-up starts exactly half an hour before I go down the ramp; if my start time is three minutes past three, I'll get on the turbo at two thirty-three on the dot.

I like to get to the bus early, soak up the atmosphere, chat with the mechanics, make sure everything's OK with the bikes, chat through my warm-up with my trainer Tim Kerrison, make sure I know about fuelling and hydration, and then go and sit down and listen to some music. At this point we get taped up by the physios using Kinesio tape; it's like putting on your armour before going into battle. Then it's a bit of stretching in the back of the bus. Get the numbers on the suit, get changed, smear on the chammy cream, leave the suit unzipped, put a vest on.

Every now and then little demons appear in my head. Something in my mind says: what if you puncture? What if the chain snaps? What if I lose two minutes? – silly little things like that. I try to put these worries to bed, but it's a constant background noise. I've stopped thinking rationally.

Half an hour before warm-up: I start listening to my playlist. It's a dance-music mix that my former teammate Steve Cummings did for me a couple of years ago at the Tour of Lombardy. I always start listening to it at exactly the same time; any earlier and I begin getting into the zone too soon.

Twenty minutes to warm-up: shoes on.

Ten minutes to warm-up: lace them up.

Zero hour: out of the bus and on to the turbo. My warm-up takes exactly twenty minutes. I've done it for fifteen years, the same ramping up in power. It's like a test on the old Kingcycle, the rig they used at British Cycling in the 1990s. I push myself up to threshold and then I'm totally in my own world. I am in the zone.

As I turn the pedals on the turbo trainer, people pass by but I see no one. Most of the time my eyes are closed. I'm

3

going through the ride in my head: sitting on the start ramp, flying down off it. I'm constantly sensing what it's going to feel like, imagining lying on the time-trial handlebars, or skis, as we call them.

I always pick a power to ride at. If it's 460, 470 watts, I'm imagining being there, at that power. In my head it's feeling strong, flowing, everything's working. It's easy, I'm floating along, I'm gliding, it's feeling great. I can sustain this feeling for up to an hour.

Ten minutes to start: off the turbo, into the bus, have a piss; overshoes on, gloves on, wipe down, sit down for a couple of minutes. Calm down.

Six minutes: Tim comes in. 'Let's go.' Clip on visor, go down towards the cordoned-off area around the ramp, find a chair straight away; keep going through the start process in my head. This time I remember to turn the chair round to get away from the photographers' flashbulbs. My eyes are closed under the visor but they annoyed me last time. Vincenzo Nibali, who is 3rd overall, is just starting.

Three minutes: Chris Froome comes down the ramp; I go up the steps. I'm looking at him in the distance and the car following him, and as they get further and further out of sight my mind gets really positive, really aggressive: I'm coming after you, I'll be seeing that soon – that kind of feeling.

Chris is my teammate but there are no teammates in time trialling: it's you against the clock and you against everybody else. You are in your own little world from the moment you get on the bus in the morning. I'm concentrating and thinking it through and at that point I don't give a monkey's about anyone else in the team and what they're going to do out there today.

In this race on this specific day Chris is like the rest of them and he is my closest competitor. And I am going after him.

One minute: clip into the pedals. Go to the starter. My *directeur sportif* Sean Yates is in the radio earpiece: 'Come on, Brad, let's go and get them.' I don't need reminding; I want to nail it.

Five seconds: throw the body back on the bike; push back on to the guy holding the saddle as if my back wheel is locked into a start gate on the track.

Three: deep breath in. Fill the lungs.

Two: deep breath out.

One: breathe in, deep as I can.

Winning the Tour de France is one good ride away.

Part One

Down And Out In London And Manchester

CHAPTER 1

THE PLANNER'S DREAM GOES WRONG

In the late evening of 17 October 2010 I was sitting in the lobby of a hotel in Milan Malpensa airport, all alone with the best part of two bottles of red wine inside me. I had just climbed off in the Tour of Lombardy, a legendary one-day Classic and the last big race of the season. Lombardy had been a complete disaster with only one rider from the team finishing – I had called it a day after getting caught behind a number of crashes. It was a low-key end to several months of total disappointment and public humiliation. I had flopped at the Tour de France. I had gone through a personal crisis. The team hadn't ridden well at the Tour of Britain, our big home race. It had been a tough first year for Team Sky, and the lowest point had come when the team pulled out of the Vuelta – the Tour of Spain – after the tragic death from septicaemia of our *soigneur* Txema

González. A *soigneur* is the person who takes care of us on and off the bike, and Txema had looked after all of us at the Tour and the Giro d'Italia. He was a great guy, and his sudden death had hit us hard.

Being sent to race the end-of-season events – Paris–Tours, the Giro del Piemonte, Lombardy – is not the usual fare for team leaders and supposed Grand Tour contenders. At that time of year we are meant to be resting to rebuild our strength for the following season. But the Sky management was grabbing at straws after the nightmare end to our year. I had been sent to Italy in the hope of picking up a ProTour point or two and to put some structure into the end of my season. If it had been down to me I'd have stopped in September, but that would have made the whole winter's training harder. I'd had no option but to go on.

The team had been booked into the Holiday Inn Express at Malpensa. There were a few of us, staff and riders, and they wanted to eat together. I didn't want to sit down and chew over the race. I told them I had found a flight that evening, got the bus to the airport, walked across to a half-finished hotel and checked in. I wanted to be alone. I was flying out of Milan the next day and here I was: absolutely wasted, on my own in this soulless airport hotel. In one sense it felt quite cheery if I'm honest: at least that season was finally done. I had put a big, fat, red pen through it.

The crisis of 2010 had been building since the summer of 2009 when I came out of the Tour de France having finished 4th, completely on cloud nine. I had equalled the British record in the world's greatest bike race, but it was totally unexpected. When I had signed with the American team Garmin in 2008 I hadn't done so thinking I would try and finish in the top five in the Tour de France the following year. Far from it. In fact, my main goal was merely to earn a place in Garmin's squad for the Tour, to be there in the mountains to work for the team leader, Christian Vande Velde, a genial American who'd finished 5th in 2008. I'd won two Olympic gold medals in Beijing, in the individual and team pursuits, which had been my only goal for the previous four years. With that in the bag, by the end of 2008 I'd had enough of track racing and I just wanted to compete hard on the road.

My previous contracts with road-racing teams hadn't been much to shout about, but Garmin felt I had potential and offered me a good deal. That in turn meant I wanted to repay them by giving it my best shot. My old GB track teammate Steve Cummings had just had a pretty good year on the road after dropping his weight, so I thought I would try and do the same and see how it affected my performance. So in 2009, I was just enjoying it and loving riding my bike again. I was in a great set-up where it was a lot of fun, people didn't take themselves too seriously and we went out and got the job done. On top of all that, I went to the Tour several kilos lighter than I ever had been, with my sights raised a bit. I'd climbed well in the Giro d'Italia, I'd gone past Lance Armstrong on a couple of mountains, and I had said publicly I would try for the top twenty in the Tour. Inside, I was thinking I might even get into the top ten. The Tour went almost perfectly: I never had a bad day, I surpassed everyone's expectations in the mountains, and, with a lot of help from the lads at Garmin, I rode into Paris in 4th overall, the best British performance since Robert Millar managed the same placing in 1984. I had surprised myself as well, and from the end of the Tour I began to think, 'Imagine what I could do if I really trained for this thing properly.'

Sky was a new team being formed for 2010 by Dave Brailsford, the performance director at British Cycling, and Shane Sutton, the head coach. Until the rest day in Limoges during the 2009 Tour de France, I had never thought of joining them; I had a two-year deal with Garmin. Dave and Shane were setting out to build a British team with the publicly stated goal of winning the Tour within five years with a British rider, and doing it clean. So they were on the hunt for a rider who could challenge at the Tour. My ride in 2009 came at the perfect time: all of a sudden Dave and Shane had the chance to launch Sky with a British leader. It was like a dream come true for everybody.

Dave came to visit me in Limoges, but I didn't want to be seen talking to another team boss. The transfer season in cycling doesn't officially begin until 1 August, so I told the guys at Garmin that I needed to get some toothpaste, hopped in a team car and drove to the supermarket round the corner from the Campanile hotel where we were staying. Dave and I had a coffee in a little café in the Carrefour and he put it to me.

'Come on, this is an ideal situation. Whatever happens in this Tour from now on, we've got a starting point. You've proved you can climb with the front group in the race. It's our goal for the next five years to win the Tour, and you can be our rider to go for the overall.'

Dave explained that they would work in the same way that he and Shane and the GB team had done on the track. Shane and Dave had guided me to my second and third Olympic gold medals on the track only the year before. I had been in that environment since I had been a junior, and had had access to the expertise within their system even when I was racing on the road. The approach that Dave and Shane and British Cycling had adopted in the run-up to Beijing was a constant search for perfection: the best equipment, the best back-up staff, the best experts to research every area from diet to aerodynamics. I knew that they would dissect what it takes to do the Tour in the same way they had done with my track events, the individual pursuit and the team pursuit. It wouldn't be easy, but it was something I understood. These guys had backed me since I was eighteen.

The critical point for me was that I would be working with the same team of backroom staff I'd had up to Beijing. Even when I was planning my road campaign for 2009 with Garmin I had had help from their dietician Nigel Mitchell; and my trainer, Matt Parker, had helped me get my 4th place in the Tour. The British Cycling staff were like my second family. I'm quite proud of the fact that I was the first athlete to be signed by the World Class Performance Plan, as it was called back then, under its first head, Peter Keen, in 1998. I've been part of it ever since as it's grown under Dave into the best national sports team in the country. I can't imagine what my career would have been if they hadn't been there. One thing is certain: I wouldn't be where I am today without them. World Class came along at the right time in my life; I could have missed it either way by five years and it would have been a completely different story.

From the moment when Dave explained about the British Cycling link, I was sold straight away. I had eighteen months of my two-year deal with Garmin to go. I loved being there; they had believed in me and had given me the chance to do something on the road. But I'm a patriotic bloke, and the chance to lead a British team in the Tour was only going to come along once. The urge to go home was too strong.

I said, 'You know I've got a contract', and Dave said, 'We'll talk, we'll work that out.' The next two weeks went by, I finished 4th in the Tour; I went straight into the velodrome in Manchester a couple of days after riding into Paris. The velodrome had been the centre of my cycling world for eleven years – it's where the track team and all their staff are based, and it was where Sky would have their office. I met with Shane, Dave, and Carsten Jeppesen, their general manager. They felt my moving to Sky would be ideal, and that was when the whole transfer process started: they had to negotiate a way for me to get out of my contract with Garmin so that I could join them.

It was all new to me – in fact, a transfer battle of this kind was almost unprecedented for cycling – and it went on for a long, long time. Much too long, as it turned out. The week after the Tour we went back to Girona, the city in south-east Spain where my wife Cath and I had set up a second home for the season, as it's the Garmin base. I went out for dinner with the Garmin team director Jonathan Vaughters. He said, 'Look, I can pay you this much, but I can't pay you it next year because I don't have the budget. In two years' time I can pay you more, and I'll match what Sky are going to pay.' Jonathan is a lovely guy – he understood me and he understood that my urge to join Sky wasn't really about the money. However, I think he was pissed off with the way everyone went about it and I think he felt a little bit threatened at the idea of losing a potential leader for the Tour.

As the deal was being negotiated, a lot of the press weren't helping either. There were journalists digging for information, ringing up Jonathan, saying, 'I heard Brad's going to Sky. Is this true?' Jonathan would then get annoyed, which didn't make negotiating any easier. At the end of November, Dave and Carsten went to New York to meet Jonathan and fought it out over six hours in an office with all their lawyers. When they came out of that meeting they'd done the deal but it was all on the basis that nothing could be said. A week later I raced at a Revolution track meeting in Manchester and I gave the press the impression I might be staying at Garmin. I had no choice but to say that because if I'd said otherwise I would have violated the terms of the deal and I wouldn't have had a team for 2010 at all. The whole thing was a mess from start to finish and when it was over and the announcement was made it was a huge relief for everyone. But that was just the beginning.

A lot of the problems that cropped up in 2010 went back to the fact that from the end of the Tour until I signed with Sky, which was almost five months, I didn't have a team. I remember coming home on 9 December having been presented to the press in London as a Sky rider, and that was it, it was all done. But then it was Christmas, and New Year, and in all that time I hadn't really started training for this big race in France that we were going to try and win.

It had all been about changing teams up to that point. I'd just been drifting along, going to all these dos – parties and dinners and the rest, all for having finished 4th in the Tour – but because I didn't have a team, I hadn't done the usual thing you do in October. Every year, when the season's finished, that's when you sit down with your coaching team to plan the next season, set out your targets and discuss how you're going to achieve them. I had done none of that. I didn't even have a proper bike to train on: I was riding around on a bike made by my old mate Terry Dolan, who has a business a few miles away from my home in Lancashire. Garmin had taken back all the Felt bikes I had been using; as I wasn't with Sky yet, I didn't have a Pinarello to ride. I couldn't go to the first Sky get-together in Manchester and I was riding around in unmarked, black kit through November and December. It was a week before Christmas by the time we got it all signed and I was told that I would be looked after by Rod Ellingworth, who was Mark Cavendish's trainer and had joined Sky as race coach; Matt Parker, my trainer since 2007, would be working with me as well. But I still hadn't started training.

On 4 January I needed to be in London for the team launch at the Millbank Tower, a massive place down on the

Embankment. I remember arriving at the hotel in London the previous night and shaking hands with a load of people I'd never met and who I was supposed to be leading. Someone told me that Thomas Löfkvist was frustrated that I'd signed because he had joined on the assumption that he would be the leader in the big Tours.

The hype around the team was immense. We had put our cards on the table: Sky wanted to win the Tour de France with a British rider within five years, and win it clean. The crowd at the launch was huge; when we came on to the stage to be introduced by Sky's Dermot Murnaghan, I was asked to stand in front of the other riders. I didn't want to at first; I wasn't keen to be at the head of it all. Already I felt uneasy about being the centre of attention. I spoke to the press there but had had no briefing about what I should or shouldn't say. I started babbling about how I would have to learn to talk bullshit; I've no idea where it came from. It was all completely new to me.

Straight after the launch we flew to Valencia for the first training camp. I was really unfit, and struggled for the first few days, but all the cameras were there and only one question was being asked: can you win the Tour within five years? But even at that point I still hadn't sat down with anyone for a phased planning session that answered the basic question: right, how are we going to do this? We simply had no time to stop and reflect.

We rushed the race programme out and then drifted along. I said I had ridden the Giro d'Italia in 2009, and that it had seemed to work really well for me, so I would do the Giro again; before we knew it we were in April, and then we were off to the Giro. I won the prologue because I'd been training for that, and was in reasonable shape until a week to go. I was lying 7th by then, but I was beginning to feel really tired, so I dropped back from the lead group on one of the key mountain stages and then rode through to the end. Even if I hadn't sat up I wouldn't have been able to stay with the leaders. The problem was that everyone was watching me; if I wasn't physically up to it, it was easier to drop back and say I was saving myself for the Tour de France rather than having to explain to everyone that night what was going on. I knew I was going to have to save myself for the Tour or I would have nothing left, but the physical damage was done anyway.

Before the Tour we went on a training camp in the Alps to look at the mountain stages but during those few days, I just felt terrible. I hadn't done the work and I didn't perform. On the day we checked out the Col de la Madeleine, one of the biggest mountains in the Tour and a key climb in 2010, Michael Barry – the Canadian who was my personal watchdog for that Tour – was supposed to do about half an hour on the front and then I'd take over. It was something similar to how we might work it on the Tour, with the lead *domestique* – team worker – making the pace to enable me, the team leader, to sit in his slipstream and save my strength. But it didn't work out like that: he dropped me at the foot of the sixteen-mile climb. Instead of me surging past him to take on the lead as he fell back, I was left behind. From there on in to the Tour it should have been apparent that I wasn't in the shape to get a podium finish. It was as simple as that.

The pressure during the Tour that year was massive. It was Team Sky's first year in cycling, the stated goal was to win the Tour, I had finished 4th the year before and the natural assumption was that I would perform better than before. The amount of media attention was immense, because no British team had been in this position. It was new to me too, and I didn't deal with it well.

The prologue was a nightmare – I wouldn't normally expect to finish 77th, even though I was riding in the rain – and for the whole race I was carrying the effects of a nasty crash on day two. I got through that, moved up to 14th overall after the stage across the cobbles of Northern France to Arenberg, and coming towards the Alps at the end of the first week I was feeling good. I was beginning to think I might be OK, even on the first big Alpine climb, the Col de la Ramaz on the stage to Morzine. I asked the team to ride on the front there, to set a decent pace, but by the time we got to the finish at Avoriaz I simply hadn't recovered. I was hanging on all the way up the final climb, counting down the kilometres until the point where I simply couldn't hold the lead group any more. When I look back now I'm amazed I clung on for so long, not accepting what was meant to be, that I was going to get dropped. As I crossed the line a journalist asked me if that was the end of my Tour. I told him where to go.

I had no option but to keep playing the game, keep telling people what they wanted to hear even though inside I knew it wasn't going to happen. I particularly remember the first rest day in Morzine, the very next day. The team was holding a press conference in the evening and I said to Dave, 'I am not going, it's just not on, what am I going to say?' His answer was, 'Come on, Brad, just head down there. Say you're going to continue riding, and just keep up that fighting spirit. The press don't like people giving up, so just keep going.'

That was what I did. I tried to fight on but it's hard to fight when you haven't got any form because ultimately it depends on what strength you have in your legs. Every mountain day became a grind as I wasn't quite good enough to stay with the first group when the racing got serious. I did start to come round a little bit in the third week and I had a couple of decent days. I was in the break one day in the Pyrenees and I had a good last time trial for 9th place. In fact, I was good enough physically to have a chance of winning it but the wind changed quite a bit so I rode in tougher weather than the guys who filled the top positions in the standings. I was the best of all the guys who rode in the harder conditions, but it didn't count for anything.

So much had changed from the year before. All of a sudden I was leading a team – or I was supposed to be leading a team – and I didn't really know how I'd got there. As far as building up to the Tour went, I had repeated the training and race programme that I had followed the year before. I thought it would work but it was all on a wing and a prayer. I finished 23rd in the Tour, which shows I was fit; what I was lacking was the last 10 per cent that it takes to compete with the best guys; for example, when we went over a certain altitude – about 1,600m we later worked out – I was struggling. As a result I was barely hanging on whenever the overall contenders began slugging it out.

Mentally it was tough. I felt I had let a lot of people down. I'm quite good at remaining positive though, and that's what I was trying to do. But throughout that whole season I felt alone. I felt I had no one to talk to; I didn't really have a coach to ring up on a daily basis, to give me constant feedback and support. My feelings finally got the better of me in the Pyrenees, at the summit finish at Ax-Trois-Domaines, where I came in 36th, four minutes behind the favourites. Unusually, I was on my own when I got back to our camper van on the mountaintop; there was a wall of press waiting for me when I came out to ride back down the climb to the team bus, which was parked at the bottom. One of them, an Australian journalist I've known for many years, asked me what had happened. I just opened up: 'I'm fucked. I've got nothing. I don't have the form, it's as simple as that. I just haven't got it as I did last year. I just feel consistently mediocre. Not brilliant, not shit, just mediocre. I just haven't got it right this year.' It might not have been my most professional interview ever, but it was almost as if I was tired of the lies. It's incredibly hard telling people what they want to hear when you know the opposite is true. I didn't want to go on flogging a dead horse.

By the end of the Tour it was clear that we needed to look at where it had all gone wrong. There had to be a review of how we had built up to it, taking in everything: my racing programme, how we selected the team, how we dealt with the media, how we rode the race. At one point late on, Dave said to me, 'Look, we know you've got the machine. We know you can do it. You finished 4th last year. We just need to figure out how to get your body working properly.' But after Paris the whole team went their separate ways: we were all exhausted, and at the end of the Tour, all you want to do is get home. I didn't ride my bike for a week and then the Sunday after the Tour de France finished, I took part in the Manchester Sky Ride, one of a series of mass-participation cycle rides where thousands of members of the public could get on their bikes and pedal along with the stars.

That night I was sitting at home when my phone rang. It was my mum and she said, 'George has had a heart attack.' I said, 'Fucking hell', or something, and I hung up on her. I had absolutely no idea what to say. George was my granddad.

CHAPTER 2

ROCK BOTTOM

When I came off the phone, Cath asked me, 'What's the matter?' and I said, 'George has had a heart attack.'

We had no idea what to do. It was about ten o'clock at night, so we dropped everything and drove to London. We got to the hospital at about two o'clock in the morning and stayed all through the night. He was on a life-support machine, so I stayed for three or four days at the hospital, day and night.

George had always been there. He was the father figure, the role model in my young life, from the day when my mother Linda and I moved in to my nan and granddad's flat in Kilburn after my father Gary had walked out on us. Gary didn't so much walk out on us in Christmas 1982 as throw us out. I wasn't even two-years-old. We'd gone from our home in Ghent to see my mum's parents, and he called my mum to say she and I weren't to come back to Belgium. He'd got together with someone else. For a while, until Mum got a small place of her own, I ended up living in a family consisting predominantly of women: Nan and Granddad and their three daughters and me. For a long time, George was the only other male in that environment until my aunties had kids. For my first eight or nine years I spent a lot of time with him, so he was like a father in many respects; he brought me up. I find it difficult to explain what he was like. I suppose everything I am, everything I say, all my mannerisms and so on, all come from him.

Granddad loved sport, so I used to go greyhound racing with him every Saturday night at Wimbledon dog track. We had a weekend routine of our own: Saturday morning I'd go and get *Sporting Life* and a handful of betting slips from Ladbrokes for him, go back home and fill in all the betting slips for the Saturday afternoon horse racing on the telly, and after that it was off to watch the dogs. Through him, I learned all about betting: how the odds work, all the signs the tic-tac men use. I guess as I got older he was incredibly proud of me, but he never showed it to me. Even now, that side of my family doesn't hold me up as anything special, I'm just like any other cousin or grandchild. They don't really say, 'I'm so proud of you', they'll still put me down or whatever – 'What've you got your hair like that for?' – which helps you keep a sense of who you are.

George had been to watch Gary Wiggins race when he was with my mum. Gary was a hard-drinking Australian bike racer who had come over to Belgium to make a living competing on the track in the Six Days in the winter and the kermesses – the little circuit races that make up the bulk of the Belgian calendar – through the summer. George would tell me about a time when Gary had crashed somewhere, and he had pulled all the splinters from the wooden track out of his back with pliers. Gary shut us out of his life from before I was two until I was in my seventeenth year, from the day he came back to London with four black bin liners containing our stuff from Belgium and dumped them at the bottom of the stairs to the flat where Nan and Granddad lived. He moved to Australia later, and briefly, in my late teens, we spent a little time together there, but we never built a proper relationship.

Gary had used amphetamines to race; he'd sold them to other bike riders, and worst of all he'd knocked my mum about. In spite of all that, George never, ever said to me what he thought of my dad until I was about eighteen or nineteen, and he told me, 'Look, he's a wanker . . .' But he never said that through my childhood years. Instead, he always spoke of him, perhaps not affectionately, but along the lines of 'He was a bike rider', or 'He did this; I remember when your dad crashed once; I remember when your dad did this race once.' I suppose he left me to find out in my own way what kind of a person Gary was. I do know, however, that from the point of view of a father, he never forgave Gary for what he did to us two.

After a few days in the hospital, the doctors told Cath and me that we might as well go home for a little while, pick up the kids and collect some stuff. There wasn't a lot more we could do, so we went back north for a couple of days and then it was back down to London. We got as far as the Tuesday, nine days after it had happened, and the doctors told us they were going to turn the life support off. His brain had been deprived of oxygen, so even if he did come round he would be a cabbage. They said, 'Look, we're going to turn it off but it might take twenty-four hours for him to pass away.' They turned it off and we sat there most of the night with my nan; in the morning he still hadn't gone. My nan said, 'Just go home, it don't matter. He knows you're here, he could be another couple of days yet. Go on, go home, I'll sit him out, you need to get home.'

So off we went. Cath and I were on the M1 about ten minutes away from Watford Gap services when my mum rang me and said, 'George has died.' We stopped in Watford Gap and had a coffee and that was it. He'd gone. I had last seen him properly the year before when we'd had a party in the golf club near our home, funnily enough on the day after Sky and Garmin had thrashed out my transfer deal in New York. He'd been ill for quite a while but he hid it well. Losing this man who'd been there all through my childhood and my teens, who had given me some stability when I was a kid, was a massive blow. It came at a time when I was struggling with my career and it left me dealing with one of the hardest periods of my life.

I'd had to go through the disappointment of the Tour, the way I felt that not everyone in the team had been there with me. I felt a bit of a failure. I felt as if I'd let a lot of people down. People were saying publicly that I was never going to win the Tour, that I had been stupid to sign with Sky, that them hiring me was a waste of money and a bad investment. I didn't know how to deal with it. Cath sometimes describes me as emotionally retarded but what she means is that I really struggle to express my emotions and I bury my head in the sand over a lot of stuff. I always try to remain positive even when I'm not feeling it inside. So if someone asks me if I'm all right, I'll tend to say, 'Yeah, yeah I'm fine.' So at the time, I just tried to take it in my stride, making it look as if I was coping with it. But in fact I was in a bit of a state with everything that had happened.

We drove home, trying to get our heads around it all, and on the Wednesday Shane rang me.

'You need to fucking get into the office.'

'What's the matter?'

'You need to get into the fucking office.'

And I started thinking: what's happened? What could it be? The next day I went into Sky's office in the Manchester velodrome; apparently they had been fuming. The trouble was that I hadn't switched my phone on during this whole period. All that time I'd had no thoughts of cycling at all; I had been on another planet. My phone had been off since the Tour, so for nearly two and a half weeks Shane or Dave or Fran Millar, the logistics manager, or other people from the team had been trying to ring and they were getting annoyed with me. They were really angry, in fact. They had no idea what had happened.

I had thought I would be in for the hairdryer treatment, but by the time I got there, Shane had got hold of Cath and she had told him what had happened to my granddad. I think that dampened it down a little bit. The line that I was given was that something had to change. I think I'd told a journalist that that was it, I wasn't going to race for the rest of the year after the Tour, I was knackered. The journalist had rung Dave and told him what I'd said and Dave was annoyed because he hadn't heard it from the horse's mouth. In the office they reeled off the names of my rivals: Cadel Evans, then the world champion, who'd had a disastrous crash in the Tour; the former Giro winner Ivan Basso; they were already back out there racing, they told me, and I needed to get out there now. Brad, they said, you don't ever answer your phone, people can't get hold of you, you're unreliable. They were very unhappy with me and I can understand why. I'm not saying they were wrong. We couldn't go on like this.

The Sky management were determined that I get back on my bike, so we had a look at the race programme. The first thought was that I might race at the Eneco Tour of Belgium and Holland, the following week. That didn't sit well with me because it was George's funeral that week and there was no way I was missing it, so I opted to go to the Grand prix de Plouay in Brittany, then the British Time Trial Championships and Tour of Britain. A week later I went back down to London for George's funeral on the Saturday. We had the wake, I had a few drinks; I was racing the following day so the next morning I flew out of London City to Nantes to race at Plouay. There I just made matters worse. I was asked at the start by French television, 'What are you expecting today?' and I let slip that I wasn't really in the mood, something like, 'I don't know, I don't even really want to be here if I'm honest.' Shane saw that and was really annoyed about it but it was the day after the funeral; I still stand by that. I was just trying to take it all in my stride as I did at the Tour, when I didn't have the form, I didn't want to be there and I'd had to keep bluffing. I already felt really insecure because I felt as if I had let everyone down during the Tour, so I didn't have the guts at that stage to say, 'I'm not racing, my granddad has just died, it's a hard time for me and I need a week or two off.'

So I got on with it. I finished Plouay, went home, back to Gerona with Cath and the kids, and I started training again; I was out on my bike every day getting in some decent work. I had the British Time Trial Championships at the start of September, which I won, and then I did my job at the Tour of Britain but, as a team, Sky didn't have great form. We won a stage; I nearly won another, but overall we weren't in the hunt. I didn't feel like a leader at that point, and there were a few things that went wrong on that race, in front of the home media and the home crowd.

For the rest of the season it was a matter of getting through. I'd already opted out of the Commonwealth Games and the Road World Championships; they were in India and Australia which was just too much travelling. But again after the Tour of Britain I didn't ride my bike for a week. I had no motivation whatsoever. About ten days after Britain finished, I was in bed and there was a phone call at midnight to the landline. Cath answered. It was Shane and he was just going absolutely bonkers.

'Where's Brad, what the fuck's he doing in bed?'

'Well, it's midnight, you know.'

Shane was with the Great Britain team and they were in Australia, in Geelong, at the Road World Championships, in a totally different time zone.

'Dave's fuming. Fran's tried to get hold of Brad and he hasn't answered the phone to her.'

Cath explained that I had lost my phone. We'd just bought our new house, I'd been up there doing some work on it and I'd left my phone in the garage when I went back to our old house down the road. It was typical of the way things went that year: the day I left my phone up there, everyone was trying to get hold of me.

Then Shane added: 'Dave sent you a text, it's pretty fucking damning, you need to go and read it.' Actually I couldn't find my phone for days so I didn't find out what was in the text. Anyway, I was dead worried. I didn't sleep all night. The next day I went in to see Fran in the team office, feeling like a little kid who's been told off. The Great Britain team are all based in the Manchester velodrome, just down the corridor from Sky, so I asked to see Steve Peters, the psychiatrist who works for the GB team, who had helped me out on occasions in the past. Steve calls himself a 'mechanic of the mind', but he has a broad-brush approach because so many of the psychological issues you have in sport go back to your personal life and your background. What that means is that if there's a big problem, a really big problem, and particularly one that concerns your relationships with other people within the team, he's the man you turn to.

'Look, Steve, I don't know what's happened but nothing I seem to do at the moment is right. I don't know whether I'm coming or going. It's just been a disaster. I'm sort of mourning a little bit and I'm trying to bury my head in the sand with it.'

'I know the situation, I've spoken to Dave. Obviously Dave

has talked to me about it, he's said, "What should we do with Brad? He's a bloody nightmare."'

'Am I going to lose my job, Steve?'

'Well, I won't lie to you, it's been mentioned.'

And that really shook me.

Steve explained to me about a few pieces that had appeared in the media. I think there had been an article in *The Times* saying I was difficult to work with, calling me arrogant. Dave had seen it and he wasn't happy about how it reflected on the image of the team. He felt I wasn't leading the squad as I should be and clearly he was right. As Steve told me, Dave had a job to do, which was to run the team, and he was wondering what Sky, as our sponsors, were going to make of their leader drawing such negative coverage.

'Steve, what do the other trainers in the team say?'

'The other trainers say, "Look at getting someone else in."'

If Sky replaced me as leader, perhaps demoting me to a team role, it would be disastrous for me: an admission that I couldn't win the Tour and that Sky had put their eggs in the wrong basket. My name would be mud. I would take a massive pay cut, but worst of all I would be branded a failure, not up to the task of being at the top of the biggest project that British cycling had ever seen. I headed for home, beating myself up and convinced something had to change.

Cath was struggling with it as well. She kept saying, 'They don't quite understand what has happened, with George dying and just what that means. Have you told them, have you told them exactly?'

'Of course not, I don't want to appear weak.'

31

The thing is, it's hard to go into the office in Manchester and stand there in front of Dave and Shane, who are quite intimidating guys, and say to them, 'You know what, I am really struggling at the moment. I just feel like crying all the time.'

I had envisaged Shane going, 'Pull your fucking self together', or something along those lines. That's what you expect it'll be like.

That seems over the top but at that time I was already feeling pretty low. Everything I did seemed to turn into a disaster of some kind. Around the time of the British Time Trial Championships I did an interview with *Procycling* magazine, where the journalist asked me what the mistakes were that we'd made at Sky. I remember talking about Garmin and how much of a good time I'd had there, how they were a great team. It came across in the interview that I was saying how great Garmin was and how Sky was too serious, for example, having the massive team bus with all its high-tech kit. Dave read the interview, was really fed up with me and sent me a text, the gist of which was, 'Nice piece in *Procycling*, slagging the team off.' But 2010 hadn't been an easy year for Dave, of course. He was struggling a bit too, because it was his first season as a team boss on a professional road-racing team and questions were being asked. He was under pressure as well.

I decided from that summer that I couldn't carry on in this way. I wasn't enjoying it. I had to make amends and I was ready to do that. That year I had shied away from a number of my more stressful responsibilities as team leader, simple things like dealing with the media. They weren't to do with being a cyclist but they were the kind of things that go towards how you are perceived by your teammates. I've always had a tendency to withdraw into myself. That didn't matter when I was an individual on the track going for individual gold medals because I only had to focus on bringing the best out of myself. Sky is a big outfit. It's not three other guys like you have in a team pursuit, but twenty-six riders plus thirty-odd staff. I wasn't carrying them with me. I didn't appreciate the knock-on effect it would have on everyone around me when I withdrew, as I had often done in the past. The possibility that I might be demoted from leadership, reduced to the ranks, was a massive wake-up call, a huge disappointment. In a word: humiliation. Dealing with it would mean growing up.

The turning point had already come. George's death had had something to do with it. It wasn't exactly that I went out and said, 'Oh, I'm going to win the Tour de France for my granddad.' It wasn't like that. His death had a huge impact on me that year. I wouldn't say it was the only thing that turned me around but, looking back, I was a changed man after that whole episode. It was more that his death came on top of everything else that had gone wrong. I don't know if it was a matter of standing on my own two feet because I had lost my father figure. I really don't know. Even now I think more than anything I threw myself even harder into trying to win the Tour as a way of forgetting about it.

Rod Ellingworth had been given the task of looking after me when I arrived at Sky; Rod is fantastic but he wasn't right for me. I felt bad about Rod because I'm not the easiest person to look after. We'd raced together in the past, but we hadn't built up the right sort of relationship as rider and coach. I think I knew Rod too well. Sometimes he'd ring me and I'd think, 'I don't want to speak to Rod at the moment.' On the other hand, I knew I couldn't do it all by myself in terms of training to win the Tour. That was partly where I had gone wrong that season.

There was only one person I knew who could put me on the right footing, who could tell me the things I didn't necessarily want to hear at times when I might not want to hear them. Only one guy would make me listen. I went into that office and I said to them, 'You know what, the only person who really understands me and knows me inside out as a person is you, Shane, and I'd like you to coach me.'

That took Shane a little aback. He said, 'I wasn't expecting that', but Dave immediately answered with, 'That's a really good idea, you know.'

Shane's first concern was that he didn't really have the time. His worry was that he was trying to run the track programme for British Cycling, and if he coached me on a personal basis then all his lead riders – Vicky Pendleton, Sir Chris Hoy – would want him as well. I left the ball in his court for a few minutes, so he could think about it. Eventually, he said he liked the idea so we came out of that office in a really positive frame of mind; we'd really sorted a few things out.

That day, Cath had dropped me off at the velodrome because I hadn't been on my bike for two and a half weeks. I was going to do a four-hour ride home, so I got changed at the track, got my kit on, and Shane said, 'I'll ride with you for a bit.' We left the track together and pedalled along for a couple of hours talking.

'What do you think about it?' I asked.

'You know, I'm really excited. I just need to think a lot about it and how we go about the process because it's not something I want to take on lightly.'

His conclusion was that he would coach me on a full-time basis, but with the support of the sports scientist Tim Kerrison. Tim had been working at Sky that year, he knew relatively little about cycling, having only just begun to explore the sport, but he had revolutionised training in Australian swimming. I said I would hand the two of them my body: 'Train me,' I said. 'Get the machine working for next July.' I had unfinished business with the Tour de France.

CHAPTER 3

TIME FOR TRUTH

'I know I've been an absolute fucking c*** this year but this is what I want to do in 2011: I want to start enjoying my racing again. I want to do Paris–Roubaix and I want to get back to finishing top ten in the Tour. And I want to start here.'

It was the end of November 2010 and I was sitting in the massive meeting room at the Savill Court Hotel near Windsor. Gathered around me were the Sky management: Rod, Shane, Dave, Carsten, *directeurs sportifs* such as Sean Yates. This was our first get-together to build for 2011. I had really thought hard about what I wanted to do on day one at the first training camp of the new season, and this room, in front of all these people, was where it began. 'Right, Brad,' someone said. And off I went. I ran through the whole thing, outlining my plan and how I was going to execute it. I wasn't going to take no for an answer.

Showing I was serious about 2011 meant doing more than merely stating my intentions to the guys who ran the team. I had brought a mountain bike to Windsor with me to use on the road, all set up with lights and mudguards, and I was out early every morning on it in the freezing cold. That was partly to make it clear I was showing willing, partly to make it clear that nothing was going to stop me doing my winter training in any conditions. The biggest gesture came at the end of the camp, when we had a big party. Everyone got absolutely blind drunk, except for me. I went to bed. The whole team knew I was happy to have a drink if the time was right, but on this occasion I made sure I didn't touch a drop and just went to bed. I had one idea in my head: I'm going to start leading this team and the first step is that I don't want to be paralytic in front of everyone.

Given what had happened in 2010, perhaps it wasn't surprising that when the team were handing out mock awards at the party on the last night, I won the one for the biggest media blooper of the season. It's not every day you give an answer like the one I'd given to Eurosport during the Tour.

'You know what, it's not that much of a disappointment,' I had replied in an attempt to be defensive, which backfired a little. 'I'm 21st overall in the Tour at the moment, you know, if I'd been lying 21st a year ago everyone would have been masturbating.'

It was still a bit embarrassing but I went up and said, 'Thanks, I'd like to dedicate this award to Brian Nygaard.' That raised a laugh or two, at least. Brian had been our media manager until he left suddenly in mid-season to found the Leopard-Trek team.

What I had said and done had worked, in the sense that everyone seemed excited by the new season. Most of all, I remember one thing. When the camp was over, I was driving home and Dave called me: 'Great work this week, Brad. You know, everyone says you've changed.' After that, I knew I was on my way.

I had begun to make a bit more of an attempt to behave like a leader once the 2010 season was done. The place to start was when I got to the winter break, the only time you can start looking ahead to the next year. With Lombardy out of the way, I had four or five weeks off. Cath, the kids and I moved into our new house and I did some work on it. We bought two dogs and I ended up walking them a lot, which helped to get my head right. Meanwhile, Shane was away thinking about the coaching, how we could improve. I remember thinking, 'This is it now. Even if I don't perform on the bike I'm going to try and lead a little bit. I'm going to answer my phone and be more proactive with the press.'

Initially when I started the process of trying to change, trying to be more communicative, trying to lead the team, it was mainly to please everyone else. If I was asked to do something, I did it. That in turn was because I felt threatened; there was a chance that I was going to lose my job. But as time went on I started getting results. People responded well to me. I'd give an interview, it would be really upbeat, the interviewer would enjoy it too, they might tell me how much they'd liked working with me and I'd feel fantastic about it. I began to realise that in helping other people I'd helped myself.

I came away from that first team meeting feeling good, but it wasn't just down to the way I'd behaved. I'd had a meeting with Shane. Clearly he and the others had done a lot of thinking too and had worked out what approach we needed to take. Tim Kerrison had agreed to start helping us as a sports scientist, which was critical, because Shane didn't feel 100 per cent confident that he could cover everything on his own. Tim had some good ideas; he wanted to bring in some of his knowledge. On that basis, they wrote me a winter's training programme.

The summer of 2010 had left me determined to change, but it had also left me at my lowest ebb in terms of self-confidence, wondering if I could really make it. Could I ever get back to the heights of 2009? Because of this it was important not to ramp up the pressure too much. So Tim, Shane and I sat down and deliberately didn't set the bar too high. We were not going to win the Tour de France in 2011. However, a place in the top ten would go some way towards getting back to being a yellow jersey contender in the biggest race in the world. I knew that getting in the top ten would be a fantastic achievement, although it had tended to be overlooked a bit, as people talked about winning the Tour or getting on the podium. This was where Tim came in. He had started looking at what it takes to get in the top ten and from what he told me I began to realise that physically I was more than capable of it.

Between the three of us we had a breakthrough, a complete change of approach. It came about when Tim looked at the margins and the percentages from the 2010 Tour de France. I had had a 'disastrous' race, yet had still finished 24th; a lot of people would give their right arm for 24th. We realised that if I had lost a minute or so less on a lot of my worst days I would have been up to 11th. So then we started looking at the data, thinking about how I could avoid losing time.

What we realised was that I would be better off riding my own race rather than trying to go with Andy Schleck or Alberto Contador when they attacked on a climb. My riding style is not explosive, but what my body is good at is riding at high intensity for a long time, without ever going completely into the red. Basically, I had to avoid blowing up. That meant I should drop off the back of the lead group if necessary, when the climbers began pushing up the intensity, because if I rode at my own tempo I would limit my losses maybe to forty seconds rather than trying to stay with the pure climbers and losing two minutes, as I did on Morzine in the 2010 Tour. With that in mind, top ten in the Tour became an achievable goal. But in order to achieve that, we began working to a rather unusual philosophy: I had to forget competing for 1st place. I had to put all Sky's long-term goals and my achievement of 2009 to one side. I had to ride my own race. Call it blue-sky thinking, call it thinking outside the box, it was Tim's way of working and it turned into the basis of how we approached the next two years.

I believed this could work mainly because I was certain that Shane Sutton was the one person who was not just going to tell me what I wanted to hear. If Shane felt this was a sound idea, he really meant it. The two of us have a lot of shared history. We go back to the days when I was a schoolboy. Shane retired from racing at the end of 1995, and at the end of the next year he became Welsh national coach. He was at the old outdoor velodrome at Leicester – it's fallen out of use now – with his squad at the 1996 national track championships. I finished 3rd in the junior points race and after I'd come down off the podium, he was crouched there having a fag, in his usual fashion, and he began chatting away, 'Oh, I used to ride with your dad', and so on. Shane and Gary had raced together in Australia and knew each other, but I don't think they got on very well when they were racing. Shane was a tough little nut and Gary was the same so they never saw eye to eye.

In 2002 Shane came on board at British Cycling to help us with the Madison – the two-man relay race in which I'd got close to a medal in Sydney. We were always struggling to qualify teams for the World Track Championships in that event, so I saw more of him. After the Commonwealth Games that year I hooked up with Cath. We'd met years before when we were both on the junior track squad, but August 2002 was when we got together; it was not long afterwards that I went to live with her in Manchester, where she was studying at university and still riding the track. By then, Shane was more than just another coach to me, he had become a friend. I came back to Manchester at the end of the 2002 season, which I'd spent racing with the French team Française des Jeux, and Cath would be at university all day. We had a whole routine of our own. I'd call up Shane and say, 'Do you want to go down the pub?' and we'd sit in the pub in Didsbury all day drinking. We'd have seven or eight pints and then Cath would finish uni, I'd pick her up, we'd go home and Shane would stay in the pub. Cath would go and do a track session at the velodrome and I would go back and meet Shane for another couple of hours. Then Cath would finish at the track, pick me up and drive me home. And the next day Cath would go back to uni and I'd go and meet Shane again. Every day it was the same during that off-season. We were mates, talking all the time. That winter, I rode some of the German Six Day races, on the tracks at Dortmund and Munich. Shane came with me as my mechanic and we had a massive laugh, not to mention some big drinking sessions; there's a bit of that culture in the Six-Days.

This might sound like a lot of drinking for an elite athlete, but I'm not exaggerating. For one thing, there was more of a drinking culture within the sport back then, certainly in the UK. The other point is that I was only twenty-two; people say to me, 'You were in the *gruppetto* with us six years ago and now look how far you've come', but they don't fully appreciate what I used to be like. Marc Madiot, who managed me in 2002 and 2003, said recently that he would never have imagined me as a Tour contender; he didn't really know me, he had no idea what I got up to in the winter. As I've explained elsewhere, I had another drinking winter in 2004 when I was trying to figure out my future after taking my first Olympic gold medal at Athens. In spite of the gold medals and even though I got close to the podium of the

Tour in 2009, I'd say it was only in 2011 that I completely understood how much you need to work to get to the very top, what hard training is, and how much of a lifestyle change is involved. I simply didn't train as much back then. I just never did the work. I've now realised what I'm capable of and I've done something about it.

Shane was the mate I'd go down the pub with, but sometime in 2003 he stopped drinking and that was it: he hasn't touched a drop since. He was working with British Cycling, but not on the track-endurance squad of which I was a part; he was quite heavily involved with the team sprinters, Chris Hoy and the others. I guess in a lot of ways it was like having a father who worked at British Cycling. He always looked out for me, although initially he wasn't in charge of me or my programme. It was always Shane I'd ring if I had any problems. The thing with Shane is that from the minute we became mates this guy would do anything for me, literally anything. Then again, if you get on the wrong side of him you've got an enemy for life. But if you're on the right side, he'll take a bullet for you.

Typically for Shane, he had established contact of a kind with Gary even though they hadn't got on together in their racing days. After the winter of 2002, when we were drinking together and became friends, Shane went off to Australia for a training camp with the team sprinters. I hadn't had contact with my dad for a couple of years but while he was out there Shane bumped into him at the Tasmanian carnivals. He came home from that winter break and said, 'I met Gary out there, he's living in Taz.'

'How was he?'

'He was in a really bad way, mate, he didn't look so well. I bought him a drink one night and we talked through a few things and he asked a lot after you, you know.'

Shane had looked after Gary because he was my dad, helped him out a bit and gave him a thousand dollars out of his own pocket and that was it; I think it was the last time Shane saw Gary, and pretty much the last I heard of him.

Six years later, when Gary died in January 2008, it was Shane who phoned me at 4 a.m. to tell me he had heard from a mate in Australia that my dad was in hospital and it wasn't looking good for him.

Later I spoke with Shane a bit more about him and he said, 'Fuck, Gary was talented, very talented, but he just didn't put the work in. And he was a big drinker.' I never knew my father as well as I know Shane; I do know he's far more loyal than Gary ever was. Shane has been my role model for the last ten years and he says I'm like his son.

When Simon Jones, my coach since 1998, left British Cycling in early 2007, Shane was brought in by Dave Brailsford to oversee the team pursuit squad. Simon had wanted us all to go on a massive training camp in Australia that winter, but I'd refused to go because Cath was pregnant with Isabella. Simon was fairly annoyed at me, and told the guys when they arrived Down Under that I would never race with them again, something that I had no option but to accept. At the start of 2007, Dave told me he was letting Simon go, and said, 'Shane's going to take over, and I'm going to bring this guy Matt Parker in, he's got some good ideas; he's going to be the sports scientist.'

Shane's first words were, 'You've got to start getting some enjoyment back into this programme.' He asked me to lead the group. And he said, 'We need to start loving our athletes a bit more.'

'What do you mean?'

'What do you need?'

He bought me a phone and a SIM card, and said, 'See this? This is the backbone. If you ever need anything just ring me and you're not paying for this out of your pocket.' Three months before I had thought I was out of the squad after I'd refused to go to Australia; suddenly I was being made to feel like a million dollars.

It can be infuriating being trained by Shane, because everything in his life is so hectic. He's got a lot going on and he really struggles when he feels as if he's not in control. He will ring me at times: 'What you doing?'

And I'll say: 'I'm having a day off.'

'What the fuck you having a day off for? You should be out on your bike.'

But he hasn't seen that I've been training for the last five days. When he's not in control and he comes in and just sees what's in front of his eyes, he can find it tough. It's just the way he is and the way he operates. He's constantly thinking about his athletes, often to the detriment of himself and his own family. There are times when you think, 'For Pete's sake, Shane, go and see your own family, don't worry about us for once.' His approach can seem extreme. For instance, he apologised to me at the start of the Dauphiné in 2012; he was really upset because he felt he had let me down. He had wanted to be at the race with me, but he'd had to go on holiday with his family to Center Parcs after being away at the World Track Championships in Australia. At times he expects you to show the same commitment as him. I'll say, 'I need to spend some time at home', and he will say, 'I haven't seen my own family for three years.' It can be infuriating. All you can say is, 'No, Shane, we're all different.'

Shane is incredibly observant as well. He's always watching and thinking. He looks at little details, like the way I am pedalling, and he'll say to me, 'You didn't look comfortable on that climb', or 'You were pushing too big a gear.' He is great at knowing when to make an athlete stop and rest. He's always saying, 'You need to recruit now.' By which he means letting the work soak in. His argument is: you need to do all this training but you also need to take the time off to let your body recover and adapt. Not a lot of athletes do this, but you need to recruit all the effort and repair all the muscle damage for the training to have any effect. If you don't rest, you don't recruit. For example, before winning the Dauphiné in 2012 I had two days off. I wasn't sure about taking two days without riding the bike but he was determined I spend some time with my family. That's what he's like. As a coach he is incredibly good at the human side of it. He knows how it feels because he's been there; he knows what six hours in the saddle feels like and he knows the mental effort it takes to ride for that length of time two days after a race.

Since the end of 2010 the way Tim and Shane have been working together is that Tim will write the training programmes and then Shane will adapt them to fit me and the world I live in. He'll simply change the details, based on his experience of bike racing and his knowledge of me. It may seem small, but it makes a massive difference to the state of mind of his riders. Tim might have pencilled in some interval training three days after I've won a big race; Shane will look at it and say, 'No, Brad just needs to ride his bike that day. He doesn't need the mental stress of doing intervals.' The outcome is the same: in physical terms I end up with the workload Tim devises, but Shane reduces the impact the training has on my mind and on my life. The key thing is Tim has never been a bike rider whereas Shane has; that means he understands what it's like and runs the programme through the filter of normal life. That's where the two of them work well together. Their skills just marry up.

Between them, Tim and Shane figure out the specific areas I need to work on. They look at everything through the year, they review what went right and what didn't. Once we've reassessed the goals and decided what we're doing next year, Tim and Shane will go away and write a plan for the season, a phased plan – like a business plan, but working back from the main goal – and Tim will look at it for weeks before coming back with another plan that includes all the specifics. One phase can be two weeks or ten days, one phase could be a week-long rest; for example, you might start off with five weeks general conditioning, getting back up to, say, twenty hours a week; phase two will be pre-race conditioning so it will be Majorca, say 1 January to 19 February. That will be working harder, starting to touch on threshold areas, and then it will be 20 February to 24 March, an initial race phase that includes Paris–Nice. It will be like that all the way towards July. That's what we've always done with the track as well, from the days when we always worked back from the date of the team pursuit at a World's or an Olympics.

Before Shane and Tim took over, I worked mainly with Matt Parker, the sports scientist who had begun working with the team pursuit squad in early 2007. Matt had always been at the velodrome; he used to test me on the rig. He looked after bits of my training until 2010 although he wasn't a constant presence like Shane and Tim are now. I'd ask Matt what training I should be doing for a particular period; he'd send something through and I'd follow it, or at least I'd follow bits of it. It was much more informal, and there was never any criticism from Matt. He was very respectful of me and he always used to say to me, 'You know yourself better than anyone.' Which is perhaps why I felt like I could do no wrong. Perhaps Matt had too much respect for me; he is a lovely guy and would never have a go at me or criticise me if I missed out sessions we'd agreed on. Whereas Shane would go, 'Why the fuck didn't you go and do that? I didn't tell you that was a key ride for the hell of it.' So that's the difference between Matt and Shane.

That's not to say a hairdrying from Shane is hard to take. He's just honest. It's always a matter of, 'Right, I'm going to tell you something now, you're not going to like it, but you need to pull your head out of your arse, all right? You know

I love you to bits, but these next three days are vital.' It's in that tone. He'll tell you you're the best athlete in the world and you've just got to get this bit right. He'll praise you at the same time as making you feel how important this is. He'll say, 'To be honest, last week you fucked up. I'm telling you that as a mate, you messed up big time, you shouldn't have gone and done what you did, but it's done now and you learn from your mistakes.' The reason why athletes like Sir Chris Hoy and I are happy to take a bollocking from him is because when he tells you that stuff you know he cares about you. He's not ranting at you because he's going to get in trouble himself or because he's had a bad day. And you know likewise that when you do well he will never blow smoke up your backside. He will say, 'Good job, mate, and you know the next three days are important; you need to get your feet up and recover.'

At other times it's swung the other way. I've been in a bit of a box physically, needing to recover, but I've still gone out and completed what's on the programme. In that case Shane will pull me to one side and say, 'You know, Brad, this is where you've got to be careful, because that's your desire to win the Tour coming through and it may be your downfall; you've still got to be very sensible and listen to your body. Just because you think, "You know what, I'm tired, I'm not going to do it today," that doesn't make you not committed or dedicated to what you're doing.'

It's quite funny when it's Shane who's telling me to take it easier because he has such a reputation as a hard nut, but a lot of the time it's Cath who ends up doing that for me. I'll say I feel guilty because I didn't go on my bike today and she'll tell me not to be stupid. She's the one who always knows me best in that sense. As an athlete you are always trying to find that balance, to walk that fine line between training hard enough and not overdoing it, so it's not enough to have a coach who simply shouts at you and tells you you're soft, now go out and do it. Getting it right comes partly down to experience, and partly to having the right people around you.

CHAPTER 4

BACK ON TRACK

One of the key things that Shane came up with in autumn 2010 was that I really needed to get back into the velodrome. He feels that track work in the winter gives you real routine, and some of the intense work we do with the Great Britain track squad is beneficial for the road. So with a view to possibly riding the team pursuit in the London Olympics – which were now just over eighteen months away – I went back to the GB squad again. That gave me a good base for what turned out to be a pretty mundane winter: I would be in the velodrome a couple of times a week doing some fairly intense workouts, I would be riding hard from my home in Lancashire and that was it.

I did what I had to do and when I began racing on the road again at the Tour of Qatar, the form was there straight away. That didn't mean I was winning, but it put me in the front group on most of the stages. The team were pleased and that began to set me up for the spring. After Qatar it was the track

World Cup at Manchester, where I joined up with my fellow Beijing gold medallists Geraint Thomas (or 'G') and Ed Clancy, plus young Steven Burke, for a convincing win that wasn't light years away from the world record we'd set in Beijing. I was getting a lot of praise that winter, which was rewarding after I had made more of an effort to be a leader. Everyone was telling me I was more communicative, a joy to work with again. As an athlete, you feed off that: if you do something and it works and you get positive feedback, you want more of it.

That spring, it all started to go right. At Paris–Nice I finished 3rd overall, which was a huge step up in performance from anything I'd done since finishing 4th in the Tour the best part of two years before. It wasn't run in my kind of weather, being cold and wet, and the guys ahead of me, Tony Martin and Andreas Klöden, were both serious stage race specialists. It was clearly a step forward: we were heading in the right direction, and that's how it continued. At Paris–Roubaix, my favourite one-day Classic of them all, I did a good job for the team, giving Geraint Thomas my wheel when I crashed and he punctured at the start of the Arenberg Forest cobbled section. At the Tour of Romandie I helped with leading out another of my teammates from the pursuit squad, Ben Swift, to win a couple of bunch sprints, something I'd begun doing at Qatar for Edvald Boasson Hagen.

By that summer, I felt I was beginning to lead the team: at the dinner table, before and after the races, when Sean Yates was talking to us in the peloton on the radio. I wasn't afraid to make it clear at the start of some events that I was just there for preparation, but I was ready to give something back as well by helping my teammates in those races. The point was that I had been 100 per cent committed throughout the season and had been communicative with the guys about that. That meant riding on the front when G was leading Bayern Rundfahrt – a five-day stage race in Bavaria – and then getting the payback at the Dauphiné Libéré when I put my hand up and said, 'This is a big race for me.'

Another big change in our approach was that I had begun racing to get results all year round, rather than just putting everything into the Tour. Again, I had learned a lot from 2010. I remember being 7th overall with a week to go in the Giro d'Italia that year, and sitting up on the mountain stage to the Zoncolan, because I wanted to save myself for the Tour. I ended up thinking that perhaps I could have managed a top ten in the Giro; it was a reminder that there are races out there other than the big one in July. For the sake of just racing for five or six days flat out, when I was in a position to get something, rather than sitting up and thinking, 'Yeah, well, you know what, I'm going to save it for the Tour,' I might have won Paris–Nice that year, for example. So I thought, holding back for the Tour is not going to change a lot. You've still got to ride the races.

In 2011 we never really backed off on any one race, apart from the Tour. The goal was always July; I wanted to peak for my best form in that month but I wasn't going to sacrifice everything for it. The Brad Wiggins of 2010 might have tapered off, gone into races like the Dauphiné or Paris–Nice fresh to get the best possible result, but in terms of the bigger picture you don't hold any consistent form if you drop off training several times in the year in order to hit one peak after another. It has to be one long build in which you race as hard as you can, you race to win with whatever you've got at the time. If it's good enough for a result, that's great.

So I raced the Dauphiné quite tired. I'd done a five-hour ride the day before the prologue time trial, and after the prologue I added on another 80km on the bike. I was riding it at the end of a six-week block of quite intensive training, first at altitude in Tenerife, then racing the Bayern Rundfahrt in Germany, where I beat Fabian Cancellara in the time trial, which was a nice little bonus. That was one of the big differences with having Tim and Shane working on my training: what they did was keep me pushing on during those times when perhaps in the past I would have felt that I needed to back off.

In spite of the fatigue I was able to produce the best win of my entire career up till then, taking the yellow jersey in the time trial at Grenoble, then holding on to the lead in the mountains. With three summit finishes before the end of the race – Les Gets, Collet d'Allevard and La Toussuire – I had to race intelligently to keep the lead I had: 1min11sec from Cadel Evans. This was where the new approach that Tim had devised came into its own: I couldn't go with all the attacks on all the climbs. I had to race my own race in the yellow jersey, even if that meant coming off the back of the group at some points. It was a great success, thanks to some selfless support riding from Eddie Boasson Hagen and Rigoberto Urán in the mountains. The Dauphiné is a major event in the second tier of stage races, one rung down from the three big Tours; that made it the most prestigious road win of my career by some margin. It took a while to sink in, although strangely I didn't feel it was a great performance.

After the Dauphiné we moved straight on to the final three-week run in to the Tour: our next destination was a training camp at altitude in Sestriere. That meant there wasn't a great celebration because we didn't have time. It was a bit like winning the first Olympic gold medal when I was going for three in both Athens and Beijing: it was put in the drawer and forgotten about because I had to focus on the next one. It was hard to do, but it worked.

By June of 2011, with that win behind me, finishing in the top ten of the Tour looked more than achievable; getting on the podium seemed to be within reach, but still with the idea of riding my own race. We had realised that the key thing was to avoid getting involved in the massive explosions at the foot of the climbs when the pure climbers would begin attacking. I had to treat every *col* as if it were a time trial, thinking of getting from A to B as fast as possible without blowing up. It was not the most attractive way to ride a race, it was not riding with panache, but that was the reality of it. We'd all like to be able to attack at the foot of a climb and ride Alberto Contador off our wheel but actually it's about being sensible, riding intelligently.

That was the biggest lesson I learned from the Dauphiné: there was no shame in dropping off the back even if you were wearing the yellow jersey, bearing in mind you could always come back to the leaders. Even when I was in yellow, the centre of attention with the cameras watching me, it didn't faze me when I decided the pace was getting too much and I had to put our plan into action, and watching it succeed boosted my confidence as well. Miguel Indurain was criticised for riding in this way throughout his career, but looking back you realise how great he was on his best days on the Tour.

This change in approach was largely due to the input we had from Tim Kerrison. I'd first met him at the Tour of Britain in 2009 when I had yet to sign for Team Sky but was being kept in the loop about what they were up to. There was a stage that started in Peebles, and Shane turned up with this lad in a Great Britain Swimming fleece. He and Dave had just poached him from the swimming team. Apparently Tim had been on his way to a job interview with English Cricket. He was going to take the job doing much the same thing with them as he ended up doing at Sky. Sky rang him on the way and he made a detour to the velodrome to see them. That's how Shane tells it, anyway: before Tim went to this interview, he and Dave convinced him to come and work with them. They told him: we want to win the Tour, that is our goal, this is what we would like you to do, and they got him on board before he could go anywhere else. On paper, Tim's job description was 'performance analyst', but first he had to find his way around bike racing.

In 2010, Tim spent the year on the road, mainly with Matt Parker, just observing. He spent all his time in his and Matt's camper van; I used to call it the Skip. Their nickname for it was Black Betty, but it was always in a bit of a state. You would go in there and you could imagine what Swampy's little tent looked like in those trees. Tim didn't open his mouth practically all year. Even now he's not a big talker but back then you would never hear him say anything. He was there all the time observing, taking it all in, learning how cycling worked. A key part of that was getting on top of how to interpret the data from SRMs, the cranks that measure a cyclist's power output. They have been an integral part of British Cycling's training since Peter Keen founded the programme, because they are the best way to measure how hard a cyclist is working, and to control the workload in training. Tim wrote a lot of things down. He could have written a book by the end of that year.

By the end of 2010 Tim had started asking all sorts of questions, simple things that would prove to be more and more important as we went along. It was stuff that an outsider to cycling might ask, such as: why don't the riders warm down at the end of the stage? Just think about it, why don't they warm down? He would be told, it's not the done thing; the riders don't want to look foolish. There was no scientific reason for not having a warm-down, it was just that no one did it. Another thought Tim had was that he felt that a team should not just be about the leader. In his view, it should be about getting all the guys to the same level as the leader they are supporting. He asked more basic questions: why is it only the team leader who gets to go on the training camps where we reconnoitre the mountain stages? Why does only the leader get set blocks of time for training while the rest of the team race themselves to death? Why don't we get the eight other guys who will race in the Tour – or as many of them as we can – to ride together all year and race in the same races, go to the training camps, go and recon the mountains together and get to know each other as a football team would? That single point made me realise that during that first year at Sky we had all raced all over the place. The first time I raced with Geraint Thomas and Edvald Boasson Hagen and all those guys was when we got to the Tour. I'd hardly seen them all year.

Tim was looking at a host of little things that traditionally no one had ever questioned. He was responsible for us beginning to use altitude training camps, with one in Tenerife in May 2011, and another at Sestriere, in the Italian Alps, that June. And he would ask: why don't teams have training camps in December? Well, we said, they normally have training camps but they're more sort of drinking camps where everyone gets to know each other and you collect your bikes, that sort of thing. January's the serious training camp. Why? Tim would ask. Why don't we do that one in November, and have a serious one in December, because that's quite an important month. Traditionally in professional cycling teams, everyone gets their training bike in January; Tim wanted to know why they couldn't get it in October and then have a training bike that they use at home? And what about specific time-trial bikes, not just for the leader but for the whole team?

Tim went away, looked at the data he had gathered from me and the other riders in the 2010 Tour and began examining the numbers. He worked out what rate you need to be climbing at in the Tour de France. That calculation was done in terms of VAM – *velocità ascensionale media* – which translates into English as 'average climbing speed', or how quickly you gain height in a climb. It's basically a measure of how fast you are going upwards as if you were in a lift, measured in metres per hour. He figured out what power output you needed to be averaging for a certain body weight if you were going to win the Tour. He wrote down all the demands of the event and we went from there. We'd not done any testing with reference to the Tour, so the first thing he did was get me in the lab. We started testing and slowly started to build a picture of what I was capable of doing and what I couldn't do.

It took a while to build a trust between the three of us. As the season went on, as the training and racing and going to altitude took effect, we started to come away with better and better results. The progression was clear: 3rd place at Paris–Nice, a time-trial stage win at Bayern Rundfahrt, the overall title at the Dauphiné. We had set off into 2011 with the idea of aiming for a top-ten place in the Tour, but eventually we realised that I could be up there with the likes of Cadel Evans and Alexander Vinokourov who were going for the podium.

There was another aspect that made us more optimistic as the Tour drew closer in 2011. Various things were coming out on the anti-doping front. It emerged that the UCI had established an 'index of suspicion' – I rated five out of ten – which at least meant they were on the case. Most importantly, they had brought in a needle ban, forbidding the use of injections across the board, even for substances used for recovery such as sugars and vitamins. British Cycling have always had a no-needle policy, it's been a mainstay of theirs; so it was something I grew up with as a bike rider.

In British cycling culture, at the word 'needle' or the sight of one, you go 'Oh shit', it's a complete taboo. When I was a kid we used to play around in a car park where there were always needles on the floor from heroin addicts who used to go and shoot up – orange needles – so from a young age my mother and others would tell us, 'Stay away from those needles, don't go near them, don't touch them.' In France you can buy them over the counter; it's a different culture. Here you buy vitamin C effervescent from Boots, rather than getting it through a syringe. I've never had an injection, apart from I've had my vaccinations, and on occasion I've been put on a drip, when I've come down with diarrhoea or something or have been severely dehydrated.

Shane kept saying to me that this was all working in our favour. As long as they kept going in that direction, deterring the drug-users, that would be great. The needle ban was fantastic, although from our point of view at the Dauphiné there was no sign of it being policed. It would have been great if they had started raiding teams to see that people were toeing the line. Medical people in our team were adamant that riders were continuing to use syringes for recovery on the Dauphiné and other races even though the practice was banned. Guys with a history of this sort of stuff weren't going to say, 'Oh, it's against the law now, we'll stop doing it.' The hardcore will continue to push the boundaries, and until someone gets banned for breaking the syringe rule I don't think it's really going to deter them. But all those developments contribute towards a team like ours, which is determined to race clean, coming away with something big at the Tour de France.

As the Tour drew near, I had dropped to my lightest climbing weight ever: 69 kilos. I'd taken it gradually down to 71.5 by the start of the 2009 Tour. That was 6.5 kilos lighter than I'd been when I rode in 2007. It takes a good deal of hard work to get it down there, but it's the most effective way of improving your performance on the road: one kilogramme less of body weight means you gain about 25sec for a given power output on a thirty-minute climb. It's not just about the climbs; every time you accelerate out of a corner or up a little hill you are hefting that extra weight. Over a three-week race those efforts add up to a huge amount of extra work. On the track you build up a lot of upper-body muscle simply due to the work on your arms and shoulders from the standing starts you do as a pursuiter. On the road it's not useful and it took a good while to work it off after I quit the track post-Beijing; one thing I did initially was have regular checks with Nigel Mitchell, the nutritionist at British Cycling, to make sure I was staying healthy. It was the biggest single change I'd made.

I'd won the time trial at the Bayern Rundfahrt, taking the scalp of Fabian Cancellara, who was the man to beat at that time. I'd won the Dauphiné, the biggest road victory of my entire career, and then I'd taken first place in the British national road race championships on a super-tough course in the north-east, where Sky had been dominant. I had been massively optimistic for the Tour when I had faced the press at Kew Gardens a couple of days before the British Road Race Championships. I told them that I'd relaunched my career and said I was ready to go. It was true: I was in a better position for the Tour than I had ever been. And I raced well to win that national title. But after that trip to the north-east I got ill: diarrhoea for two days. As a result, I couldn't travel to the Tour until right up to the last minute. I think I got in on the Wednesday night, and then we were straight out, doing team time-trial training on the course for the Sunday's stage, and I felt dreadful. I was quite close to getting dropped. We did more team time-trial work on the Friday but I'd regained some of my strength by then.

Since the previous Sunday's win, it had all been a mad rush. By the time the Tour started six days later, I actually felt as if my form was dwindling a little. It's more in your head than anything physical. I remember getting to the Vendée for the start, and doing the press conference on the Thursday. Everyone around me was saying, 'Oh, it's great, things are fantastic, never been this good, it's a great position we're in.' I, on the other hand, couldn't sit there and say, 'I've had stomach trouble the last couple of days, I don't feel great on the bike.' It was all a bit like 2010. I was still talking it up at that stage because I didn't want to admit to myself, 'You know what, I'm a little bit worried about this.' So you put on a front for the press.

There is a lot of speculation about how I would have fared in that Tour, but I never felt great. I felt a bit weak, although I got through the first stage in decent shape. I was strong in the team time trial the day after and then I was poised in 6th overall. I was in a good position for the rest of the week but I never seemed to be in control of it. That was what was going through my head, but Shane was saying, 'No, don't worry about how you feel, what the numbers are suggesting is something else.' I always wonder what would have happened once we hit those mountains: whether I would have been in the front or not.

On the stage to Châteauroux seven days in, I wasn't well placed in the peloton as we began the final 50km into the finish, which can be a sign in itself. As always, everyone was trying to stay in the front. But I kept slipping to the back. I had no fight in me that day.

On the flat stages, you rely on your teammates to pull you forward; if the peloton is travelling at 50kph, you have to ride at 55–60kph to overtake the other riders; having someone in front of you to cut through the air means you save energy. With the help of the other guys in Sky, I'd get to the first few rows of the peloton, but then we'd drift back a bit, and I would think, 'I can't be bothered to go round the outside again and fight my way up to the front one more time.' And before you knew it we'd be down the back. Eddie would be saying to me, 'Come on, we need to move up.' He would take me up back to the front, we'd drift a bit, then there we'd be at the back. Next time it was Juan Antonio Flecha; they were all trying to take me up to the front.

We're moving up, moving up, moving up, we're about halfway up the field and then before I know it I'm on the deck, the team doctor, Richard Freeman, is coming over to me, I'm clutching my shoulder; I can feel it isn't right. I can't get off the floor for love nor money without it being agony. It's game over.

But what I'm feeling is bizarre: the minute I hit the tarmac, I feel something that could almost be described as close to relief. Phew, I'm not going to have to see just how good or bad I am.

CHAPTER 5

BREAKTHROUGH

When we bought our new house at the end of 2010, one of the things I did early on was get myself a shed in the garden. It's about five metres by five, made of wood, and it's big enough to take a bike and a turbo trainer plus a couple of heaters and a sound system. I can still see the sweat stains on the carpet from the hours I spent in there in August 2011, sitting on the bike, spinning the turbo and dripping like a wet sponge. There was no alternative if I wanted to perform in the Tour of Spain, the Vuelta, which ran from mid-August into early September. And I had no option other than to ride the Vuelta if I wanted to have any chance at all of getting anywhere near the podium in the 2012 Tour de France.

From the minute I crashed out of the 2011 Tour de France on the road to Châteauroux I began thinking about what to do next. I was sitting in the airport waiting for the plane to take me home to Cath and the kids and I was already talking to Tim. It was an obvious question: what are you going to do?

And we both knew the answer. Do the Vuelta. You've got to do the Vuelta now. The Tour of Spain is the third Grand Tour of the season, after Italy and France, and was moved to the end of the year a while back, to offer a chance for anyone who'd flopped or crashed out of the Tour to get their revenge. I'd never ridden it, so I was kind of looking forward to it, there was a bit of novelty there. I'd crashed out of the Tour, so I'd be on the comeback trail, which meant there would be no pressure. I could just go there and race. The Vuelta was vital in terms of preparation for 2012. The physical demands of racing a three-week Tour are unique, and I needed to get through at least one in 2011 to maintain the level I needed to be at.

I had about nine days off after the crash, then I started riding my bike again. Tim put a training programme together for me to get me up to the start. I knew I was still in pretty good shape, as I had been going into the Tour; it wasn't just going to disappear overnight. It was the first real injury I'd had as a pro, the first since I broke my wrist in the winter of 2001. A lot of people – Dave, Shane – commented on how well I seemed to be dealing with it, but I just didn't let it trouble me too much. I'd won the Dauphiné, I'd moved forward and felt I was starting to make progress. It was a good place to stop and take stock; there were no regrets about the Tour, because I had no idea how it would have gone.

I held my weight down, looked after myself, and went to the Vuelta with no real ambition other than to race as hard as I could and see what happened. That was where the shed came into its own. I had no time to go back to altitude after the Tour, and in Lancashire I didn't have any mountains to train in, so a lot of the work was done on the turbo trainer, which is a tripod with a weighted roller on it. You slot your back wheel into the tripod, settle the back tyre on to the roller, then ramp up the resistance to the required level, and you pedal away. With a broken collarbone to heal, I couldn't get out on the road initially, so I did a lot of the specific training in the shed.

The heat was a massive issue in the Vuelta a España; it was one of the weak areas I had identified after the 2010 Tour de France where I had been struggling through a very hot July as well as with the altitude. We had already begun thinking about it before the 2011 Tour. Tim said that you could acclimatise to heat in the same way as to altitude, but you needed to do specific work at high temperatures. So we devised training sessions in a heat chamber, which just happened to be my garden shed. We put some heaters in there and a humidifier, getting the temperature up to thirty-five or forty degrees, and I would sit on the turbo for anything up to two hours, just riding the bike. We aimed to do three or four sessions a week, and eventually put them on the end of training rides on the road. It was every bit as uncomfortable as I needed it to be, so I couldn't do any sort of efforts or anything. Pedalling in there was quite enough. As well as being valuable acclimatisation, there was a mental side to it: this was something I was able to do with a broken collarbone because I could just sit on the turbo without having to put weight on my arms, and I could still feel as if I was doing something towards the Vuelta.

That Vuelta was funny. Although physically I was not in the shape of my life, I was still in a good place. What Shane and Tim were trying to emphasise to me was that being in that Vuelta was as much about 2012 as 2011. If I wasn't in contention there was no question of throwing the towel in and climbing off. I needed those three weeks of racing and I went into it with the attitude, 'Yeah, right, I'll be the team leader, I'll take the responsibility that comes with that, and let's have a crack at it. Maybe I'll end up in the top ten, who knows, let's see what happens.'

We just took it day by day, and the first day was terrible. In the team time trial in Benidorm we finished 3rd to last, partly because Kurt-Asle Arvesen crashed early on, which disrupted us all, but ultimately because we didn't go fast enough. However, we didn't dwell on it, we just thought about the next day, when Chris Sutton won the stage for us. Four days in we went up the Sierra Nevada, 2,000m high and the first summit finish I'd done since the Dauphiné; I finished with a front group up there, so that gave us a bit of confidence. We could see that Chris Froome and I were perhaps not the best but better than most on that climb. Another five days in, the day before the individual time trial, we had a summit finish at La Covatilla, and that was where Chris and I ripped it up. There were just a handful of us left at the top, so we knew we were in the mix, and it went from there.

The day after that we had the time trial at Salamanca. And there, maybe, I made a bit of a mistake: I went out to try and kill the race but I went too deep. I led at the first checkpoint, then faded to 3rd behind Tony Martin and Froomie; I definitely didn't ride it right, given we were racing at altitude in blistering heat. That put Chris in the race lead, but at the next summit finish two days later, a gruelling 19km climb to Estacion de Montaña Manzaneda, he slipped back after responding to a series of attacks, and I went with the leaders. That put me in the leader's jersey, a position I had never expected to be in. From coming into the Vuelta feeling that if I could get a top ten that would be great, out of the blue I was leading the race and looking as if I was one of the best guys there. Suddenly I started to think in those terms: I can win this.

If it hadn't been for the stage to the top of the Angliru in the last week, I'd have been close to winning that Vuelta. But that finish in Asturias is one of the hardest and steepest in bike racing. For nearly four miles the climbs are averaging a gradient of one-in-seven, there's one section where it is close to one-in-four, and other bits are around one-in-five. I still finished 5th there but that's where my weakness emerged. It was just too severe for where I was physically. Both Juan José Cobo of Spain and Froomie were stronger than me, although Chris did his best to keep me up there for as long as he could on the climb. That settled it, really. From that point on, the race became about keeping a place on the podium, which I managed, running out 3rd overall behind Cobo and Froomie, although Chris won the mountaintop finish at Peña Cabarga to close to just 13sec behind Cobo.

One of the questions that came out of that race was over Sky's choice of leader. Both myself and Chris had been in the mix for the win. He had led after that strong time trial, I'd taken over, and then he had been stronger on the summit finishes at the end. The basic problem was that we were all going into new territory, both Chris and me, and the guys managing the team on the road. I even asked the team at one point whether I should ride for Chris. And they said I shouldn't, because they were not confident Chris could last the distance. Up to that point Froomie had never done anything like this before, so there was no reason to believe he could sustain it. Even Chris was surprised: he'd been so inconsistent with his performances before then, thanks to the bilharzia parasite that had affected his health. So I guess I was the safer bet for the team. It was a difficult call.

Merely getting on the podium was success in itself, although it was a huge disappointment at the time to me. Shane put me straight: 'No, you'd have took 3rd coming into this race, don't talk stupid.' But I'd started to believe I could win the Vuelta, to dream of that win. The point is that you don't think at the time, 'I've got the jersey, but you know what, I haven't really got the condition, I haven't done the work coming into this.' You just race for the moment. When we got to Madrid there was a bit of both disappointment that I'd lost the Vuelta, and also a feeling that looking where I'd come from, 3rd wasn't too bad. It was from that point on I thought: 'Well, if I get the preparation right next year, and I don't have a broken collarbone for six weeks before it, maybe I can win the Tour.'

After the Vuelta I felt like a completely different rider. I'd got my first podium finish in a Grand Tour – a very big step in a mountainous race, after breaking a collarbone and being handicapped in what training I could manage beforehand. I'd proved that I was capable of racing as well as I had in 2009. That had been a big question mark up to that point: was I ever going to get back to that level? What's more, I'd done it in a different race, and one that was extremely tough. In some ways I had always had in the back of my mind the possibility that my 4th place in 2009 might have been a fluke, or perhaps I was wondering more, how on earth did I get there? But I'd done it again in a race I had not even expected to ride until six weeks before, so obviously my confidence was sky high.

Part of that was down to the way I'd been climbing compared to the other riders who were in the mix. Even with what physical ability I had at the Vuelta, I had finished 5th on the Angliru, which I would never have given myself half a chance of doing a year before. We hadn't trained for that kind of climb at all. We hadn't done any torque work; we hadn't looked at power output at a lower cadence than I usually ride. I think for the last three kilometres of that climb I averaged 56rpm, rather than the usual 90 or 100, and we hadn't trained for that. All the training we'd been doing was for 6 or 7 per cent gradients, which is what you hit in the Tour, not for close to 25 per cent. In the Tour the climbs are longer, but they aren't as severe.

We had also made a massive discovery. The conventional wisdom in cycling is that you need a decent number of days of racing in your legs before you go into a three-week stage race, but because of my collarbone we had had no option other than to go against that. After the Dauphiné in early June

71

I had raced just seven days before I started the Vuelta: one day at the British national championships and six at the Tour. On paper it didn't look good for Spain, but what we found out that August and September was that as long as the training is right, you perhaps don't have to race as much as you might expect. For the first time, I'd begun to look hard at what I got from racing. Shane and Tim had introduced me to TrainingPeaks, which is an online coaching platform that enables the coaches to communicate with the riders. From the start of 2011, all my data went on to it – I would download all the information on every training session from my SRM cranks, which measure power output, while the SRM unit also measures pulse rate, pedalling cadence, speed etc. That meant Tim and Shane could assess what I'd been doing; the software gives you what they call TSS – Training Stress Scores – showing how hard you've been working. I'd never done this before; we'd always used SRMs with the Great Britain track team, but had never had a system that evaluates and gives you a weekly score. And I'd never done it specifically for the road.

If you take a flat stage in a stage race, you might get a TSS of 150 because you've been sitting in the wheels all day doing nothing; I can go out from my home and do a six-hour ride with specific blocks of intensity, have a TSS of nearly 300 and be absolutely knackered. That's a harder day than if I'd gone and ridden a flat, long one-day race such as Paris–Brussels. People think that as Paris–Brussels is nearly 300km it must be a hard race. In fact, it's not: it's flat, you're sitting in the wheels, you've got a tailwind; you're hardly doing anything.

In terms of the workload, in a Tenerife training camp we can do the equivalent of two weeks' racing in a Grand Tour, but in a much more controlled environment. The hardest training day we had there was at TSS of 350 or 360; not as hard as the toughest one-day Classics such as Paris–Roubaix, but the beauty of a training camp is you can go and do that, then do it again the next day. Tim can dictate exactly what we're getting out of it, whereas in racing, you don't know what you're going to get from day to day. The Ardennes Classics, Liège–Bastogne–Liège and Flèche Wallonne, used to be almost obligatory for Tour contenders, but we didn't do them in 2012; you sit around for four days in a hotel, you do this massive one-day race, but you might crash having only ridden 100km, and all of a sudden you've missed five days of training.

Here's an even more important point: the fitter you get the less the races take it out of you, which in turn means you have to train even harder. You get into the depths of the season, as we did later on, and you find a one-week stage race such as the Dauphiné has hardly touched the sides, because you're so fit by that point. By the end of the Dauphiné it was tough on the boys, but not on me sitting in sixth wheel all day.

You assume racing is harder than training because as a cyclist it's engrained in you from when you are a kid. I used to assume that after a stage race I'd have three days off to recover, three days of café rides. When we started working together in 2011, Tim got me out of that; I'd say I needed to recover, he'd tell me the race hadn't been that hard. I had to get out of a lifelong habit of thinking you don't need to train in summer because the racing takes care of it.

The Vuelta was the eye-opener: I'd finished 3rd after three and a half weeks of quality training. And the training hadn't even been about the Vuelta; we went to the Vuelta to prepare for the world time trial championships. From there we thought: more training next year, more quality work on the things that we can control. It's about specific things: Tim might say, 'We need to train your threshold, increase your threshold.' I might spend ten minutes at threshold in a four-hour bike race; we might as well go and do an hour of that in one day, in twenty-minute blocks. So the philosophy became: don't go to the race to train, but train first, go to fewer races, and go there to win.

CHAPTER 6

BROTHERS IN ARMS

Before we could work that through, and before I caught up with things over the winter, there were two big jobs to be done in Copenhagen. First up, the world time trial championships, a race I'd never quite got right. As long ago as 2004 I had finished 5th behind Michael Rogers in Madrid, while in Mendrisio in 2009, one of Fabian Cancellara's many wins, I had been in 3rd on the road when my bike gave out on me. I knew that I had a medal in my legs at some point; it was simply a matter of getting the build-up right.

For a good five years, Fabian had been the man to beat in time trials, the best in the world by some margin. He'd won the World's in 2006, 2007, 2009 and 2010 and the Olympic gold in 2008. He was the one who had raised the bar in the discipline. In fact, he'd raised it so high that he became dominant to the point of making his opponents look almost ridiculous at times, such as at the World's in 2009. It was only in 2011 that people started to get the better of him, riders such as Tony Martin of Germany, while I had finally managed to beat him earlier in the year at the Bayern Rundfahrt. The World's in 2011 in Copenhagen, when Tony took gold and I rode to silver, was the first time he'd been beaten in the championships since 2005 (he didn't ride in 2008). That made the time trial a huge day for me. I'd been knocking on the door for a few years, just trying to get a medal, and it set us up with a perfect platform for 2012, when I was aiming to go for the Olympic gold in London. Coming off the back of the Vuelta, that Wednesday in Copenhagen closed the season brilliantly: I'd won the Dauphiné, crashed out of the Tour but come back at the Vuelta, and now I'd broken my duck here at the World's. There was just one job still to do on the Sunday.

I'd had a fair few text messages that year from Mark Cavendish. Before the Tour began, the messages were all really encouraging: 'I hope you do well, I think you can win this.' And when I crashed out he sent me some lovely texts while he was still on the race, just saying, 'I hope you're all right, I'm gutted for you', and that sort of stuff. It was just nice, typical Cav, typical of how we get on. Cav is like my younger brother. We fall out, we make up, we take the piss out of each other, we say this and that, but the relationship is never going to go away. It's like that with my own brother Ryan, who is eight years younger than me and is now living in Milan teaching English. We can go for months on end when I don't happen to talk to him and then it's like we saw each other yesterday. It's just the relationship we have.

The first time I remember bumping into Cav was in the corridor at the Manchester velodrome some time in 2003 when I was in there training for the world pursuit championship. Cav was in the academy and they were in there trying to set their individual pursuit times – back then you used to have to meet a certain standard to get on the programme. He came up to me; he'd done the time he needed to do and he was really made up about it. He'd have been seventeen or maybe eighteen. The next year, 2004, we rode a criterium, a city-centre circuit race, in Calne; I was riding for Crédit Agricole at the time, he was there with the academy. I got 2nd and won a box of Go gels as a *prime* – one of the prizes they give out for first across the line on certain laps during the race – and I remember in the HQ afterwards I gave them to him. They'd have been twenty-five quid's worth, and he was so grateful I'd given him these gels because at the academy they had to buy that kind of thing for themselves. I reminded him of that in 2011 and he said, 'Oh yeah, I forgot that, I'm going to put that in my book.'

In 2005 I rode the Giro; after that it was the national *criterium* championships at Otley, where I led him out and he won it. By 2007 he had turned pro, he got his first big win in Scheldeprijs and he was getting established as a sprinter; he started saying to me, why don't you come to T-Mobile next year? We both rode the 2007 Tour, then started doing some Six-Days together that winter as preparation for the Madison at the World's and the Olympics, and then I joined T-Mobile, or HighRoad as it became. So we spent a lot of time at training camps and races; we used to room together. In 2008 we won the Madison together at the world championships, did Romandie and the Giro in the same team, shared hotel rooms all through those. Then it was the Beijing Olympics, where the Madison was a disaster because I wasn't at my best, and Cav was extremely unhappy as it was his only chance for a medal, and he was really pumped for it. After that we didn't talk for five years, or so it would seem if you believe what you read in the papers.

After Beijing, I didn't speak to him until I saw him in Qatar the following February, but I did get a text from him a couple of weeks after the Olympics: he said, 'How are you doing and have you sobered up yet?' In 2009, when I was with Garmin and he was at HTC, we would talk about cycling but never mention the Olympics. That's something we have never, ever discussed. So through 2009 we had a few little spats but it's not a problem. When he does something I don't like I just say, 'Oh you dick', and likewise he'll say it to me. That's part of the relationship we have. That's how we get on.

We had a bit of a spat on the Tour in 2009. Cav had the hump a couple of weeks in, because he had been docked some points in the green jersey by the *commissaires*. A few days later we rode a stage to Le Grand Bornand in the Alps. Thor Hushovd, who was Cav's big rival for the green jersey, and who had benefited when Cav was declassified, spent most of the stage at the front, and took loads of points towards the green jersey. At the end of that day Cav said a whole load of stuff about Thor in the press and I put on Twitter: 'Great to see Thor answering his critics in his own way by putting two fingers up at them.' So Cav said to me,

'Oh, thanks for that,' and I told him he had been a bit of a tit. There had also been a dispute between Garmin and HTC – on the same stage where Cav was declassified – when their rider George Hincapie was close to getting the yellow jersey and Garmin chased him down. Cav had been pretty unhappy about that as well, so we didn't talk for about a week. We were always avoiding each other. So then we didn't talk during that Tour until the end, on the penultimate stage up to Mont Ventoux. Coming up to the mountain the race split in the crosswinds when we put the hammer down. Cav got up to the front group, I remember going up to him, riding up the side of this echelon; I just put my hand on his back and he put his hand out and we shook hands. It was like saying sorry. Then we went up the Ventoux, I nailed 4th place overall, and the next day on the roll-in to Paris we were talking for ages. There are some lovely photos of us from that day chatting and laughing together.

In years to come, I know I'll look back and be proud to tell my grandchildren I rode with Mark Cavendish, the greatest sprinter of all time. A large part of that comes from the World Road Race Championships in Copenhagen, where the Great Britain lads put in one of the most dominating rides that event has ever seen. But it was a special time for me too. I'd come out of that Vuelta and my self-belief had gone up, I got my medal in the time trial, and then in the road race I had a role to play. My job was to do the last lap, to keep the pace as high as I could, and make sure that the peloton was all together when the final build-up to the sprint began.

Earlier in the year it didn't look quite as simple as it turned out to be. In all the discussions about the World's with guys like G, Ian Stannard and the others, and the discussions with Rod Ellingworth – the manager who masterminded the whole thing – I didn't quite know what to think. But as the year went on, it became more clear-cut. Cav said he would love me to ride, which was probably what made the difference; and I thought, 'OK, I'll do the road race.' But earlier in the year, I don't think I really believed it would be possible. It wasn't that obvious to me how we would manage to keep the race together to ensure there was a bunch sprint for Cav. No team had managed anything like it for years. But once we did it, we realised we had been part of something very special; that feeling is one I'll never forget.

During the race, there wasn't a lot of time to take it in. We had jobs to do, so we were concentrating on remembering the plan and realising it. Personally, I was just counting down the kilometres until I could open up. I felt the urge to go early. I was constantly thinking, 'I'm going to go now.' David Millar was the one who was captaining the team on the road that day; he was always sitting behind me and he was continually talking to me: 'Not yet, Brad, it's too early, we need you on the last lap, wait, wait, wait, wait . . .' Dave was instrumental in our success; he'd become a father earlier in the month and wasn't on his best form, but his guiding role was superb. He kept me on a leash. I didn't want to be in a fight on the last lap; without him I'd have gone too early and ripped the race to bits.

Dave kept a cool head throughout the race, and on the last lap I was able to go for it. That turn I did felt fantastic. I was just super light on the bike. I always thought I had it in me but I had that rare feeling of grace, of confidence. I was convinced that no one would be coming past me, I had that kind of cocky attitude, a bit like Bernard Hinault used to have. I was swerving across the road going into the climbs, messing up any accelerations from behind. It was like the stuff I used to do on the track, a bit of showboating almost. Physically, what I had to do was commit every bit of energy I had for as long as possible before someone came over the top of me. I didn't expect to last as long as I did. I think I did 8km on the front, 8 or 10km. At the end I felt incredibly proud that I'd done my job, and I'd not let Cav down. I'd committed to the job and I'd done it. And then I crossed the line and realised that we'd won and that sparked off a whole different set of feelings.

Sometimes in the past when I'd been in a winning team it had been a simple matter of, 'Oh, that's a good job, I've done my bit, it's great you've won.' But this time it was much, much more than that. I did it for Cav. Since mid-2011, with him it has always felt special. He's so gracious, so grateful for everything you do for him. When you are committing to do your job for him, you know he's not going to let you down. That's inspiring in a way because you know he really needs you on the road when you're doing your utmost, and he looks after you as well when it's all over.

I can't remember what he said afterwards. He was very emotional when we saw him in the bus, but it was a while until that happened, because he went straight off the podium to the doping control and press conference, and all that time we were in the bus drinking champagne. So it was at least an hour before he came back to us and we were all a bit silly by then; he was just very emotional. He thanked us all individually, we had another team photo on the bus; then we all went back to the hotel. We were all a bit dumbstruck, all a bit in shock. I don't think we fully appreciated what we'd achieved. Cav's gold medal was a victory for all of us.

The spirit that we built for that race was special, and it had come through when we had the team meeting before the start. We had to discuss what would happen if Cav punctured in the last lap and the thought was that all the attention would turn to G. We began wondering whether we should try and set up the finish for him or something like that but I said, 'Look, we start as a team, we'll finish as a team. We're all here for Cav, we've all agreed to ride the World's to help Cav win. If we do the whole day for Cav and he punctures on the last lap, we all stop, we all wait and we all try to get back. We'll finish as a team that way.' The attitude in that team was the same as if we had been going into war. We weren't going to leave anyone out there on the battlefield.

That week in Copenhagen was just the best way to end the season. Afterwards, Shane was emphatic: 'Just five weeks off now, this is part of next year, don't touch your bike for five weeks, enjoy yourself a little bit but look after yourself and when we start back on 1 November we're starting properly.' There would be no question of having a month getting back into things. I had to be ready to start training hard on 1 November 2011. That was when 2012 began.

Top Left: Me and my dad, Gary. He was a decent cyclist in his day and in all honesty he was probably better on the bike than he was as a dad

Top Right: Getting to grips with an early time-trial bike

Left: Other kids were into football, but my bedroom
walls were filled with posters of my cycling heroes,
like Indurain and Museeuw

Right: Too cool for school

Left: Lap of honour in Sydney with Paul Manning, Chris
on and Bryan Steel

m Left: Fighting back with Rob Hayles in the Madison in
s after Rob's crash

Triumphant after the individual pursuit in Beijing

The 2010 Tour de France was a struggle, although Cadel Evans (left) doesn't seem to be finding it easy either

ly training days with Sky after its foundation at the start of 2010

Previous Page: Where's Wiggo? See if you can spot me
at the start of the 2011 Tour…

Left: Cav triumphs in Copenhagen, one of the proudest
days of my cycling career

Top Right: I'm leading the train with Steve Cummings
and G on my wheel

Bottom Right: The 2011 Vuelta podium with Juan José
Cobo and Chris Froome

Moves had been afoot to bring Cav to Sky for a while. There were already mutterings in March or April 2011, and I remember talking to Cav about it. I encouraged him to come, saying it would be great to have him at Sky because at that time I was still finding myself, trying to become a real leader. I spoke to him a couple of times during the 2011 Tour; at the start of the Vuelta we were still discussing it. He had been talking about trying to get his main lead-out man Mark Renshaw to come as well; he was upset that Renshaw had gone to Rabobank. I didn't see him again till the World's and even at the World's he hadn't signed. Then I remember Dave ringing me a couple of days after the World's and saying to me, 'You know what, Brad, what would you think if Cav didn't come to this team? It's becoming a bit of a pain in the arse now, there's so much riding on it.'

Eventually Cav did sign and all at once the game changed: the questions started about whether we were going to try and win both the yellow and green jerseys in the Tour de France – which is a massive task for any team to take on – or were we just going to support Cav to win the green? The week it was announced, it was big news everywhere and Dave called me, saying, 'There's been a lot of hype about Cav this week, I just want to let you know you're still up there, high on our priority list.' But at that point I was so engrossed in my training from 1 November, looking towards the Tour, I just thought I would keep training; that was my goal and I would let it all happen. Whatever ended up happening in the team's selection for the Tour was a long way in the future. Then it started becoming apparent in January that we were going to try to win the yellow and green jerseys, so the questions started again: is it possible? Can you do it? Can you win yellow and green in the same Tour?

I never felt my position was threatened by Cav coming to Sky. I could understand that he was coming to the team as world champion, so he was in a much stronger position than me. I'd crashed out of the Tour in 2011 and perhaps that had been my one opportunity to do something. There was a part of me that thought it was bound to happen at some point. It was always inevitable Cav would end up at Sky; now he was world champion and he had won the green jersey last year so I couldn't blame them for wanting a piece of that. I just reminded myself to put my head down, concentrate on what I was doing and get the training in. July was a long way away.

I had several goals for the early season, so there was no point in expecting the managers at Sky to come up with a strategy for the Tour back in January. What I had to do was concentrate on performing in those races I'd picked, do my job and see where we ended up. All I had to do was make sure I was ready for the Tour when they started picking the team. I spoke to Cav a lot on training camps and there was no friction; it was always pretty clear that we would have separate programmes for much of the season. He was actually very encouraging whenever I spoke to him, saying that he thought I could win the Tour. There was never a point where he seemed to think it was not going to happen. He was probably one of the most supportive riders around me in 2012. But that's just him, that's a sign of our relationship. It's the kind of champion he is. He came into Sky as world champion and winner of the green jersey in the Tour, yet he was still ready to sacrifice some of his results for what he thought I could achieve. What really sticks in my mind was the first time I met him after he'd signed for Sky, at the training camp in December in Majorca. I'd last seen him perhaps two months before that when he'd just won the rainbow jersey and it suddenly felt like we were still in Copenhagen. I remember talking to him about the World's. We said to each other, 'God, that was good.'

Part Two

Little By Little

CHAPTER 7

TEARING UP TRADITION

There's a stiff breeze blowing in central France as we head towards Orléans on the second stage of Paris–Nice, but I'm already on cloud nine. I'm lying 2nd overall after the prologue time trial. I was storming there, would have won quite easily, but Gustav Larsson of Sweden went off in the dry and I went off in the rain. From the moment I finished that I thought, 'Bloody hell, this is looking good.' We know the race is going to split in the crosswind at some point today, so this stage is about sustained vigilance. I have to keep my eyes open and not get caught if it happens.

Sure enough, not long after the feed, the gaps begin to open at the front. We've got about 100km to race, we're on a typical French *route nationale*, dead straight, with trees perfectly spaced every 20m, and a farm building every couple of kilometres. Vacansoleil are the team who commit first, driving at the front. Almost the whole peloton goes into the left-hand gutter to try and keep out of the wind. As most of the guys immediately dive left, those who've got the strength try and go into the wind down the right to get into the first group. There are about twenty or twenty-five pulling clear, the next echelon not closing on them. If I want to win Paris–Nice, I need to be in that front group. I'm about forty riders back; I'd rather go up the outside even if I'm fighting against the wind, it's better than trying to hide in a wheel. I go right to find the open road.

I'm sprinting up to the back of the front group, across the gap to the back of the line; keep looking at those wheels a few yards in front of me, and that's it, I'm there. Next up, Tom Boonen appears; he's come from twice as far back in the main bunch as me. I can't help thinking, 'Bloody hell, Tom's going well,' and sure enough, he wins the stage, then goes on to land a bunch of Classics later in the spring. It's not easy at first in the group; in fact it feels really hard for twenty minutes as my body recovers from the effort I've just made. But I'm where I need to be.

On a windy day, once you're in the front group it's simple, it's making it there that's the hardest bit. When you're in the lead group it's just a case of going through and doing your bit, team time trialling the last 100km. G has made it as well, and then I know: with his help I'm going to take the leader's jersey. I'm not thinking about the stage win, I'm just keen to contribute to the work and drive the group if need be. I know I'm going well, better than most, when I pull off after a turn at the front of the line and no one is there to come through, in fact there's a gap behind me, even though I haven't been pushing myself flat out.

The last intermediate sprint comes up, and I get myself in the right place to start sprinting for it; I don't quite know why. Whether I get that sprint or not, I can take the jersey at the end of the stage, and there is still the time trial up the Col d'Eze to come on the last day. That's six stages away, but it's my insurance policy. The sprint comes into view; no one else is going for it, so I give it a push, and that's a useful two-second time bonus in the bag. I was wondering how I'd sprint after all that explosive training this winter, to develop the top-end power for the climbs when the guys like Contador attack. Now I know. I feel confident, with good reason. The winter I've had, the tests I've been doing, the numbers we've been crunching: everything has been telling Shane, Tim and me that my form is better than it has ever been. But we're working towards July. I haven't peaked for Paris–Nice. This is all part of the process. After all, I'm still in a building phase.

The 'Race to the Sun' was where the winning streak of 2012 began, but the process of getting there started five months earlier, on 1 November 2011. After the world championships in Copenhagen, I took five weeks off. I didn't ride my bike: I worked in the gym a little, did a bit of walking with the dogs, didn't drink loads of beer and only put on a couple of kilos, which wasn't a huge amount. On 1 November I was ready to train and it was no effort: first week fifteen hours' riding; second week, eighteen hours; third week, twenty-one. Before I knew it, we'd got to Christmas and I'd put in nine weeks of good, consistent, on-the-ball training. Sky went to Majorca the week before Christmas for the team training camp and I turned the wick up a bit: forty hours in seven days out there, six hours a day with Eddie Boasson Hagen. For someone who works in an office, that's like pedalling every hour of the working day. It's not the kind of week you can do off the cuff; you have to build into it, which was what I had been doing over the previous six weeks.

I didn't just spend that winter on the bike. I made sure to be in the gym three days a week from 6 a.m., working to a strength programme devised for me by Mark Simpson, British Cycling's conditioning coach at the time. One of the things that had been flagged up at the Vuelta, specifically at the climb of the Angliru, was that because I'd broken my collarbone, my left arm was very weak. That meant I couldn't work hard enough when climbing out of the saddle. All-round, I didn't have enough upper-body strength to deal with the steepest climbs. It's always been known that steep climbs aren't for me; I struggle on them.

Tim and Shane's view was that at some point I was going to have to perform on those climbs if I wanted to win the biggest race. My answer was that I've never been great at it; my core strength has never been that fantastic; my upper-body strength has been poor at times and I've never worked on it. I had always been known for my good pedalling speed on the track, but to perform on some of these steep climbs, you have to work on your power and your torque, producing that power at a lower cadence. That was why we had started looking into torque sessions for time trialling, and that was why I had to get to the gym. It was not only to get the power back in my left arm but also just to increase my general physical fitness and strength. I had to do it without bulking up, without ending up looking like a panel beater, becoming stronger physically without putting any muscle on. I felt a huge difference straight away.

The gym work was a classic case of the three of us working out where I had a weakness and refusing to be reconciled to it. A lot of athletes will simply accept that they aren't so good in certain areas rather than trying to do anything about it. You can't just say for the rest of your career, 'Well, actually, you know what? I'm not that good at climbing.' If that's the case you have to work on climbing. The art is to work on your weak areas without losing what you're good at, and that's very much what we achieved in 2012. Personally, I used to really struggle when the climbers started attacking at the foot of a mountain. I lacked the explosive power to deal with it. That and my lack of power on the steep climbs; these are all weaknesses you show in public – 'Ah Brad, he likes a consistent pace on these climbs, he does struggle when they start attacking.' They're things that everyone knows about, so why not deal with them?

This change in attitude came partly from Tim asking all his questions as a non-cyclist coming in from another sport. Cycling is very traditional and set in its ways about how you train. Since I was a kid it had always been the same: cyclists had October and November off, we would start training on 1 December, and that would be runs to café stops – the social side of cycling – using fixed wheel if need be. On 1 January you up the miles and intensity a little; you start doing longer rides to cafés, sprinting for road signs. In February and March you enter your first races; you know it's going to be bloody hard to blow out the cobwebs. It's always been the same. That is the tradition of cycling. Tim came along and asked why we didn't train at the same high level for twelve months of the year. Swimmers do it and rowers do it. People in cycling say you shouldn't be doing interval training in December, you'll be blown out by July. Why? It's just tradition.

The attitude I took to my training had changed significantly as well. I specifically said to Shane and Tim at the end of 2011, 'I don't care what you ask me to do, I have a lot of faith in you because we've come on a lot this year, I just want to win the Tour de France.' I told them that I didn't know how long I would be able to go on training for the Tour and living the life it demands. It's too intense and it takes too big a toll on your life and on everyone else around you. I felt I was willing to give it a shot in 2012 because I had a decent chance to win the Tour and I might never win it again. This might be my one opportunity.

I'd always led my programmes in the past; I had always said I want to win this, I want to win that, win this prologue time trial here because it gives me a bit of security if the main event goes wrong. For 2012 I told them, sod it, I want to win the Tour, I'm the gerbil on the wheel. I want to be uncompromising, so you guys write down what you think. You work out the training programme; you know I trust you, just do it.

Using TrainingPeaks, Tim would work out my training for the day – times, power outputs, cadences – he would upload it, and I would get a notification telling me to go and read it in an email. It's a far cry from the mileage chart that they used to print on the *Cycling Weekly* centre-spread at Christmas every year, which I coloured in religiously until I was about sixteen.

So the schedules came in, week by week. I just did exactly what I was asked, then each day I downloaded the SRM file from the box on the handlebars – the little computer that records power output from our cranks, pulse rate, cadence and so on – and put it into TrainingPeaks for Tim to look at. For once I wasn't interested in the details. I had 100 per cent faith in what Tim and Shane put down on paper. I gave them total responsibility. That in turn made them think about it, and that is where a lot of my faith in them came from. I knew that they had put a lot of brainpower into it; they hadn't just written it up sitting on the toilet.

In the midst of all that we came up with a race programme as well. I remember sitting in the office in Manchester with Tim next to me, saying, 'You know, I think I can train harder than I race sometimes.' It was something that we'd realised the previous August when I rode well in the Vuelta after six weeks with no racing. That's why I decided to race less in 2012. We decided to include two Tenerife training blocks because training there had worked so well in 2011; that took up four weeks, because they have to be at the right times and there are only so many times in a year you can go there. We worked back from the Tour. We considered doing the Tour of Switzerland but I wanted to go back to the Dauphiné. That's a race I really like; after it there is a nice gap up to the Tour, so you can tweak things if you need to. Before the Dauphiné there was Tenerife; before that camp I liked the idea of going to the Tour of Romandie. I hadn't been to Romandie for a few years; it normally comes down to the time trials. I could probably win those so would have a good chance. Before that we had originally put in the Tour of the Basque Country, but I said I would rather go and do another training camp in Tenerife, so we did that before Romandie; before that was the Tour of Catalonia, Paris–Nice and the Tour of Algarve.

So then they said, what are your goals in those races? Working from the start, at Algarve the aim was to play a team role but try and win the time trial; as for Paris–Nice I said, 'Well, I was 3rd last year. I'd really like to have a crack at that and go for the overall classification because the last few days finish with a time trial so I've got a good chance of placing well or maybe winning that, so I'll accept responsibility as leader.' At Catalonia I wanted to play a team role again; Romandie I wanted to win; Dauphiné as well. Those were the goals for the year.

One of the biggest things for us was to move away from the cycling tradition of racing yourself fit, riding races purely as training. So going to those races, and taking the responsibility as leader was part of the process; race practice, you could call it. Paris–Nice, Romandie and Dauphiné are all only five, six or seven days long, so it's not as if you've got to lead for three weeks each time. The idea was to go to those races, perform, treat each one as if it were a Tour de France in miniature, lead the race and get the team around me to do the job as they would in the Tour. When it came to July, getting it right would not be just a matter of being in perfect form; it was as much about leading the team and getting used to leading overall and all that went with it. It was also important not to disrupt the build-up for the Tour; what that meant was that, although I might have only been at Paris–Nice at 95 per cent of the form I went to the Tour in, we still went there as if I was at 100 per cent and raced with that.

At Algarve I won the time trial – by less than a second – from Tony Martin; Richie Porte from Sky won the overall, and I was 3rd. It was key to help the other guys like Richie and Eddie win in their own right. Their sacrifice was going to be a huge part of me winning the Tour de France. The competitive part of me wanted to race for the win in the Algarve but I had to think of the bigger picture. If I said I was in a team role, I had to act like it; my teammates had to realise that if I said I would ride in a certain way, that's what I would do. I had had a great winter, starting training early on, so I was still in better form than most of my rivals, even though I was still building, gradually, towards the Tour. It's not as if I was winning those races by minutes – I was winning by a few seconds, certainly at Paris–Nice and the Tour of Romandie. I kept telling people, 'You don't realise what's still to come, this is just the start of it.'

Paris–Nice was more than just a physical test. There were other things that I was worried about more than the climbing and the time trials. The route wasn't the problem; the issue was that I really struggle in cold weather, and on some days, like the fifth stage to Mende, it didn't get above zero all day. Simply staying warm enough so that I didn't crack was a bigger challenge than the physical demands of racing. The cold and wet is something I've always struggled with. I've no idea why. Some people prefer it but I find it affects my legs more than anything; once they go cold, or they get wet from the rain, they just shut down.

Paris–Nice was everything to me at the time. I was racing for those six or seven days with no thought about the Tour. Once we were in the race there was never any question of thinking, 'Whatever happens here, if it goes wrong, it doesn't matter because we're training for July.' I wanted to win Paris–Nice that week, and that was that. I thought, 'All this crap about saving it and not showing your aces too early, you could still be in the same position physically, not show the world how you are, yet you've still got to manage that form on the first of July, so why not just race and try to win?'

At Paris–Nice I was in slightly different form compared to the Tour. I was still two or three kilos over the weight I wanted to be in July; that gave me a little more explosive-ness, and the weight I was at that time was good for the weather. Having the extra kilos on meant I wasn't getting as cold and it didn't matter because we didn't have to go up climbs for thirty, forty, fifty minutes on end. The Paris–Nice climbs were more explosive, short, 2 or 3km like the one at Mende.

As usual in a stage race, once I'd got the lead it was just a matter of going day by day, the team taking the strain, then I was finishing it off at the end; keeping in touch on the bunch finishes, hanging in on the big climb at the end of the stage to Mende. Perhaps what I didn't expect was having to answer so many questions about what I was doing. Time after time I was asked whether I had peaked too early; time after time I had to explain it all. Trying to convince people how we were going about it turned out to be harder than the race itself. It really was a strain. It felt like dealing with a five-year-old, telling them why they can't go in the garden when it's raining. It was like talking to someone who doesn't speak your language and you don't speak theirs, and you're trying to ask how to get to the toilet, 'le toilet?' I was continually trying to explain that we were training for July and it was possible to race to a high level all year, but it was like talking to a brick wall at times.

What wins you the Tour is all the work you put in over the whole year, all the background training. That is what allows you to be at your best for twenty-one days in July without having one bad day. Over the course of the season, there is not a huge difference in power output; what changes is that your weight goes down gradually, but most of all you improve your ability to maintain that power one day after another. In March, you might have that form for one day, or a few days, but you wouldn't be able to manage to go out on a time trial like the one from Bonneville to Chartres after three weeks of racing and produce the kind of power I managed there for an hour and five minutes. That's the difference.

It wasn't as if I had 50 watts more in me in July than I had at Paris–Nice. It's more marginal than that, because to win Paris–Nice you still have to be bloody good. Winning something like that would be the peak in most people's seasons. It's not as if I won it at 80 per cent. I probably raced the Tour de France in 2009 at the form I was at in Paris–Nice in 2012; I might have been good enough to come 4th in the Tour in the shape I had there, but obviously it's that last 5 per cent that's going to push you on to the podium in the Tour. So at Paris–Nice I was in bloody good form, at 95, 96, 97 per cent, but that last few per cent is going to come from the fine-tuning, the last bit of weight loss, being acclimatised to altitude, being acclimatised to the heat. That's what gives you the ability to race day after day for three weeks: the seven, eight months of training before it. It's such a different way compared to how we used to do it. Rather than starting the season in a really bad place, overweight, then building all the way through, I started at about 95 per cent.

I only competed in five races before the Tour in 2012, so it was not as if I was racing week in week out. I raced Paris–Nice, we had a week off, then we went to Catalonia; there it was just a case of riding the race and letting the mountainous terrain give me a workout. This should have been a classic example of using a race as training, but it went belly up when the final stages were snowed off. So I went home, Tim devised three tough six-hour rides, and I ended up putting in more work than my teammates did that weekend racing in the Critérium International on the hilly roads in Corsica. Then we had four weeks left until Romandie. We went away, did an altitude camp, so by the time I got back to Romandie I was ready to go again. Romandie is five days' work, then it's all over, and after that we had five weeks to the Dauphiné. Critically, it was not as if I was going from one race straight to the next, burning my mental reserves up as I did so.

The idea of racing yourself fit is a curious one. What Tim identified is that when you race a lot, there are times when you don't work your body hard enough. You de-train. The trouble with racing is that sometimes mentally you can't be bothered to compete so you just sit in the peloton and it becomes a way of getting the hours in, cruising along. It can end up a bit like sitting on the rollers.

That's even the case in the Tour. The first few days of the Tour should be relatively easy, sitting in the peloton for 200km in a flat stage. If there's a wind or bad weather that changes it, but the first 200km you're just sitting in, chatting with your mates. It's the last 50km that are bloody hard because you have to stay in position, the speed goes up massively, and by the end of the stage when they download the SRM boxes from your handlebars you learn that you've only averaged 190 watts for the day. You could go out and do a five-hour training ride harder than that.

That is precisely why at Sky we still did some bloody hard rides up to five days out from the Tour, rather than backing off for two weeks beforehand. Tim was saying that you could get to a point ten days into the Tour and find that all of a sudden you haven't trained really hard for a month so you've de-trained before you hit the mountains. That means that when you start making those really intense efforts it comes as a massive shock to the system. If you were in the last week before the World Road Race Championships, three days out you'd go and do a big effort, a big ride.

Clearly, we got our preparation for the Tour spot on, but what made all the difference was having people like Tim in the background, asking those questions. Building up to the Tour was about defying tradition, not being scared to try out new ideas. I think we were vocal about this in the first year of Sky, when we were determined that this was what we were going to do. That was always Dave Brailsford's goal for the team: changing the way we think, defying received ideas, asking why's it always been done like this. The most obvious example, and the simplest one, is warming down at the end of the stage. How many teams are doing that now? But when we started warming down in 2011 everyone laughed: 'What are they doing? Look at them idiots.' But it makes total sense: you warm up, so why not warm down? At times the overall philosophy didn't work, or we started to look stupid, but we are still sticking with it, and we are still learning from our mistakes. The difference is that now it's all working and people are praising Dave and everyone else. I think we're setting a precedent for how it's done in the future.

Another radical change in the way we built up to the Tour was our two-week training camps at altitude in Tenerife, staying at the Hotel Parador on top of Mount Teide, the volcano in the middle of the island. We did one camp in April, but the second one in mid–late May six weeks before the Tour was probably the most important. Quite a lot of Tour de France mountain stages finish high up so the main goal was to be able to perform at altitude without any drop-off in power. Another massive plus of Tenerife was that we were pretty secluded, with no distractions and nobody about. That meant we could get the work done – plenty of climbing, key blocks of specific training – and sleep every other hour. It was ideal.

The altitude training dated back to the big rethink of 2010. Tim's view was that in that Tour I had been really struggling with the altitude, especially whenever the race went over 1,600m, which he calculated was eleven times. He said, 'We've got to train for altitude', but he was also asking the question: 'What do we need to do at altitude? If we're going there for two weeks we've got to know what we're doing.' So Tim went to Tenerife in January 2011 to check the place out. He went around all the roads, looked into how other people were training at altitude, and came up with plans of what he thought we should do. He really did his homework. We went there straight after the Tour of Romandie in 2011, did two weeks and realised we'd latched on to something. We felt we had to do it again in 2012, more and better, so we planned two camps. We had gone to Sestriere in 2011, up in the Alps on the border between Italy and France. That didn't work out so well, because the weather doesn't tend to be as good as in Tenerife and you have no choice but to ride down from the resort to train. In Tenerife you can do a two- or three-hour ride at 2,000m, if that's what the trainers feel you need.

From each camp we did at altitude, we seemed to be getting a bit more information to make the next one better. There is a difference between training at altitude, which can be pretty damaging, and acclimatisation to altitude, where you just let your body adapt to the thinner air. There is a well-known benefit from being at altitude: as your body adapts, it naturally produces more red blood cells, increasing your body's capacity to carry oxygen to the muscles and improving your performance that way. This is what most people think of as 'altitude training', but this wasn't our goal. What we wanted to do in 2012, with the core of the Tour team at those camps, was acclimatise; get our bodies used to performing in that thin air so that we would all be able to do it at the Tour.

The toughest thing with training at altitude is getting the right balance: Tim had decided that the issue was doing enough work to get an improvement in performance, but without overdoing it, given the demands altitude makes on the body. You can't fail to get the efforts in when you're in Tenerife because the climbs up to Mount Teide last for a minimum of 30km: a camp like this is where you always do the hardest work of the year, because there is no compromise when you are away from home, it's just you, your teammates, and the trainers. As for acclimatisation, just being there and sleeping there is enough. We ended up training mainly on the roads down below, then riding up to the hotel again. We didn't stay up on the top and train hard at 2,000m because that's quite damaging to the body as your system fights to work hard in spite of the thin air; that's probably the most destructive way of training because, in addition to the effort, you are taking more time to recover due to sleeping at altitude. But if we had an easy hour or two on a rest day, we didn't bother going down.

The goal in the plan was to do 100,000m of climbing between March and June. That sums up that period. If you worked it out it was about 10,000m a week – a little bit more than the equivalent of going from sea level to the top of Everest. It was clear that if I was going to win the Tour I was going to have to do a lot of climbing, so at first just going up the hills would help in itself, but later on the work I had to do on those climbs was very specific. In Tenerife in April, between Paris–Nice and Romandie, we were doing five or six hours a day, just putting in a lot of mid-range effort. It's the kind of climbing you'll do on the Tour on the first climb of the day when a team is riding tempo on the front and there are three *cols* to go. We were putting down a big fitness base so that when we came to Tenerife the second time, we were even fitter, so we could tolerate doing the really high-workload stuff. At the second camp, in the big, intense sessions, we might do as much as an hour and a half of threshold, working at the point where your body is producing lactate as fast as it can process it – in other words, the point where if you go any harder you crack rapidly. That would all be on climbs: pure hard work.

The critical thing is that I couldn't have done any of this without all the background training going back to November. Everything I did from then onwards was building on that foundation, with the workload continually getting longer and more intense; that meant when I got to Tenerife in late May I was able to train so hard that I could not only finish the efforts, but I didn't dig myself into such a hole that I needed a week off when I got back. That is part of the philosophy that swimmers train to: daily grind. It's bloody hard work.

After one of those rides we do in Tenerife you feel incredible satisfaction: that's another day in the bank. To take one day in the second camp as an example, I was doing the last effort, we'd done five and a half hours, the average temperature had been thirty-five degrees all day. We got to the last climb, we'd done 4,000m of climbing, we had one more twenty-five-minute effort to go, and three of the guys were wasted – Froomie, Richie Porte and Christian Knees – they couldn't do the last effort so they rode up the climb to get home. Me, Mick Rogers and Kosta Siutsou did the last effort; those are the moments when you realise, if I can do this one now, that's the Tour winner. We used to get days like that on the track where that's the difference: whether you can do that effort or not.

The last stint we did was twenty-five minutes, starting at 1,500m altitude and going to 2,200. We would ride one minute at 550 watts, basically prologue power, which you can sustain for a few minutes, then four minutes at threshold torque – 50rpm at threshold, maybe 400–440 watts depending on the altitude, which is bloody hard to do because riding in the big ring, say a 53x16 gear, at threshold on a climb is like going up a steep hill in your car with your foot to the floor in fourth – then down to the little ring to start again and do 550 watts for one minute. So five sets of five minutes, alternating normal cadence and high power for a minute, low cadence and threshold power for four. We'd already done five and a half hours, one hour at threshold, so the last five minutes is horrible; you're at 2,000m, you can hardly breathe but you realise that in the Tour you will be glad you've put yourself through this.

It's hard to put into layman's terms how you feel. It's a nice way of being wasted. When you are fit and your form is great those efforts are hard in a very sweet way. Sometimes you haven't got the form and you are suffering, but if you are hurting when the form's good, it can be an incredible feeling. When you are getting dropped in a race it's horrible, a lot of people who ride *sportives* and so on would be able to relate to that. But when you are off the front as I was in Paris–Nice that March or leading a time trial, it's a different kind of pain altogether. At the top end it's a very sweet pain. It's mixed with the endorphins you get from the effort; it's what makes you able to push even harder. I've been at both ends of the spectrum.

I quite like the boredom when we're on camp in Tenerife. It's quite peaceful, and when you're training that hard it's nice to come back and not have any distraction. There's no sitting on the Internet and we haven't got Sky television in the room so you find yourself doing the most basic things: reading a book or watching DVDs. We tend to watch a lot of films and that's about it really. You're living like a monk. It's not even somewhere you could bring the family as there is nothing for them to do. You feel you are doing something that no one else is doing. It's the most extreme thing and I like that too, the sacrifice of it. Training to win the Tour takes a lot of sacrifice in all our lives – by the other team members, but most of all by my family. You get to a point in your career – I had it with the track – where you tell yourself you are no longer going to compromise. I didn't want to look back in ten years' time and wonder what I might have achieved. I don't want to have any regrets.

CHAPTER 8

THE MIDAS TOUCH

At the Tour of Romandie I couldn't help feeling that something special might be on its way. I was growing in confidence. At times, what was happening seemed almost too good to be true. There were days on those roads on the west side of Switzerland in late April when everything I touched seemed to turn to gold. Sometimes I felt as if I could do no wrong. It was a feeling I had never had before. I had sensed it at times on the track maybe, at an Olympic Games or a World's, but had never come anywhere near it when competing on the road, not even in 2009. I was starting to feel almost untouchable.

Romandie began well for us when Geraint Thomas used his pursuit skills to win the prologue; again I was a victim of the weather. It started raining ten minutes before I got to the start line, and I finished 11th. Without that, I'd have been very close to G, so from that moment on I knew I was in bloody good shape. I actually suspected it from the days after

I'd come back from altitude training. The first stage was when eyebrows were raised as I managed something I hadn't achieved since I was an amateur: a bunch sprint win.

That day into La Chaux-de-Fonds was a tough stage. We went up some decent climbs in the finale and it whittled the group down quite a bit. There weren't many bodies left at the end. I had a little bit of swagger about me, a feeling that, 'Yeah, I'm here to win the race', so I put the boys on the front early on to ride tempo behind the break. When a team does that it's always a statement of intent – 'We're going to take responsibility and try to win this.' Ultimately, it was our *directeur sportif* Sean Yates's decision to take control, but it was also an example of how I was beginning to ride like a leader: I put my hand up, saying, 'I want to win it, I will take the responsibility.' In doing that, there's a thought process you have to go through. You think, 'Right, the break's up the road, BMC aren't going to ride because Cadel Evans has said he's not here to win the race, there are no other big sprinters here, so we're going to have to take it on, and we're going to have to ride.' You think: 'I'm quite happy with that, let's do it.'

We lost Cav over the climbs, so he wasn't there to go for the sprint finish. After we got over the penultimate little hill with about 20km to go, I punctured; there were a few attacks while I was getting a wheel change, which meant that as well as the adrenaline you get after a chase through the support cars, I had the hump a little bit when I got back to the front. As soon as we came back, we hit another climb, then another descent; I lost all my teammates, which left me alone with about 15km to go, so I ended up closing gaps on my own. That all made it a really tough finale. The peloton lined up for the stage finish with about 3km to go; I was about fourth wheel behind a little train from Rabobank, sitting there expecting to be swamped by whichever team was going to lead out the sprint. We got a little closer in; nothing had happened. Liquigas went over the top with about a kilometre and a half to go, so I swerved right and got on to their train. Everyone was just pinned to the wheels because it had been such a hard ride through the stage; we got into the final kilometre, no one came past, so I thought, 'Sod it, I'm going.' I put my foot down at 500m from the line, just went as hard as I could, and no one came round. That was that: it was a good ten years since I'd won a race in that way. It didn't happen entirely by chance: I'd led out Rigoberto Urán in one stage of the Tour of Catalonia, a few guys came past me and I ended up 16th; since that stage I'd been thinking I should have just gone for it.

The win earned me a useful time bonus that, together with the fact that G had dropped out of the lead group, put me in the leader's jersey for day two. That was pretty satisfying, but there was more to it than that. I was surprised at the win. I knew I was fast enough to win a sprint, I knew I had the length for it – it was about a 20sec push, and in training we do up to a minute in those efforts – but I was amazed that having led out for so long no one came round me. I'd won Paris–Nice, gone away, trained, come back, won the first stage in a sprint finish; it was all too good to be true. I was really happy. The press were wondering where it had come from, but I was surprised people didn't realise I had that kind of speed in me from racing on the track. After all, that was the same kind of flat-out effort I would make when we were full on in a Madison and I was going for a lap gain, as I did with Rob Hayles in Athens and Cav at Manchester in the 2008 world championships.

It was a new experience. I'd never won a road stage at a major race. I was always expected to do the business in the time trials. Generally, I can't stand bunch sprints. I'm one for racing in a straight line – which is funny, because on the track in a Madison I find it easy to manoeuvre. But when you win in that fashion there's an element of adrenaline, a real rush, because it all happens so quickly. You don't know you're going to win until a few metres before the line, whereas in a time trial you've got a long time to think, 'I'm going to win this, I'm still the fastest time, I'm going to win this.' In that one, the cut-and-thrust meant I had much more of the feeling of racing my bike; the race was on for the last 20 or 30km, and I won it. It felt like being a junior again.

There were other things to take home from Romandie. This was the only race that Mark Cavendish and I would ride before the Tour de France, so it should have been a test outing to see how we worked together. It didn't quite end up like that, because it was an extremely hilly Tour and there was no stage flat enough to be a sprint finish for Mark. He was struggling a bit at that time – he was training hard for the Giro so he came to the race quite tired – and he had a tough time in the hills.

However, there's always teamwork to be done. The duties

for our team riders, the *domestiques*, include carrying bottles for everyone from the team car, carrying clothing to and fro as the weather changes or the race hots up, waiting for the leader when he punctures or stops for a piss, or simply sitting at the head of the peloton, forming a 'train' together to keep the pace high. The first day I had the yellow jersey, Mark wanted to work with the rest, in spite of the fact that he was wearing the rainbow stripes as world champion. So he came up with bottles first, then he started riding on the front with the other guys. I went up to Graham Watson, the photographer who is always in among us on his motorbike at the races, and I said, 'Got to get a picture of this, Graham, I want to show the kids one day, the world champion riding for me.'

Romandie was Sky's best performance as a unit in any stage race since we had started out as a team. There was one point where I was sitting in the line, watching Richie Porte, Mick Rogers, Cav and G driving along ahead of me. The quality of the riders helping me out made me look twice: a triple world time trial champion, an Olympic track champion, the world road race champion, and one of the best young cyclists Australia could produce; all up there, all on the front, all putting their necks on the line for me. As a team, we dominated all week; G won the prologue, I won two stages, and Richie and Mick finished 3rd and 5th overall behind me.

The five days were a good test for a rider preparing to go for the overall at the Tour de France: an uphill time trial, a prologue and some hilly stages. It wasn't just a matter of putting the team on the front and controlling it; I had to nail the final time trial as well to regain the lead from Luis León Sánchez of Rabobank, who had won the penultimate stage to take the jersey from me. The time trial was 16.5km around the resort of Crans-Montana, but it wasn't flat. On paper I had a good chance of taking back the 10sec I needed to win overall, but nothing can be taken for granted. The climb up towards the finish was a tough one, and my chain came off at the bottom, as I shifted from the big chain ring to the little one to get into a lower gear. I tried to flick the chain back on by hand, but it wouldn't go, so I had to stop and let the mechanic do it. In the past I'd have lost my temper and bunged the bike into the ravine by the road, but this was different. In 2009 at the World Time Trial Championship in Switzerland exactly the same thing happened: my chain went and I chucked the bike away in disgust. Here, I remember thinking, 'This could happen in the Tour, deal with it.' So I did; I went on to beat Luis León by 1min23sec, which is a big margin in 16.5km, and it earned me my second major stage race of the season.

It was a bit like the first stage I won; I punctured, a few guys in the field were attacking while I was getting the wheel changed; I may have been annoyed but I didn't start blaming anyone. I came back and got on to the front, and thought, 'Right: I'm going to win this stage.' That wasn't a conscious thing; it just happened and I dealt with it. In those situations it's not as if you are expecting an incident of this kind, thinking, 'Right, if this happens I'm going to count to ten.' You just deal with it on the spur of the moment; it's not rehearsed. Both those little events were unexpected, and you either react to them in the way that I did, or you lose it. And that's a mind-set, a pathway. Keeping an eye on the bigger picture shows your focus and confidence. There's a bit of everything happening as you gain maturity as a leader. Age comes into it, a sense of security as well, but there's an element of taking responsibility for everything you do. After the work the team had done, paying them back by throwing my bike on the ground wouldn't have gone down well. The chain derailing was a small incident at the time but, looking back, it seems like a significant milestone.

During all the races that I won, there was no huge adulation from those around me. There were no great big pats on the back from Tim and Shane. Shane would always say, 'Good job that, this week you need to look after yourself, you know you need to do this that or the other,' and Tim would just say, 'Good job, Brad', and that would be it. There was no stating that this was a landmark, no sense of what a huge milestone one particular win or another might be. It's amazing to think now, but at the time it all seemed as if it was meant to be. That time trial was typical. I remember finishing it and expecting Tim and the others to be saying, 'Bloody hell, that's good', but it wasn't like that.

After that time trial, I said something to Tim about how I could have done without the chain coming off, and his answer was, 'Well, you've got to give them a bit of a chance.' There was no big deal made of any of the wins; it all just felt as if it was meant to be. It was like being in a football team in mid-season: great victory, but we're playing Manchester United next week. If you compare my cycling season to winning the Premiership, getting to 22 July in the yellow jersey was the equivalent of hitting the end of May with 100 points to Manchester United's 95. If you beat Chelsea along the way that's fantastic, but you don't dwell on it. You go on to the next one. It's only when you look back that you think, 'Bloody hell, that was good.'

I was pretty tired after Romandie. We'd had a massive April; we'd done a lot of hours, and I had had only five days at home to recover before we travelled there. As a result, I didn't feel great in Switzerland even though it went so well. I wasn't comfortable and had to dig deep at times, for example to win that first road stage. I'm not used to being out of my comfort zone like that. But that was the plan: the early season wasn't about winning Romandie, it was about building to be at my best at the Tour. So Romandie was part of the workload; the good thing was that, in spite of the fatigue, we still won the race. It showed how far we had moved on.

I had a massive downer after Romandie. I felt like packing it all in, simply because I looked at Twitter for the first time in a long while. While social media is a great way to keep in touch on the net, it has a downside that most people in the public eye experience: users can say pretty much whatever they like about you under the cover of a pseudonym. They can target you, but you don't know who they are. It was about this time that a group of people 'out there' began making insinuations about drugs. What was being said made me begin to think, 'What I'm doing at the moment, I'm quite dominant here; I'm winning bunch sprints and it does look a bit suspicious, I guess.' I started thinking that I didn't want to win the Dauphiné Libéré, because if I did win it they would say that I was doping for sure. Then I began thinking: imagine if I win the Tour – what will they come up with then? I started saying to Cath, 'Forget this, I can't be bothered. I don't want to win the Tour because I can see what's coming.' So I had a week off the bike after Romandie. I spoke to Shane; he got pretty annoyed and said to me – among other things – 'You have just got to ignore those people.' I said, 'Yeah, but I'm human. I can't just take it on the chin all of the time.'

I spent a week in Majorca with the family, and started riding my bike a bit, and then I went to Tenerife. I hadn't done much for two weeks and I had begun to feel really guilty. When I got there, I thought, 'It's been so perfect up to now; perhaps this is when I'm going to lose the Tour.' It was hard to deal with at the time, and I spoke to Tim about it. Tim's view was, 'You're gonna get this, you're gonna get this.'

When that little crisis came I didn't deal with it by taking to drink or anything like that – that was a phase I'd gone through back in 2004 and it was very much a phase. Instead I immersed myself in time with the family. As usual it was Cath who took the brunt of it. She's on Twitter, so she's vulnerable – people think they can have a go at her too. And at home my being unhappy and angry impacts on her, so it's a big strain. We began to realise that it was part of dealing with success. You don't expect it but there is a lot of other stuff that comes with winning bike races. It wasn't nice at the time, but I look back now and I think, well maybe that's part of the process, maybe it's not just about leading races but about dealing with all the other hassle that comes with it. So I thought, 'To hell with it, I'm not looking at the computer.' I got to Tenerife and I threw myself into the training there. You're cut off, you're remote and that is probably the best environment. You're among like-minded people and you get down to business again.

That period in Tenerife at the end of May was the last big spell of work we were going to put in before July and the Tour. We were doing back-to-back days of heavy training, putting in six-hour rides, climbing at specific power outputs, working hard all round. We then had nine days until the Dauphiné to back off and freshen up, to let the training work through. Six weeks was still a long time until the Tour, but in terms of building a base, which we had been doing since the start of November 2011, those two weeks in Tenerife at the end of May were the last big block of work we could do, because of the time it takes for the work to be absorbed. During that fortnight our workload was getting on for the equivalent of fourteen days' racing at the Giro or the Tour, but in controlled conditions.

The Critérium du Dauphiné, or Dauphiné Libéré as cycling traditionalists call it, was not quite like the other events I'd raced in 2012. It was the moment when the season became truly serious. We came to the start in Grenoble having done that Tenerife camp, so that was all the work done apart from fine-tuning. We all realised that now we were into the last period before the Tour. We had won Romandie and Paris–Nice; at that stage the season had been perfect and I was already the Tour favourite, but the other Tour big names for

July – Cadel Evans, Vincenzo Nibali and Andy Schleck – were all going to be riding at the Dauphiné. It was the first showdown close to the Tour where what happened really mattered. Up to that point nothing had been particularly significant because Cadel had had a different schedule; you couldn't read too much into the racing he had done. He was sure to have improved since Romandie and would be getting into his Tour form.

This all put the Dauphiné at a different level compared to the other races. At Paris–Nice or the Tour of Romandie, if something happened, no matter how disappointing it might be on the day, in the long term it didn't matter because the season was all about the Tour, whereas this was the race where you needed to show off a little bit. In addition, for the first time in my career on the road I was going back as defending champion to a stage race I had won. I certainly felt I had to step up; it felt different from the minute we started the prologue. I was last off because of being the previous year's winner, which was a different experience altogether. As had been the case in the prologues at Romandie and Paris–Nice, the conditions were changing all the time during the day. There were thunderstorms, and although I had a dry run the wind had changed quite a bit, so in the circumstances finishing 2nd by 1sec to Luke Durbridge of Australia was a good enough ride, considering he had started ninety minutes earlier than me. I'd gone considerably faster than everyone who'd started around me; as at Paris–Nice and Romandie, it was another sign that I probably would have won had I gone off with the fastest guys.

The minute I'd finished I began thinking, 'I haven't got the race leader's jersey, it's the perfect position to be in.' I did manage to take 5sec out of Cadel, who had chosen to start earlier and went out at the fastest time of the day. Ever since we all got it so wrong at the prologue of the 2010 Tour, when I went off early because we thought the weather would change, I've opted to accept the responsibility of starting last man in the team, no matter what the conditions. You accept who you are and you take what you get.

The next day was a little different: Cadel won the stage after getting away close to the end, but he wasn't far ahead and I took the jersey. It sounds strange, but I was a bit gutted. It meant the team had to ride on the front for two days more than we had wanted, and I was not keen to be wearing the jersey going into the long time trial on day five because I didn't want to have to wear the race leader's skinsuit.

That sounds fussy but it's a good example of how the smallest things can affect you when you race. As is the case in all the races run by ASO, the company that runs the Tour, Paris–Nice and most of the biggest races in France, the leader's kit is supplied by Le Coq Sportif. Their skinsuits don't suit me, because they have panels on the arms where the logo of Le Crédit Lyonnais, the race sponsor, is printed. The logo has to be printed a certain way so they put in the panel, which is stitched across the top of the biceps. I had noticed it after the Paris–Nice time trial; it's uncomfortable, because when I get into my tuck position the stitching pulls my arms and I get a lot of cuts right into the flesh. It's purely down to my body shape.

I knew that my time-trialling form was there from the prologue. I was even more certain after day five, the 42.5km *contre-la-montre* to Bourg-en-Bresse. I nearly caught Cadel, who had started two minutes ahead of me, and that felt like the first time I had really put the hammer down before the Tour. As far as the time trial itself went, it was ridiculously windy, the worst I've ever done. At times it was touch and go – I was right on the limit of being blown off. Andy Schleck did come unstuck in the wind, breaking his pelvis, which put him out of the Tour. It wasn't a shock to me that he lost control, because you didn't dare take your hands off the bars to take a drink, and there were times when you had to come off the tri-bars to keep command of the bike. I'd ridden a couple of shorter time trials, 10-milers, in horrendous winds in England – including one just before the 2009 Tour – which were good practice as it turned out.

I didn't set out to catch Cadel: I always expect to catch the rider in front of me, but that simply reflects the state of mind I have for every time trial I ride. There were some lovely long straights on the course, rolling straights on the run-in to the finish, so I knew I'd get within sight of him. I expected to be at least a minute faster than him on that day, having taken 5sec out of him in a short prologue, so to get him in sight and nearly catch him meant it was job done. I tried not to get too fixated on it though. If you were watching it, you might wonder why I didn't catch him, as I had him in sight for so long in those final kilometres. I kept to my rhythm, I didn't want to take too many risks on the corners and he finished strongly. It's not a case of thinking, 'Oh yes, I'll catch him now'; at that point you are both trying to empty the tank, you're an hour into the stage and all you can do is to ride your own race.

It was every bit as important to have beaten Tony Martin by 34sec; I'd only very rarely got past him before he became world champion in 2011; in 2012 I'd beaten him just the once, at the Tour of Algarve, but that was by milliseconds. We'd been chasing him since he had raised the bar at the World's the previous September and putting over 30sec into him meant it was paying off. There was another side to this win: I had to be careful how I dealt with beating Cadel by such a large margin. I know I'm not that good with the media, but on this occasion I may have got it right. The journalists were trying to turn our sporting rivalry into a personal battle, and they were asking me whether this was making a point or not, a big statement that I was better than the defending Tour champion. It was important to make sure I was very respectful of him in all the interviews I did. It was also vital to keep in mind that things can change: at a similar time trial in 2011 I put a fair amount of time into him, but he pulled the best time trial of his career out of the bag to win the Tour six weeks later.

After that we had only to defend the jersey. Compared to the previous year, when I had been a bundle of nerves, I was far more confident, and the team was better prepared after the training camps. The real statement for the Tour came on the second-to-last stage, a full-scale day in the Alps culminating in the Col de Joux Plane, a brute of a climb which is shorter than the usual Alpine *col* at just over seven miles, but hits one-in-nine in places. The bottom of the mountain was almost impossibly hard, with Eddie setting an incredible pace. For the first 600m I didn't drop below 500 watts. After that it was a matter of the team riding as they had done in training in Tenerife, where we had practised this: hitting a climb, three guys in front of me, each of them doing 3km as hard and as long as they're capable of, and then peeling off.

I didn't look around a lot and I remember Sean saying through the radio, 'Nibali's gone' and 'Vanendert's gone.' He was just talking me through all the riders who were going out the back as our guys set the pace, and eventually there were only eight left in the group. On those climbs you're concentrating so much, but even then the little doubts come in. You think, 'Right, what if Cadel attacks now at this pace?' but then I look back and realise I was doing 450, 460 watts, so if someone was going to attack at that pace it would have been ridiculous, they would have had to be going so hard to open even a tiny gap.

Because I was sitting in second or third wheel all the way up the climb, I never turned round. I try never to look behind on a climb, so that then all the other riders get to see is my backside. Sometimes you're sitting there thinking, 'This is getting tough', but I've been told I don't really show it when I'm on the rivet, and I guess that's a good trait to have. You don't need to assess the others: if you're feeling it then they're feeling it. It wasn't until I looked at the photos afterwards that I could see just how much the other guys were grimacing behind. I had a decent lead in the overall standings, 1min43sec on Cadel, and I knew the race was over once we got down into Morzine, because the day after should be pretty straightforward; that meant it was just a case of counting down the kilometres. On that kind of climb the pain is similar to that in a time trial, but with the difference that you have five hours in your legs when you hit the climb so there's a bit more fatigue in there. It's not easy, it's not painless, but with the team in control it's pretty businesslike.

As I've often said, I know my cycling history. I've always been into it, since I was a teenager watching videos of the Tour de France rather than doing my homework. So the night I won the Dauphiné, I asked the journalists in the press conference a question: who was the last winner of Paris–Nice and Dauphiné in the same year. A lad from *l'Equipe* called Alex said it was Eddy Merckx. I smiled straight away; it was Eddy, and before him Jacques Anquetil – another five-time Tour winner – and they both went on to win the Tour in the same year. I thought, the three of us now, it's a nice little club to be in.

There is so much focus on the Tour. It's the only race that the media and public really pay attention to, but I have a soft spot for those other great events that tend to be forgotten a little bit when the Tour comes round. What I love about races like the Dauphiné is their tradition: the list of winners that goes back years and years and includes a host of great champions from the past. Apart from me, the only British riders to have won it are Brian Robinson and Robert Millar; they are names you want to be up there with. No one had ever won Romandie, Paris–Nice and Dauphiné in the same year; that was a little record of mine that made me hugely proud.

Whatever happened at the Tour, I would always have those three stage-race wins.

Rather than thinking about the bigger picture, I tended to live for the here and now when I was in the races, which is one reason why I did so well in them, I think. But after the Dauphiné one part of the bigger picture became clear: we had an incredible team for the Tour and I was going to be the favourite. Everyone was saying it. I knew it. I would have to deal with it.

CHAPTER 9

THE WINGMEN

One thing that makes the Dauphiné difficult to read is the fact that there are a lot of guys in the field fighting for their Tour de France places, particularly among the French teams who leave it late to name their line-ups. Sky didn't do it that way. There wasn't that much to be decided about the team that they chose for the Tour. The core group that had trained and raced with me all year selected itself, and as a star in his own right Cav was always going to be added to that list.

There was, however, what seemed to be quite a heated debate among the selection panel – Shane, Dave, Rod, Sean Yates and Carsten – about whether or not the ninth rider should be Bernhard Eisel, Cav's right-hand man. It was tough on them and I wouldn't like to be in the position of having to do what they had to do. I stayed out of it. I felt we both deserved back-up. Cav had raced his heart out to finish the Giro, he had nearly won the points jersey, he had won three stages. I was the favourite for the Tour but I wasn't going to start making demands about who went in the team. I respected Cav, he'd respected me; I thought the best thing was just to let the selection panel decide who went.

The riders who missed out were Danny Pate, Juan Antonio Flecha and Rigoberto Urán but the issue confronting the selection panel went back to the question that had been asked when Cav was signed: could we race for both green and yellow? As the season went on it became more and more clear that I was the favourite for the Tour. It was not a done deal, but it was highly likely that if we got it right I would win overall. That left the selectors with an obvious dilemma. Bringing Cav to the Tour raised the question of who they should bring to back him up, and in the end they opted for Bernie over Danny Pate from the climbing group. But that was fine with me, Bernie and I go back ten years and he was magnificent for me throughout the Tour.

I made my intentions clear with Shane and Tim as to who I wanted around me, my key figures: there were seven of them, the core group of riders who had been with me all season.

The thirty-one-year-old MICK ROGERS was to be the team captain on the road. The tall and studious-looking Australian is a triple world time trial champion, and he has always been a bit of an idol of mine. In 1997, when we were kids, we raced the Junior World's together in South Africa; Mick won the points race, where I came 4th, and he was 2nd in the pursuit. Later on in that year he was 2nd in the World's junior time trial in San Sebastián, so as far back as that, I was thinking, 'Wow, this guy's good.' Mick turned pro at

Mapei; there was a lot of talk of him turning out to be Australia's first Tour de France winner, and he kept doing quite well in the Tour in his early years – not brilliantly, but always in the top forty. We were teammates in 2008 at T-Mobile but he was ill with glandular fever that year and then he spent two years at HTC alongside Cav, after which I was keen for him to join me at Sky. I said to Shane in the winter of 2010 that I wanted him by my side in the Tour because he's such a calming figure. He's a great team captain, very vocal, and in the 2012 Tour he called the shots on the road. He was really involved in what we did each day, always speaking up in the bus when Sean discussed strategies for the day. He's also the guy who judged the pace up the climbs, getting us to ride at what he felt was the right intensity, and he would calm us down when it began kicking off a bit and the others started attacking.

RICHIE PORTE was the other Aussie in the group. I didn't know him very well until he came to the team in 2011, although we'd raced the Giro together in 2010, when he came 7th, led the race for a couple of days and won the young rider's jersey. From day one this year when we were in the Algarve together, we just hit it off as we got to know each other better. We roomed together on the training camps in Tenerife, had the same programme all year; by the end, it was apparent that he believed I could win the Tour and he was fully behind what I wanted to do. There was no hint that he might want his own opportunity. He's just a lovely guy who I get on very well with on and off the bike. He's also a huge talent. I think he had a bit of a tough time at Saxo Bank after riding that great Giro as a first-year professional. He had a bit of a poor season the year after, played a team role for Alberto Contador when he won the Giro in 2011 – although Alberto was disqualified much later after his doping ban – and I think his confidence took a bit of a knock around that time. Richie is a phenomenal climber, and a great time triallist as well; he's been invaluable this year. At the Dauphiné he did a lot of damage on the climbs, especially on the Joux Plane at the Morzine stage. And he was good enough to win in his own right: for example, coming 1st at Algarve.

KOSTA SIUTSOU has the same devoted attitude: when he came to Sky he said to Dave, 'I just want to ride for the team – whatever you want me to do I'll do.' He's from Byelorussia, via Italy, and when we first met when I was at HighRoad in 2008, he didn't speak a word of English; he's improved to pidgin now. He's a very old-school Eastern European, likes his long five- or six-hour rides; when we were training in December in Majorca he started coming down to the gym with me at 6 a.m. and he was doing it the Russian way – squats, weights and everything. He's an incredible bike rider: he's won a stage in the Giro, and finished top ten there; he's a former under-23 world champion, and he came 16th in the Tour in 2008. A lot of team riders are super-talented athletes in their own right, but don't want the pressure of leadership; he strikes me as being like that. He's happy in the service of others as long as it brings him security and a job.

CHRISTIAN KNEES is another with a great record; he finished in the top twenty in the Tour in 2009, which is quite a result for a big lad like him. He's a double German champion, another lovely guy, and he was phenomenal in that Tour. People never really noticed how much work he did in the first week. For the first five days he was constantly riding in the wind at the front of the race. He'd be on the side of the train leading the bunch, whichever team was riding, with me in his wheel keeping out of the wind. We realised that after five days of that we simply had to give him a rest, because he was not going to make it through the Tour if he kept doing that. But we got to the first hilly stages and he was doing it again there. Christian was the man of the match in the Tour.

Another contender for that title, though, is BERNHARD EISEL. Bernie is just a joy to be around. The last couple of years he's been pigeonholed a bit into his role as head of the lead-out train, Cav's right-hand man. He is the guy who will ride early on to make sure the sprint happens for Cav. When Cav gets dropped, Bernie drops back. They go on holidays together. They're the best of friends; wherever Cav goes, Bernie will go with him.

However, Bernie is a hugely talented bike rider, a very fast sprinter and one-day Classic star, who won Gent–Wevelgem in 2010. He's another one who came out of Mapei's youth squad, like Mick, and we roomed together all through 2003 when I joined Française des Jeux as a new professional; he was in his third year. We did the Giro together that year, he came close to winning a couple of stages, and he was already up there in the Classics alongside riders like Andrea Tafi, Johan Museeuw and Peter van Petegem, which was quite something for a twenty-two-year-old kid. He lost his way for a few years with FDJ then he went to T-Mobile, found a role there, and the last few years at Columbia and HTC he's always been under Cav's wing.

Once we got into the 2012 Tour, as well as doing the job for Cav in the final kilometres of the sprint stages, Bernie seemed to have a presence when he was around that could make me feel special, like a million dollars. I could see why Cav loves him so much. It's hard to put your finger on it but, for example, on day one, we were riding to sign on in Liège and there were hordes of people trying to get there. He was behind me, but came past and said, 'I'll ride in front of you to make sure that you don't get knocked off your bike.' It's little things like that. He's just a very caring person. Throughout the three weeks of the Tour, he was always in the same good spirits every morning, always smiling, always joking, never down about anything. When we had the jersey he was constantly riding on the front. He seemed to be relishing it. He always knew what pace to ride, never panicked in any situation. Just before he was going to get dropped he'd swing over and it would look as if that was his job done, but two minutes later he'd be back up the front with nine bottles. In the first five or six days of the Tour when it was crazy at the front, he knew exactly where to ride to keep me out of trouble. He lacks confidence in himself and his own ability, which is surprising because from the outside you think he is an incredibly confident guy. I did get the impression that he was a bit insecure about his selection. I think it was Dave said that to me, that Bernie was questioning whether he was good enough to be there, whether he was just there because he's Cav's wingman, that sort of thing. It took a while for us to boost him a bit.

Although twenty-five-year-old Norwegian EDVALD BOASSON HAGEN wasn't racing with the climbing group all year, he was a rider we simply had to have with us in the Tour. I've been saying for years that Eddie is one of the most talented young bike riders of his generation if not *the* most talented. The only potential downside is that he can do everything and there is a risk that he may never end up specialising in one thing. He is capable of winning Classics, prologues and shortish time trials; he can get wins in bunch sprints like he did at the 2011 Tour in Lisieux and he can land stages from a break as he did in the last week of that Tour. On top of all that he can climb with the best of them in the mountains. We all saw what he did on the Joux Plane in the Dauphiné; in the Tour he rode the whole of the Col de la Madeleine, on the biggest day in the Alps. That's one of the toughest *cols* in the race and he is supposed to be a road sprinter. He is just phenomenal and he is an absolute gentleman off the bike. He may well be too nice at times but he is a lovely, lovely guy and invaluable.

The team had learned their lesson since my broken collarbone in the Tour the previous year, so CHRIS FROOME, the climber from Kenya, was there as back-up after his 2nd place in the Vuelta; he would step up only in an extreme case, basically if I crashed out. Chris had had such a rapid rise; he had started the Vuelta of 2011 without a contract for the following year because Sky had been ready to let him go. He had been very erratic before that Vuelta; we would feel he might be physically capable of something but then he would bomb. At times, it's been frustrating for the people around him. His performances were up and down due to the bilharzia parasite; he got on top of that in 2011 and became more consistent. Chris has got some funny stories about situations he's been in out in Kenya – people knocking him on the head and nicking his bike and so on – and he came to road cycling late so he's raw in his talent and can seem quite naive at times, or less knowledgeable about the history and culture of the sport. I remember at the end of the Vuelta in 2011 we were coming into Madrid for the finishing circuits and he came up to me and asked: 'Will Cobo attack?' You think, 'Are you serious? Why would he attack? He's got the leader's jersey.' But that lack of experience is also his strength, because he has absolutely no fear; he's not intimidated by anyone.

As the race went on we became joint leaders, because there was never a position where he had to ride hard for the team; when he did ride, it was more to distance people who were threatening him overall, such as Vincenzo Nibali. I wasn't surprised how well he went at the Tour; I knew he was capable of it.

The group had been handpicked over a couple of years to get to the point we were at in 2012. The riders we selected as climbers at the start of Sky hadn't lived up to expectations so there was a rethink after that first Tour in 2010. They started off by bringing in Mick Rogers, who'd had a great year, and

Rigoberto Urán, and slowly developed it – they were interested in Richie that year as well but couldn't get him out of Saxo Bank. It's like forming a soccer team. If someone takes over Barcelona it takes time to buy in the players you need; Manchester City is the classic case of that. It's a continual process of building. You have to be constantly looking forward rather than just sticking with the group you've got; by adding to it, you keep everyone on their toes. There have been cases where you see a team re-sign the Tour squad for two years, but people become not exactly lazy, but set in their position. If you keep adding to the team there's no complacency, it goes forward all the time, and people are always wary of their place. And that goes for me as well.

I can't say enough about the quality of what we called the climbing group within Sky; it consisted of guys who on their day were all potentially capable of challenging for a place on the podium in the Tour de France. Mick's finished top ten in the Tour and top ten in the Giro, Richie's run top ten in the Giro, Kosta as well, while Froomie had that 2nd place in the Vuelta, and maybe could have won it. All of these riders were superbly talented, which helps explain why we were so dominant in the mountains. If you put all those guys together, get most of them training and racing as a group all year, and get them committed to one cause, you end up with a dominant climbing group. It was similar with CSC when they had Frank and Andy Schleck, Carlos Sastre and Ivan Basso. A group like that feeds off each other; you create momentum, you become your own little unit. We all clicked and the core of the group had raced and trained together all year as well, which I think made a huge difference.

The climbing group's performance on the Joux Plane in the Dauphiné had highlighted the team's strength, but what it didn't reveal was the depth of the commitment they showed for the whole nine months, right up to the end of the Tour, and beyond, in some cases. Riders like Mick, Kosta, Christian and Richie in particular, as well as Froomie, had totally bought in to what I was trying to do, to win the Tour in 2012. On top of their work in the races, they accepted that trying to win the Tour meant they had to sacrifice practically their entire season as a result, just to do that for me. They would need to put the same training in as me, make those same efforts emptying the tank in Tenerife and Majorca, all to be as good as they could be just to help me. That was a massive commitment from those guys and it's something I will never forget.

It's hard to know what to say when other people show that measure of dedication to your cause. It's kind of humbling to think that they all did that for me. I know they get paid to do it, but you cannot forget that those guys are capable of winning races themselves. I'll be forever grateful for what they did and I don't think I could articulate that in an email. Just saying something like, 'Hey, guys, thanks for last month, it was fantastic' wouldn't do them justice, so it might take a while before I'm able to express my gratitude completely. It must be a little bit like when someone saves your life. I'm sure that's not the best analogy but I do wonder how you ever repay those people for what they did. Saying thank you isn't enough;

that's the way I feel about it. I guess the fact they were willing to do it is a mark of how my leadership skills have come on and I suppose in a nice way it must come down to the fact that they like me. That's a wonderful thing to feel.

CHAPTER 10

WORKING CLASS HERO

As the Tour approached, I was having similar feelings to those I remembered from before the Beijing Olympics. I really felt this could be my year. It was simply the way I'd felt all season; that was how it had been back in 2008, in the weeks leading up to the Great Britain cycling team's epic medal haul in Beijing, with my personal gold medals in the individual and team pursuits.

Four years on, there was a similar feeling of momentum gathering. There had been no upsets, no major setbacks, barely a day's training lost for any reason, which is rare when you are pushing your body hard for nine months. There had been two glitches, but they were not big ones. At Paris–Nice I had started getting a cold because of the freezing conditions there. My body just let go and when I got home it felt as if I was going to get really ill, but then I went to Catalonia and I was fine. I came back from Spain having pulled out because of the heavy snow on the hardest mountain stage, thinking,

'Shit, I'm going to miss a couple of days' racing.' Tim and Shane simply said, 'No worries, you can train harder than that.' So we put two or three days together, and I actually trained harder than I would have raced.

Shane is always saying, 'Don't make the small things into big things, and don't let the big things become small things.' What that means is that you just deal with what comes at you along the way, never getting too carried away with the highs and never getting overwhelmed by the lows. All year I had been trying to hover along in a stable state without making a big issue of anything. So everyone was saying, 'Sky look amazingly strong, with a team like that Wiggins is going to win the Tour'; but that didn't create any more pressure. I'd built up to the point where it wasn't a surprise. It wasn't news to my ears because we'd been training all year as a team to be in a position to go to the Tour as favourites. The feeling was simply that we were on track.

That didn't mean we took anything for granted. There is so much more involved in the Tour than with any other bike race. There were all the problems that could arise in the first week and there was the question of how much more Cadel might improve. That mattered because I had been close to my best in the Dauphiné. In the three weeks before I travelled to Liège to start the Tour, it was just a case of sustaining the form, dropping a tiny bit more weight, backing up a bit in the training and letting the effect of all the work come through. During the Dauphiné we still hadn't seen the effects of the last training camp in Tenerife. Clearly I was in the ballpark and we'd done all the work; I had got the team I needed around me, and that meant we were in a position to win the Tour de France. But we were all too well aware of what had happened in 2011. I couldn't just sit in the bunch and wait until the mountains and assume it would all go perfectly.

Before the Tour, eight or nine days out, I had to do a big media day while I was putting in my last training in Majorca. At a time like that, I see those things as just getting in my way. I had five and a half hours' riding to do that day in the mountains, and we had to start the press conference at lunchtime, so I had to go out at 7 a.m. and do my training. I was on the go for twelve hours, speaking to what seemed like every man and his dog: the BBC, Sky, Sky Sports, ITV, l'Equipe and two teleconferences for the newspapers. I was out of the hotel at 6.45 a.m., with five or six camera crews following me, got back at 1.30 and was full-on until 7 p.m. with interviews. Then the next morning I was down at the beach at 8 a.m. doing a photo shoot for l'Equipe.

But I was very confident. All the data was suggesting I was in a great place, the family were in Majorca with me and I was really enjoying it. Shane is very good at preventing me from 'testing myself' in training. The big risk is making efforts that you think will reassure you of your form, but which can actually be quite damaging. Instead, it was a matter of 'putting the hundreds and thousands on top of the cake', as he likes to say. There is always a little fear that something is going to go wrong at the last minute, but then you think, 'What if that did happen? I can't control that.' You have to have the confidence to keep up the momentum. The Tour was just another race, exactly the same thing as I'd done all year. I'd just gone through one phase of training and racing after another and now we were finally there. My win in the Dauphiné didn't tell me that all I would have to do was turn up at the Tour and I could win, but it was proof that I was going to be able to dig deep physically as a result of all the work we had done since last November.

Before Beijing, in the Great Britain team we had been aware of the expectation, we knew we were the favourites, but we also knew that we had to keep concentrating on what we had to do. I felt poised for the Tour, hopefully to make history.

After the Dauphiné finished we spent a night in Châtel and drove part of a couple of Tour stages: the route of the first long time trial from Arc-et-Senans to Besançon and the first summit finish at La Planche des Belles Filles. By now I had seen most of the Tour route, but it was a bit of a blur. I didn't see the use in having the route for stage 10 or 11 at the front of my mind because it was too much information. There was no need to know yet. It was too far away, and the race was simply too vast.

There was one thing I did have in my mind all through the spring and early summer: stage 20 of the Tour was a 53.5km time trial from Bonneval to Chartres, which we had looked at before Paris–Nice. That was a key stage for me. But as of mid-June, I was looking no further than the prologue time trial in Liège, rather than worrying about what was beyond that. The fact that I take the race from day to day means that I only remember the stages we have previously looked at when we actually get to them. When I finish a day's stage in the Tour, I look at the route and see what we've got tomorrow, and Sean Yates will say, 'That's the climb we did when you had to change the wheel at the bottom' or 'That's the stage we rode a hundred kilometres of the day after the Dauphiné finished', and that helps me put the pieces in the jigsaw. That's how I deal with it.

Sean has been the lead *directeur sportif* at Sky since midway through 2010 but he and I go back a long, long way. That was underlined by something I put in the post to him between the Dauphiné and the Tour. Back in 1997, when I was fifteen years old, I made the trip to the British Cycling Federation dinner during the off-season, to be presented with the trophy for the juvenile points race. It was Sean who was handing out the prizes; I still had the photo of us together at the dinner. I made a point of sending Sean that picture after the Dauphiné and I said to him, 'I bet you never thought that kid would become a contender one day.' He laughed, but that's just his way.

As is the case with Shane Sutton, Sean and I share a lot of history. At the Tour of Flanders in 1996, when I was just fourteen, I went up to him at the start and asked him for his autograph. He was one of my heroes as a kid; I grew up watching him. Back then, Robert Millar, Chris Boardman and Sean Yates were the Brits in the professional peloton, and for various reasons Sean was the fans' choice. He wasn't a big winner, although he won a lot of decent races: the GP Eddy Merckx time trial, the Tour of Belgium, a time-trial stage in the Tour de France at a record average speed and he wore the yellow jersey for a day in the Tour in 1994. He wasn't a Chris

Boardman, who was picking up prologue time trials left, right and centre. No, he was Sean Yates, a working-class hero. At that time cycling wasn't mainstream, so he wasn't a household name, whereas Chris had a higher profile, thanks to his Olympic gold medal. Sean was dearly loved within the cycling world though, I think because he was someone the British cycling public could associate with; he'd come from where they were, their world of club time trials and winter runs. I liked the fact that he was ordinary and unpretentious. By the time I knew him he drove an old Land Rover – the flash motorbike from his younger days had gone – and he was still competing in events like the North Road Hardriders '25', a classic grassroots time trial in Hertfordshire, simply because he loved to race. He'd ridden the Tour de France a dozen times but had no airs or graces.

Sean's last season as a full-on professional was 1996, but he has never properly stopped racing since then. By 1999, when we raced together at the Good Friday Meeting at Herne Hill – the old Olympic track in south-east London – he was competing again. He had made a comeback in 1998 to ride the Tour of Britain for the Linda McCartney team – sponsored by the vegetarian food company owned by the late wife of the former Beatle, and the last serious attempt to get a British team in the Tour before Sky came along – where he ended up as *directeur sportif*. They were the coming team in Britain, with high ambitions for the Tour de France; I was the junior world pursuit champion by then. At Herne Hill we raced together in the team pursuit. The teams were a mix of young riders and stars of the past like Phil Bayton, Ron Keeble and Ian Hallam – all names that are mainly forgotten now but which will mean a lot to British fans over a certain age – so I was in Sean's team. I remember he said to me afterwards, 'I was really struggling to hold your wheel.' He was lovely. He wasn't behaving like a lot of old pros when you're that age, who seem to be trying to put you down a bit: 'Don't get too big for your boots, this means nothing in the juniors, you've still got to break through.' He was really praising me: 'You're going to be really good one day.' And I was thinking, 'This is Sean Yates telling me this.' I remember it really sinking in: Sean Yates said to me I'm going to be really good one day.

At the end of 1998 after I won the Junior World's, he asked me if I would like to join McCartney for '99. I said no, I'd love to, thanks, but I was going to stay with British Cycling. Peter Keen had started the World Class Performance Programme and I was going to go with them. In 2000 McCartney had grown, with Sean hiring the Olympic bronze medallist and Tour stage winner Max Sciandri. I heard that Sean wanted to ask me to join, but he didn't because he knew I was on the Olympic squad and wanted to ride the team pursuit in Sydney. After the Olympics that summer, where I got a bronze medal in the team pursuit and came close to a medal in the Madison, he rang me on the landline at my mum's, because we didn't have mobile phones.

'Right: do you want to go pro with us next year? We're going even bigger and we've signed Íñigo Cuesta, Kevin Livingston and all these other guys. We can pay you thirty-five grand.' I just thought, 'Wow, thirty-five grand and a pro contract. Flipping great, I get to be with Sean Yates!' and that was that.

I signed with Linda McCartney. They sent my race programme through, saying, 'This is what we think you should do next year.' On 4 January 2001, I loaded my Fiesta up at my mum's and drove to their base in Toulouse. I drove down there with one wing mirror because someone had wiped the other one off when it was parked in London, but it didn't matter because the front-left passenger seat was full of stuff anyway. I took bedding, pictures, virtually everything I owned, left at six in the morning, went via the Eurotunnel across to France, drove down and arrived there at ten at night. Julian Clark, who ran the team, took me to my apartment, installed me in there and that was it: I was a pro in the Linda McCartney team. Although I never got as far as actually being paid.

I trained down there for a couple of weeks and in late January we flew back to London for the team launch. We were staying at a hotel in Cobham; that was the first time I saw Sean again and that was where it all came unstuck. He'd just got back from the Tour Down Under in Australia, found out there was no money because the expected sponsorship hadn't come through, and the team was dead in the water.

Luckily for me, the GB squad took me back, but I didn't see Sean again until April when we went to the Circuit des Mines in France; he was with a little squad called iteamNova and I remember chatting with him about McCartney.

In 2003 he signed with CSC as *directeur sportif*, and I saw him at Paris–Roubaix; I told him I'd finished 49th the week before in the Tour of Flanders. I remember him saying to me, 'That's a good ride. If you've got the legs to do that in Flanders you've definitely got the legs to do that in Paris–Roubaix.' I started drifting a bit really between about 2004 and 2005 when I had my years at Crédit Agricole, not doing much in terms of results, but I'd chat and have a laugh with him all the time when I'd see him at races. I never asked him, but I remember feeling almost embarrassed about myself and my performances. I'd be there going out the back of the bunch in the Tour of Germany and he would come past in the team car and I'd think, 'I wonder what he thinks of me now.' So we've gone full circle: from this kid he says is going to be good one day, through those years when I was massively underperforming, having been an Olympic champion, and then to being favourite for the Tour de France and the Olympic time trial, all in the space of ten or twelve years. It's phenomenal. It's been an epic cycle.

But Sean hasn't changed through all those years. He's still the same as a *directeur sportif* as he was when he was a rider. He never talks about himself. He was legendary as one of the hard men of the sport, but if someone's pulled out of a race because they've got cold or it was too hard, he'll never say, 'Oh, when I was riding, I would never have done that.' He's always sympathetic. He'll say, 'OK, you know how you feel.' He's always got a lot of empathy with everyone.

It's a big job being a *directeur sportif*; in the old days the DS ran everything at a team, from budgets to training and tactics. Now, mainly, a DS has to plan the tactics beforehand, make sure the riders are fully supported while the race is on – that means keeping them fed and watered on the move – and figure out the tactics on the hoof as the race unfolds. I remember talking to Dave Brailsford about Sean; I said, 'He's bloody good at his job' and Dave replied, 'He's unbelievable. You don't realise how good he is until you are in the car with him on one of these stages.' Sean is capable of doing everything at once: driving the car, talking to us on the radio, talking to someone else on the phone, handing out bottles and gels as the guys come back for them. In a time trial he has a list of things you're coming up to, he's got this all written down: 'Descending through a village, there's a sharp right-hander, eighty, a hundred metres to go before this village there's a slight pothole on the left.' He's like a vocal GPS system for the riders.

Sean is the best DS I've ever had. He's unbelievable. He goes to extremes for us, taking time out to go and look over the stages like he did with me in 2012. He shows as much attention to detail in what he does as we do in what we're doing on the bike. He absolutely loves it so I can't imagine what he felt being a British DS in a British team with a British rider going for the Tour de France this year, and following me in the race that he loves the most, those time trial stages. I think he really gets a kick out of it, because time trialling has been his passion for the last forty years or more.

As a DS, he's just completely on the ball. There are times when crucial decisions need to be made on the road – such as, shall we ride behind a break or not? – and there might be a disagreement. At times like this, Sean will make the call and put his balls on the line. It's never about him. There was one occasion I saw a while back, in a race where he made the snap decision not to stop for a rider after a puncture; Sean felt he needed to be up the road with the front group as soon as possible because we had a rider there who looked good for the overall, but who had no support. He took a lot of flak from the one who had punctured, because the rider felt he could have won the stage, but in the meeting Sean stood up and said, 'I know you're pissed off at me but I did what I thought I had to do at the time. You're going to have to deal with that, and you can continue to be pissed off with me, but I made a decision at the time in the middle of all this madness and I think I did the right thing.' Where a lot of people would have apologised, he didn't give a monkey's whether the rider liked him or not. He just wanted to do his job. The episode was over and it was time to move on.

There are a lot of DSs who will stand behind the finish line jumping up and down when one of their riders wins something, but you won't even see Sean. He is happy to spend three extra days on the road driving home from a Dauphiné or a Paris–Nice, to check out three of the Tour stages that are in that area. He'll stay locally, ride the stages on his bike, and then he's got all that information for us. But he'll never tell you he's done all that. There are times when he hardly sees his own family for months, but his life is cycling and he loves it.

There are so many stories about Sean: he has a massive reputation. Someone told me how when Lance Armstrong first rode with Motorola in the early 1990s he was terrified of Sean. Our time trial coach at Sky, Bobby Julich, told me another one like that. He turned up at Motorola, newly turned pro, and they were at the Tour of the Mediterranean. It must have been '95 or '96 and he was rooming with Sean. He was so scared of Sean – you know, the legendary Sean Yates. Bobby was reading his book in the hotel room and Sean was eating garlic, which was one of the things he was reputed to do. Nothing to do with Dracula; it's supposed to ward off colds. Bobby was frightened to do anything, so he was lying there in his tracksuit, with his book, at ten o'clock at night, and Sean decided to go to bed all of a sudden: 'Goodnight', and he turned the telly and the lights off. Bobby was lying there and he hadn't even got his pyjamas on or brushed his teeth. Sean had just turned all the lights off and Bobby was still reading and was terrified; he had no idea what to do. So he put his book down and lay there for a few minutes and thought, 'What shall I do, put a light on, wake this guy up?' He said he scrabbled around in the dark, got his pyjamas on, went into the toilet, slowly shut the door, brushed his teeth, came back out and got into bed, all as quietly as he could, and lay there trying to go to sleep for an hour because he wasn't tired. He said he expected Sean to get up as abruptly in the morning as he'd turned the lights out at night. He thought it would be 'Get up, out of bed, lights all on, I'm getting up,' but he woke up and all he noticed was the hotel-room door quietly shutting. He realised that Sean had just gone to breakfast and then it dawned on him: Sean had got up really quietly, gone to the bathroom, got dressed in total silence and gone out. He said it was just bizarre. There he was, petrified of Sean and yet out Sean had gone, clearly making a massive effort not to wake him up.

There's another story about when they were riding team time trials at Motorola. Sean was legendary on those stages;

the other guys used to be really afraid of how hard he would make it for them. In one of them, Andy Hampsten, who was the Motorola leader at the time, wasn't able to come through. Every time Sean did his turn and put the gas on a little, Andy would be screaming at him to slow down. Eventually Sean cracked; he turned round and said, 'Fucking Andy Pandy', and from then on that's what he kept calling him.

There was a tale George Hincapie told me about the first time he raced with Sean at Motorola, in the Tour DuPont in the USA. It was probably 1995, Sean was riding on the front, the pace was full on up these rolling hills, and George was struggling a bit, maybe forty, fifty riders back in the field. He said at one point he looked up and he could see Sean peeling back off the front and coming back down the line. Sean saw George and he said, 'Hey boy, what the hell are you doing there? Get to the front you . . .' And the thing was that George didn't argue with him, he just did it. Sean had that authority and respect from everyone. He led by example. But he's not an intimidating person at all, in spite of that aura he had.

Sean never tries to push himself forward; he never does what some former riders do, which is to tell you how good they were in their day. He tells his stories and he's clearly proud of what he did, he really is, but he doesn't try to put himself in the limelight. I know that everything I'm doing he would love to be doing too, but not in a way where it's about him. He would love to have been out there with us, riding on the front at Paris–Nice, Romandie and Dauphiné, the way he did at 7-Eleven and Motorola.

When he does his job he just wants to see the riders

succeed. He's never critical. All he asks of people as a *directeur sportif* is 100 per cent commitment, to give their all, and as long as they do that he's happy. As we went into the mayhem of the Tour de France, it was Sean who would be guiding us from the Team Sky support car. And I wouldn't have asked for anybody else in that front seat.

The particular feeling of confidence I have had in my best years is a hard thing to explain. It's not confidence that you are unbeatable but confidence that you have done the work to the maximum of your ability, and all you have to do now is empty the tank, be the best athlete you can, and accept what you get from it at the end. I knew coming up to the Tour that what was ahead of me was not going to be pleasant, but it was what needed to be done. It was certainly not going to be nice. In fact, it was going to be horrible. There was going to be no showboating on climbs; it was going to be a matter of suffering in the last kilometre of a mountaintop finish when the guys around me were getting dropped.

I knew I had done the work that would enable me to do that. Going into a race knowing you've got the form is completely different to when you don't know and you're just hoping you're going to do well. The interest from the media was quite enjoyable at times in 2012; I kept reminding myself that I was the favourite for the Tour and everyone was saying that. There's not many people who go into the Tour de France with everyone saying they are odds-on to win. It's quite a big mantle to wear because you have to deliver, but I was confident we could go on as we had all year. I was trying to enjoy that experience as much as possible rather than let it get to me and say, 'Uh oh, I don't want to be the favourite.' You have to accept it and get on with it. It wasn't going to change how we were going to race. The year before I was trying to shrug it off a little bit; I got a bit defensive when I was asked about getting on the podium – I'd had so much of it in 2010. It was the total opposite this year: everything was based on logic, evidence, rational thinking and questioning. So if you're asked, 'How do you feel about being favourite for the Tour?' you can only say, 'Well, I have won all these races this year. It's reasonable to say.'

I felt relaxed and businesslike. There were good reasons to be confident: the team we had built, the way the guys in that team had been riding, the fact that Andy Schleck wouldn't be at the Tour and neither would Alberto Contador who had been banned since February, which meant that there were two less riders to worry about. All those factors add up and give you greater confidence and belief. They don't create pressure. I never started thinking, 'Oh no, everyone's going to be watching me.' Pressure is what comes when you realise you haven't done the work and think, 'I may fail at this.'

Things had gone just as well back in 2009, but there was a big difference in 2012. Three years before I had nothing to lose because nothing was expected of me; in 2012 the stakes were far higher. In 2009 I could have cracked on the Ventoux the day before Paris, finished 9th overall, and still have run top ten in the Tour, which would have been fantastic. I was in that relaxed state of mind you have where there is nothing to lose and everything to gain. By the last week of that Tour I was going to finish top ten in the Tour whatever happened; no British cyclist had managed that since Robert Millar in 1989. Now, however, we were trying to win the Tour. Finishing 2nd would have been a fantastic result, finishing on the podium at the Tour would have been great, but we were trying to win the Tour. There was a hell of a lot more to lose; if I flopped the inevitable questions would have been asked – Could you have done less in March? Did you peak too early? Is that the reason why it didn't work?

What lay ahead in the next three weeks was completely different to what I'd had to do in Beijing. Racing on the track is largely a numbers game, certainly in the timed events and sprints where Great Britain excels. You know if you have a certain power output in training, that that will give you a certain time for a certain distance on race day and you can win, because no one else out there can do 4min13sec for a 4,000m pursuit, for example. It was the same with the team pursuit, and it's similar for Sir Chris Hoy, Jason Kenny and Philip Hindes in the team sprint. They know the time that means a medal.

The data we had been working on for road racing in 2012 was not power output or speed, but VAM (see page 59). The average VAM for a big climb on the Tour in 2010 was 1,530–1,600: 1,530 on Plateau de Beille, 1600 on l'Alpe d'Huez.

VAM is a measurement that has to be treated carefully. It depends on the length and steepness of a climb – a shorter, steeper climb, such as the summit finishes in the 2012 Vuelta, will have a higher VAM, well over 2,000m/hour – but it depends on wind, heat, altitude and whether you are solo or in a group. What can be said is that in comparable conditions for the same climbs, VAMs are lower than in the recent past, pointing to cleaner cycling. On the penultimate day of the Dauphiné, on the Col du Joux Plane, we had been climbing at about 1,630 VAM. The critical thing for us is that there aren't many riders these days who can go that fast, and there weren't many who had been able to stay with us on that stage. So that gave me confidence that physically I was in the right place at that time.

The catch, however, is that the Tour is not just about the numbers. Our job now was to take those numbers, the physical ability they represented, and perform day after day after day. Whatever the numbers may say, no matter how good they look on TrainingPeaks or on your SRM box, there are things in the Tour that you simply can't control, which I was very much aware of after 2011. There are things you can do to make it less likely that you're going to crash: for example, you can stay closer to the front in the dodgier stage finishes. You can get riders in your team to put you in a better position in the bunch. But sometimes in the Tour you just need luck on your side, and that's the one thing you simply can't account for. But there was no point worrying about whether I was going to crash out of the Tour or whatever. I never ever started to think about it. If something was going to happen it would happen and I would have to go home.

That sense I had that things were going my way was reinforced the moment I landed in Belgium to begin the Tour.

I'd done all that work. I was fine-tuned. I was ready to go. My body was in good shape. Given all that, I took a private jet to Liège as an investment. I made a point of paying for it myself because, having done everything I had done, there was no point in compromising it by getting a low-cost flight to the back end of beyond and spending half a day travelling.

So I went out training that Wednesday, did my fine-tuning on the bike, then took a jet out of an airfield close to my home, straight to Belgium. And it was funny, I arrived, there were a few cameras snapping away and the *soigneur* from Sky who collected me said, 'Cadel's just arrived.' He had flown in ten minutes before me, in his own jet as well, but my *soigneur* said that no one was there from the team to pick him up. He was getting really irate. We got straight in the car and drove past Cadel standing there with his bike next to him, I started thinking, 'We're at the Tour, here we are.' And I got the feeling the race had started on the wrong foot for Cadel, even if in a very, very small way.

CHAPTER 11

BACK IN THE MADHOUSE

Seraing, 29 June 2012: the first 'proper' stage of the Tour has finished. I'm feeling furious as I climb off my bike at the top of the hill, hand it to the mechanic and climb into the bus. I'm raging. The insanity of the early stages of the Tour has been rammed home: I have just been reminded it's not going to be easy. I'm in the form of my life. All I've got to do is get to the open road and I can win this race. I'm confident of that. It's infuriating to think I've got the legs to win the race but there are going to be so many other things coming into play in the next few days: people not giving a damn; people coming out and chopping you so you go down and then that's your Tour over. I could lose all this because of some idiot; and I might never get this opportunity again.

There is an element of luck in this: it's a dogfight. I don't like that side of it. I like having an open road and letting my legs do the talking. There are riders who are going to get dropped and they are getting in my way; it's a selfish way of looking at it but that's how it is. I could lose all this in one little crash. Mick Rogers was riding right behind me; someone rode into him with 20km to go and that was it; Mick lost four minutes. Your Tour could be over on day one through something as simple as that.

In the first week of the Tour there are times when it's an absolute lottery whether you crash or not, unless you are in the very front line of the peloton. I had left the Tour in an ambulance in 2011, but that wasn't on my mind: this was the year that counted. That's why I was raging. I couldn't help thinking, 'Oh God, I remember what the Tour's like. This is going to be how it is every day now.' I was coming in as favourite; part of me thought the other riders would give me space. In all those other races we'd been given quite a bit of respect in the opening stages, so it was a bit of a shock on day one: you know what, actually no one cares. There was a lot of frustration. I realised: 'You're going to have to fight for this. Not in the physical sense as in when they start attacking you, but you're going to have to get stuck in in these sprint finishes and give as good as you get'.

The opening phase of the Tour is always crazy, chaotic and nerve-racking, and the 2012 race was no exception. Each year you come away from France and you forget how it is, because it's only like that at the Tour. It's never quite as hectic at other major races. Each year you hope it's going to be better, you think the Tour was mad because it was a certain year, or because you were somewhere particular like Brittany where the roads are narrower, but every year it ends up just the same. It's something we are used to, but it's still incredible when you come back to it. My goal for the early part of the Tour was simply to get to the point where the way was clear in front of us. That meant either the stage finish at Planche des Belles Filles after seven days, or the time trial in Besançon nine days in. So we were in for a week of mayhem.

For once, the waiting game for the couple of days before the prologue time trial wasn't too tense. I always room on my own when we have nine riders at a race, so I have my music and everything with me. I like being in my own space, just enjoying my own company. The night before the prologue I was sitting in my room listening to The Jam. John Dower, who was making a film about my year, asked me, 'How do you feel at the moment?' and I remember saying, 'I can't wait.' I was feeling 100 per cent confident and I was enjoying being favourite for the Tour. I knew I'd done the work and performed. All year, I hadn't lost a race that I'd gone for, and that was a nice position to be in. The form guide showed I was on top of everything, so it was just a case of going out and doing exactly what I'd done before. I was relishing it, thinking I might never be the favourite for the Tour again: it is the stuff of dreams. As a result, at times I felt as if I was the one in the middle of all the chaos trying to calm everyone else down. In the pre-race press conference in Liège there were so many people there, and me saying, 'Just get a grip, it's only sport.' There were all these people fighting for that one interview, and I wanted to say, 'We've got three days to go guys, let's relax; yes, I'm the favourite for the Tour, it's brilliant, I'm honoured to be here.' It was madness. And I felt like the sane one in the middle of it.

I was probably more relaxed than I've ever been going into the prologue, which took place over 6.4km in the centre of Liège. I had been so consistent in these shorter time trials in 2012, in spite of not having trained specifically for them. Bizarrely, when I used to train to try and win them, I had been less reliable. The day was all about winning the GC (general classification) race within the prologue. I knew I was the best over the distance out of the guys going for the overall, so it was almost a question of how much time I could take out of the others. I had the fastest time on the board for a while, until Fabian Cancellara came in and did better, but he wasn't expected to feature over the long-term as he struggles in the mountains. Critically, Cadel ended up ten seconds behind me. The first skirmish was over and I'd gained time on all my main rivals, which set me up for the next few days. That created a little bit of a hierarchy within the peloton straight away, and with the other Sky riders packing well behind me – Eddie 5th, Froomie 11th and Christian 26th: we were well placed in the team standings. That in turn meant our support car would be close to the front of the convoy – in the Tour the order of the cars is decided by the team rankings – guaranteeing us quick service if we had any problems. It's a small thing, but they all count.

The madness began on Sunday afternoon as we came down the canalside into Liège towards the finish of the first stage, which was a few kilometres uphill into Seraing. Froomie and I went through the same pothole in the road; he punctured and lost over a minute, but I managed to avoid a flat. I was a little further back than usual when the hammer went down, but Bernie moved me up close to the front, and then I was able to work my way up the outside once we all started going up the hill to the finish. That was quite a good test; I knew I had got myself to the front quite comfortably on the hill when everyone was going flat out for the finish. Looking back, I probably could have gone with Fabian when he, Peter Sagan and Eddie attacked for the stage win, but I played it safe and stayed with Cadel.

There are various reasons why the first week of the Tour ends up the way it does. First up, there are two hundred bike riders wanting to ride at the front of the peloton. There's no significant hierarchy in the first week of the Tour, so everyone feels they've got a chance to win the stage or get in the break: no one team has control because the overall contenders haven't emerged. Crashes are the main worry. There are percentages involved; you can place yourself in the bunch, but you can be last or first in line and stay upright; anywhere in between, maybe not. Your Tour could be over in the first week, not necessarily because you fall off and break something: if there's a crash in front of you and you can't get past it, you can lose a couple of minutes before you know it.

The stress is not so much when you're just riding along; that's like training, just chatting. The problem is when you're doing 65km per hour down a hill with hundreds of thousands of people along the roadside, there is nowhere to go and you are in the middle of the peloton. Then it's hard not to think what will happen if someone goes down. That's when you start braking and drifting back, that's when you try to get to the side and move up. It's horrible. I don't mind admitting I'm scared at times when the race is like that. When a crash does happen, the first you know about it is when you are on the ground with a broken collarbone or something. It's not as if you see it coming. You don't have time to think about it; you react to it when it happens.

Over the last few years it's become apparent that the only way to avoid falling or getting held up is to ride on the front; that's what most teams try to do now. This is where you get the trains going, as a whole team lines out to make the pace with their protected rider or riders at the back of the string, and the peloton sheltering behind. Riding in the trains is hard work on a team. There is a lot of concentration involved and it doesn't always help: if you start doing it other teams will take it up as well, because everyone starts panicking. Suddenly everyone wants to get to the front, because they sense something may be happening. That's when the craziness starts. As you get closer to the finish it gets worse and worse, to the point that something has to give and then there's a crash.

So all the guys who are going for the overall want to ride at the front of the bunch to keep out of trouble, and all their eight riders are trying to ride there to protect them. You might have five or six GC guys; straight away you've got forty or fifty riders in the front. Then you've got the sprinters' teams with their eight riders in there, so that's another forty guys. That makes nearly a hundred, or half the peloton, wanting to ride at the front. If you imagine walking down Oxford Street the last weekend before Christmas at the height of the shopping period and how close you are to people there – that's how close we are. We are talking shoulder to shoulder, with no margin for error.

This year, towards the end of the stages in the first few days of the Tour, there would be a team taking up the chase behind the break in the middle of the road and nine times out of ten you had BMC on the right-hand side of the road making a train with Cadel on their wheel. We would start doing it on the left, getting our train going, and you might have Lotto and GreenEDGE in the middle setting it up for the stage finish. At times there would be four or five trains at the front; behind that everyone would be trying to move up on those trains or on the outside of them. That's where you started getting all the nutty things happening.

The crowds are one thing that make the Tour more stressful than other races. You've got more spectators than at any other race and they narrow the road even further; they've all got a phone or a digital camera or an iPad taking pictures of the race, so their hands are protruding towards the peloton, and that's another few inches taken up, so it's difficult to move up the outside of the bunch. I think sometimes the fans don't realise how close to us they are and how fast we are moving. People have got prams in the road, they jump back and leave their pram out there; they jump out of the way and leave a guy in a wheelchair sitting in the road, or a tripod with their camera on it. It's just chaos. All the riders are trying to avoid crashing by being on the front so the peloton turns into an arrow head, racing along, with all that going on at the sides of it.

In the first week of the Tour, each day is different so there's no set pattern to the stages. Stage one had a hard uphill finish so all the guys going for the general classification were up there, all the climbers as well as the riders going for the stage. Stage two into Tournai, when Cav won, was calmer, because there are only certain sprinters who have a chance in that kind of finish, so at least in the final five kilometres the guys going for the overall tend to slip back a bit. That's not to say the sprinters don't get scared as well. I remember Cav and I talking about the sprints one day and I said, 'Go on, you love it, don't you' and he answered, 'I don't, that's just it, I hate it. I hate doing the sprints.' You just assume that he loves it, getting up there at the finish, because it looks so spectacular and thrilling, but he hates risking his life. He's had a few crashes this year and I think a couple of them really knocked him for six. The one he had on stage four of the Tour in Rouen was pretty horrendous – someone dropped a bottle as they were lining up for the sprint and he ended up with cuts and grazes all over – and the one when Roberto Ferrari moved off his line in the finish straight in the first stage of the Giro was really nasty.

The first bad pile-up was on the Tuesday, coming into Boulogne; we were descending on a country road and they started falling at twentieth wheel from the front, and that was it. Apparently that one happened because someone else tried to move up right on the edge, someone else just moved to the right and the first guy went into the grass, tried to jump back up into the road and then bam. You're going downhill, doing about 60 or 65km per hour, it's narrow, only one lane. You start seeing people braking up ahead so you slam up, people

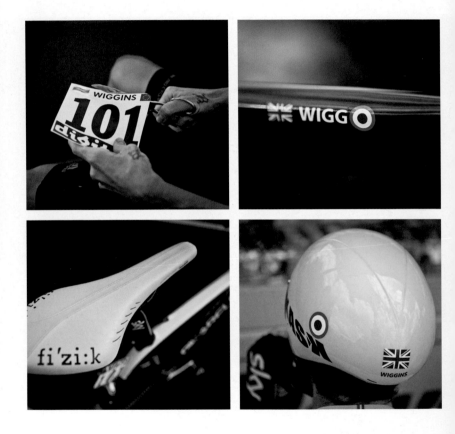

up against you hit their brakes and skid, people are all around you hitting the floor. This is what happened here, and it blocked the road completely. I didn't think twice: I got off my bike, put it on my shoulder like a cyclo-cross rider, and ran down the verge into a field to get round as there was no way through all the guys on the deck. I just got back in, and the guys behind didn't. I had to do it – if you stand on the road you're going to wait there for a couple of minutes, and a lot of people didn't come back from that crash. At the time I didn't think I might have lost the Tour, but when I got to the end and I saw how few there were in the front group, I realised it certainly was one of those moments.

That ended up being one of my hardest days on the Tour. For a little while it felt like touch and go, as immediately after the crash I was the only rider from the team in the front group. I was thinking, 'I'd better not puncture here.' It was about 20km to go, and I'd never have got back in. That could have been a couple of minutes lost all of a sudden. The other big problem was that I didn't take in enough food during the stage with all that was going on. Usually I eat as much as I can, constantly. I have a routine: every twenty minutes, eat something or take a gel. Rice cakes are what I tend to have with me; our chef Søren makes them, like rice pudding congealed into little squares.

But there was no time for that: even before the big crash, the stage had turned into a complete scramble. The crowds were huge, the roads were narrow, you couldn't move up for fear of hitting a spectator, there were small crashes going on so you were constantly chasing back to the bunch; with all that to think about, I kept forgetting to eat. I got really cold that day and I was struggling at the end. I had nothing left when we hit the finale. Without a doubt I would have lost time on Cadel Evans and the others on the climb to the finish. Luckily for me, however, I was caught behind yet another crash right at the end. I say lucky because it came inside the last 3km – the point after which they give you the same time as the lead group if you are held up in a crash. Losing five or ten seconds at that point would have been a huge blow.

The big Boulogne crash was where we lost Kosta with a broken shin. I saw him in the hotel after the stage on Tuesday and the big picture was the last thing on my mind. You don't think, 'Shit, we're a man down', you can only express sympathy for a guy who's broken his leg and will be healing for three months. There's nothing you can say to a guy in that situation; I told him not to worry about us. You have to keep in your mind that it's only a bike race.

At Sky we were dithering at times in that first week. It wasn't until the stage into Saint-Quentin that we said, 'Right, one day we are going to come unstuck and lose this.' Cav had had his crash in Rouen the day before. With 25 or 30km to go we were all at the front doing our job and it started getting hairy, I slipped back a bit in the bunch and we all split up. We couldn't move up, any of us, it was about 60km per hour, going down this descent. I remember sitting there with Christian thinking, 'If there is a crash now, that's it. It will split the peloton and we're not going to get back.' I couldn't move up the side of the bunch because everyone was wall to wall; I was just sitting there, in the form of my life, I couldn't move up; I thought, 'If something happens now, my Tour is over, because of someone crashing in front of me, not because I haven't got the legs.'

Nothing happened; we went down into Rouen and then the big crash happened with Cav. Fortunately it was within 3km to go and I crossed the line thinking, 'You were lucky there, Brad.' I said to Sean that night we'd been great until 30km to go when we'd lost it; that was where we said, 'We need to take this on a bit more at the back end.' The day after, Saint-Quentin, that was it, we team time trialled for 25km and I gave a bit of a lead-out to Cav at the finish. On that stage, in fact, we were killing two birds with one stone: we were covering my backside against crashes but we were also keeping Cav up in the front for the sprint. We were all super-happy with ourselves.

The crash that made the biggest impact in the first week was the 'massacre' on the way to Metz, which happened about 25km out from the finish and cost several contenders their chance in the race. We were doing 70km per hour down a long straight road, with the trains on the front of the bunch; apparently the crash was started by a guy who used to be in our team, Davide Viganò. His team leader, Alessandro Petacchi, decided to remove his overshoes; he took one off, gave it to Viganò, took the other one off and Viganò took his hands off the bars, sat up to put them in his back pocket, touched a wheel and that was it: bang, carnage.

Just before it happened, I was twenty riders back in the bunch, and I remember thinking, 'This is ridiculous, this is getting crazy.' The crowds were closing in on us from the sides of the roads. I thought: 'If there's a crash now, I'm down, there's nowhere to go.' I saw an opening, I went right up the outside with Christian Knees on my wheel; we passed the GreenEDGE train on the front and got in the slipstream of the motorbikes. We were doing 75km per hour behind a motorbike, so I stopped pedalling, looked round, put my hand out and apologised to GreenEDGE for overtaking them. That was just a matter of respect; telling them I wasn't showboating when they were riding at the front.

At that point the crash happened behind me, right where I had been sitting. You think: 'Was that fate?' There had been a split second when I thought, 'I'm in the wrong position here', so I moved up and got myself out of it, then the crash happened. Eddie Boasson Hagen was in the middle of it; I had been sitting on his wheel and if I hadn't moved up that would have been my Tour over there and then. We'd tried to do the same thing as at Saint-Quentin a bit earlier, we'd all got a bit dithery, I'd shat myself and moved up with Christian.

I went through that Tour without a single puncture or crash. Was that luck? Or was that me being on the ball, completely focused and putting as much thought into every single stage as if it was the only one that counted, in a way that I hadn't done the year before? It made me think of something Chris Boardman said. He was asked to sum up what quality it is that makes me a strong Tour contender.

He said, 'It's hard to put your finger on one thing, but as I've found out over the last ten years, the thing that makes Brad good is his ability to learn.' I think that's quite a reasonable summary. My crash in 2011 was definitely a lesson. You think how many guys going for the overall got wiped out in that one crash at Metz: Frank Schleck, who had finished 3rd in 2011; the Giro d'Italia winner Ryder Hesjedal; one of the best climbers, Robert Gesink; another Giro star, Michele Scarponi. So perhaps that was the day when I won the Tour.

After the Dauphiné, Sean and I had gone and looked at the stage finish at La Planche des Belles Filles, high up in the Vosges above the town of Nancy. From the prologue onwards it became apparent that I was going to take the jersey there, as long as I didn't have any problems in the first week. There was no way Fabian was going to be able to get up the climb with us. In all the races we'd done up to that point it had become clear that the most efficient way for me to climb was just to ride as hard as possible at the bottom to put everyone in the red. Then I could ride what amounted to a time trial up to the top. So, working back from the finish, we would have to hit the last hill with our climbing group on the front. We would deal with it in the same way as we had training in Tenerife: full on up the climb with three guys in front of me, each of them doing 3km at threshold or as much as they were capable of, then peeling off. That was how we had always intended to ride in the Tour. In training I had it hardest because I had to sit through all the stages: Kosta would go first, 3km above threshold, Richie would take over – Jon Tiernan-Locke was with us at that camp, so he did it as well – then I would have to take up the last few kilometres.

The goal for the stage was to hit the climb, 8.5km to the finish, with Mick on the front, then Richie, Froomie and me. It wasn't super-long so we would ride above threshold: bloody hard. Mick would go as hard as he could which would probably be a kilometre and a half, Richie would take over and do the same thing, then Froomie. Eventually we would get to the summit and there shouldn't be many other guys left with us. The worst thing for me – or it used to be in the past – is when riders hit a climb and everyone stops and looks at each other, then someone launches, then everyone reacts; we all go up to him, get back to him, it stops again, someone else attacks. That's how the Alberto Contadors of this world climb, whereas all this year, in all the major climbs we had done – at the Dauphiné, at Mende in Paris–Nice, in the Algarve when Richie won – we had hit the climb hard, running the race straight away. That's how we know we can get to the summit in the most efficient way possible.

Planning a finish like this is just a matter of working back in stages from the goal and figuring out who does what in each section. Sean looks at the route and then they'll have a chat in the bus the night before – Sean, Rod, Dave – and they'll have in mind what they want to do. They'll come up with a strategy and they'll present it in the bus to us in the morning. We'll have our own input on it but nine times out of ten we all agree; then we try and implement it. We'll say the way we need to do it is to keep Mick, Richie, Froomie and Brad for the summit; we'll say, 'Eddie it's your job to take it up from that last climb and do the descent, Christian, you're on bottle duty all day and if you can pace the guys going into that second last climb your job is done, Bernie, go as far as you can, Cav, you're on bottle duty as well,' and that's it.

So that was the goal at La Planche des Belles Filles; it was then a question of getting into the right position. Sean had worked it all out because he had recced the route a couple of times. Before the final ascent, there was a climb that dragged up for a while, followed by quite a nasty, fast little descent. We knew we needed to be in the front for that descent, and the best man for that job would be Edvald. So working back from that, Christian and Bernie could do the job to get us there early on. We decided that 500m from the summit we were going to hit the front with Eddie, and he was going to go full on down the descent, take it to the foot of the climb, with the peloton in one line. Then Mick would take over followed by the three of us. That's exactly what happened.

While all that was going on in the race, I was sitting there in the line. I was in a perfect position, because I was at the peak of my fitness. You're completely in control, but you realise you're going bloody fast. You're composing yourself, getting ready, getting ready. You are almost waiting for someone to come up and come round you, and swamp you. Once a stage is done, you look back with the lads, and you say, 'Ah, I thought someone would have come over the top', and Eddie might say, 'When I swung off the front it was in one line, everyone was pinned on the wheel.' It's at that point you realise just how good your physical shape is. What tells you you're better than everyone else is the fact that you're still in control at those moments whereas everyone else is on their limit.

When we actually hit that climb to La Planche des Belles Filles, Mick was doing his thing and it was bloody hard, but you're composed and you think, 'Yeah, I can take this up a level, it's not a problem.' Then you get a kilometre, two kilometres into the climb, Richie takes over, two and a half, three kilometres into the climb, you're halfway up, Richie's on the front, you're working hard, and you're thinking, 'I'm still in control of everything, I'm nowhere near getting dropped.' Then you watch it on the telly in the evening and you look at the back of the group and it's decimated. You watch Andreas Klöden, Frank Schleck, all these guys who've been on the podium at the Tour, struggling. You think, 'Bloody hell, that's how hard it was for these guys,' but when you're sitting there in third wheel you don't see anything else but the team. You don't realise what's going on behind you. Shane's always saying to me, 'If you were hurting, imagine what the rest of them were feeling.'

So going up there, with the pace we were setting, no one was going to attack. At the end, bizarrely, Cadel tried to get away but I didn't know why he did that. He pressed on through a little flat bit, took the corner first into the last steep part of the climb, then just stopped. It was really weird, but there were a lot of things he did in that Tour which made me wonder a little. At Planche des Belles Filles he showed he didn't have the legs straight away; at the time you're thinking, 'OK, maybe he just misjudged it.' But it wasn't the last time he tried something and it just didn't happen for him. Then on that final ramp, Froomie pulled away in the final metres to win the stage. We had done the job.

When I pulled on the yellow jersey a little while later it felt as if nothing else mattered. Regardless of what might happen in the rest of that Tour de France, I'd taken the yellow jersey. Up to that point, it had all been about the process. We knew we could win the Tour, but, for me, to get through that first week unscathed, to get to that point where we arrived at the climbs, to race a summit finish in the Tour de France, and pull on the yellow jersey that was an incredible feeling. Wearing the *maillot jaune* had been my dream from when I was about ten or twelve, so to have gone through all that and achieved it was something that's hard to put into words. I realised that a couple of hours later, when I got back to the hotel and Scott Mitchell the photographer came in. He captured the moments from arriving at the hotel, walking into the lift, going up, going out of the madness of the Tour de France into my hotel room, and just sitting there with the jersey draped across the settee next to me with the realisation that I had taken the yellow in the Tour. He captured all that, and yeah, it was a nice feeling.

To join the handful of Britons who have worn yellow – Tom Simpson, Chris Boardman, Sean Yates, David Millar – was a big moment and I knew what it meant. I phoned Cath, phoned my mum; there's not a lot to say other than 'Did you watch it?' I'd never had a yellow jersey in my hands; I'd never been in a team that took the jersey. I didn't take it in my stride. I was trying to soak that up, the whole day: regardless of what happened in the rest of the Tour, I'd taken the yellow jersey in the Tour de France. You'll be able to say that for the rest of your life when you go down the café on your bike: 'I took the yellow jersey in the Tour.'

At times I'd reflected on 2009, thinking, 'I could have led the Tour for a week or more back then, we messed up and I may never have the chance to take the jersey again.' I had come 3rd in the prologue in Monaco; all we had to do was keep it together until the team time trial, and if we could beat Astana, I'd get the jersey. Alberto Contador had been 1sec ahead of me in the prologue, he missed the split on the second stage and if I'd made the split I'd have taken the jersey and probably held it until the end of the second week. I'd have had the jersey at the Tour for ten days. I always thought I'd missed an opportunity there.

Cycling is a unique sport. It's the only one where this idea exists, that it's an achievement in itself to take the race lead in the biggest event even just for a day. Wearing yellow in the Tour is not like leading the Premiership, or being in front at the Masters for a day, or first man in the London Marathon at the five-mile point. I remember watching Sean take it in 1994 at Rennes, when he held it for only one day. I was fourteen, seeing just what it meant, not even winning the yellow jersey at the end of the Tour, but just wearing it for one day. What makes the yellow jersey special is that you get to keep it for the rest of your life. You can put it in a picture frame or whatever you choose to do with it to remind you: I held the yellow jersey in the Tour de France.

CHAPTER 12

IN THE FIRING LINE

My first stage in the yellow jersey was a hard day into Switzerland, up and down constantly, finishing at the little town of Porrentruy. Physically, it included the hardest point of the whole Tour for me. It was a short day, just under 160km, so the race was on from the off, but the support I had from the boys was unbelievable, particularly Christian Knees. We hit the last climb before the drop to the finish and Lotto really pushed us hard. Jurgen Van Den Broeck was still annoyed from the day before because he'd dropped his chain on the run in to Planche des Belles Filles, so he got his teammate Jelle Vanendert – the little climber with the moustache who won the stage to Luz Ardiden in the 2011 Tour – to make the pace on the front and between them they ripped the bunch to pieces.

There were only five or six of us left over the top on that last climb, a short steep one. I felt I was close to getting dropped off the group towards the end. But I was riding a super-light bike and a few days later I realised that it had cracked under the bottom bracket so it was flexing like crazy and that's why I was finding it so hard. But that's the point about the Tour: the race is never done and dusted. Something can always happen. After that little moment I felt fine, and we had a healthy scrap into the finish, Van Den Broeck and Cadel attacking, me chasing them down quite comfortably. It was like being a junior again, racing for the hell of it.

I didn't give much away when I had that brief crisis on the climb. I don't think Cadel can have known how I was feeling; he shouldn't have been able to tell. I remember as we went over the top, Nibali looked round to see if he was there; I shut my mouth as if I wasn't hurting, and then he turned to the front again. In that situation, you just try and soak up the pain, not show it. There's a lot of that in cycling. There's a lot of bluffing midway through the Tour, because you don't want to give anything away. You don't want to give anyone a reason to think, the next day, 'I'm going to try and attack although I normally wouldn't.' You always want to keep them thinking, 'Damn, he looked strong there.'

With that Swiss stage over, I began thinking about the next key day: the Besançon time trial. I just wanted to get back to the hotel and get on with preparing for the time trial. Coming on top of La Planche des Belles Filles, Porrentruy had been a hard day, and I didn't want to stick around at the finish doing all the press interviews. But as the yellow jersey of the Tour de France, you have no option.

The doping insinuations on Twitter had begun after the

Tour of Romandie, and they had continued after Sky had dominated on the Joux Plane at the Dauphiné. So I'd been thinking about what to say for some time. There weren't any direct accusations: it was more of a nod and a wink, knowing comments. I don't often lose my temper, but this had made me angry. I think if only people understood what I have to put myself and my family through in order to win the Tour, and if they realised what I have in my life that doping would lose me, they would probably think differently.

I knew that if I went well at the Tour these accusations were going to happen more and more. I was waiting for it. I had decided that when the question was asked I wasn't going to give it the old, 'I can sleep at night with a clear conscience' and all that sort of crap. The response had been in my head a fair while: I thought, 'I'm just going to give them the kind of answer they'd expect if they asked me in the pub.'

After the stage into Porrentruy a journalist came out with it direct in the press conference: what did I make of the insinuations on the net that Sky's performances were reminiscent of those put in by Lance Armstrong's US Postal Service team? I knew what he meant: were we doping?

I told him this: 'I say they're just fucking wankers. I cannot be doing with people like that. It justifies their own bone-idleness because they can't ever imagine applying themselves to doing anything in their lives. It's easy for them to sit under a pseudonym on Twitter and write that sort of shit rather than get off their arses in their own lives and apply themselves and work hard at something and achieve something. And that's ultimately it. C***s.'

And with that, I got up and left the caravan where we do the written press after the stage. There was, I'm told, a small ripple of applause back at the main press room, which picks up proceedings from the caravan through a television feed.

I never intended it, but for some people that statement has become a bit of a John Lennon moment. Someone came up to me recently, with some great big yellow posters printed out with that quote on it, then a little dash and my name. I signed them; it seemed a bit like 'Peace is War'. In years to come, maybe you'll see that answer in a book of proverbs, signed Bradley Wiggins.

I wanted to nip the accusations in the bud straight away. When someone asked that question, I just went for it; I don't see why I shouldn't be allowed to do that. Even if we are athletes in a public position, we are also human beings. I think people in the past have set a precedent for how to handle these situations. For example, Lance Armstrong seemed to enjoy the confrontations with the media in a way; he liked to fight and when they asked him about doping, it was just another battle for him. I don't get angry in public very often – there were journalists there who reckoned they'd never seen me get mad before, not once in ten years – but there was a good reason for my anger.

I've always tried to be genuine, and I will continue to be. That didn't have to change just because I was trying to win the Tour. A lot of people may not like it, but there are some who do appreciate it. It goes back to what I've always said about being a role model. I'm only human. I don't claim to be someone I'm not. I'm not a well-trained corporate dream who says all the right things to the media. I'm a bit like Cav; we both speak from the heart. We don't always say the right thing and what we do say doesn't always go down well. However, that's what makes some people like us, even if we are hated by others, and we'll both continue to be like that.

One thing that people have to understand is that I don't want to be cast in the role of a moral hero. During the doping affairs in 2006 and 2007, the years of Operación Puerto, Floyd Landis being disqualified from the Tour win for testing positive, and the Rasmussen, Vinokourov and Cofidis affairs, there seemed to be an idea out there that I was spearheading a massive campaign for anti-doping. I remember *Cycle Sport* did a piece in 2006 with me on the front cover headlined: 'The Whistleblower'. I was happy to talk about it but that wasn't how I wanted to be seen. I didn't want the attention. That explains a little bit why I went completely the opposite way for the next few years and said, 'I'm not going to say anything about this any more, because I don't want to be seen as a whistleblower.'

For that reason, there are journalists who have got the hump with me, thinking I've gone completely the opposite way. It's not that simple. Just because I've given my opinion on something doesn't mean that I want my views to be seen as the opinion of a group or a nation. I don't see myself as a leader in that sense, or a campaigner. The things I do on the bike make me a leader within my team, but off the bike I just feel like one of the lads at the dinner table. I'm not a leader in the bigger sense.

*

When I turned professional back in 2002, I was aware of what was going on. I didn't see anyone doping but suspected people were dabbling in lesser stuff. I would see what some riders would do off the bike when they were partying and would wonder what they got up to on the bike. You're quite easily influenced when you are young – one way I look at it is it's like the pressure there is to smoke when you are a teenager – but I was lucky: I got together with Cath in 2002, based myself in Manchester, ended up some distance away from European cycling and realised that there were things in life that meant more to me than my cycling. When I turned pro I was aware that at some point I might have to make a choice one way or the other; if I wanted to win races I might have to do this. But fortunately I never had to make the decision. If I had, I would have retired by now.

That's why I never condemn anyone. I look at David Millar, who lived in France from the age of nineteen, and I can see how he fell into it. You have to look back at cycling in the late 1990s and early 2000s: it was completely different. It's not the same for today's generation – the young British guys like Luke Rowe and Ben Swift – because it's not a choice they have to think about. Where I was lucky was that I had the track to go back to; British Cycling and their culture was a continuous thread through my life. I would go to the world track championships with people like Sir Chris Hoy, Jason Queally and Craig MacLean; Dave Brailsford was always there, and Shane. Having them there to go back to was like when other kids are caught smoking behind trees in the playground; you go home to your parents and they let you know the difference between right and wrong.

I get incredibly angry when I'm accused of doping, or even when it's merely implied. That accusation is like saying to someone else: you cheat at your job; you cheated to get to where you are now.

I made a particular effort to explain it to Hervé Bombrun, a journalist from *l'Equipe*. I'm good friends with him, so fortunately I was able to make my point without him punching me in the face.

He asked me: 'What is that anger all about? It's all right you saying all this kind of stuff but—'

'Have you got kids?'

'Yeah, I'm married with kids.'

'What if I said to you they're not your kids?'

'What do you mean?'

'What if I said, your wife had an affair at the time, so she got pregnant by someone else?'

'No, it was definitely me. I know they're my children.'

'Well, no, I don't think they are.'

So he started getting upset, and I explained, 'Look, it makes you angry, doesn't it? It makes you want to come out fighting. It's like people telling me I'm cheating at what I'm doing; it gets me angry.'

'*Ah oui*, oh gosh.'

When you haven't cheated, and the accusation is plain wrong, it gets incredibly frustrating. I don't believe in beating about the bush, and I can't sit there and watch people giving evasive answers. As for the tone of my reply in Porrentruy, I know the words I used may have shocked some people, but it can be hard to know what to say straight after finishing one of the hardest races you've ridden, when you're knackered and when you've already spent thirty minutes answering questions.

I can understand why I was asked about doping, given the recent history of the sport, but it still annoyed me. I'd assumed that people would look back into my personal record; there is plenty I've said in the past that should make it clear where I stand, such as at the start of the 2006 Tour when I turned up for a first go at the race and Operación Puerto kicked off, what I said when Floyd Landis went positive that same year, and what I said when I was chucked out of the race with the rest of Cofidis after Christian Moreni tested positive in 2007. On the way home after that one I put my Cofidis kit in a dustbin at Pau airport because I didn't want to be seen in it, and swore I would never race in it again because I was so sick at what had happened.

Nothing has changed since then. I still feel the same way and I stand by what I said. I also feel that people need to look at how the sport has changed, where I have come from, and how I've progressed. They see me put in a great time trial here and there: I can do it because I've worked hard to close the gap on the best guys, Fabian Cancellara and Tony Martin. What seems to be forgotten is that the margin between me and the best guys hadn't been that large in the past, even when I wasn't putting in anything like the effort I have in the last couple of years.

Over the years I had put down a few markers as to what I

could do. I was 5th in the time trial in Albi in the 2007 Tour, behind Alexander Vinokourov, Andrey Kashechkin, Cancellara and Andreas Klöden. The first two later tested positive for blood doping so I was effectively 3rd, two weeks into the Tour, at a time when I wasn't concentrating on the race. I had the engine, as you would expect from a world and Olympic pursuit champion; and it showed that year when I won the prologues in the Dauphiné and the Four Days of Dunkirk and a stage in the mountains in the Tour de l'Avenir. As early as 2005 I was 7th in the World Time Trial Championships in Madrid; Vino and Kashechkin were in front of me again.

It is only now that we have a much clearer idea of what was going on in the sport back then. Compared to today, it was a different era. Personally, I used to find it tough. You'd be trying to negotiate a contract, say £50,000 a year. I had two kids to worry about and a livelihood to earn, and all the while there were people beating me because they were doping. In 2007, for example, I remember telling the press after Vino tested positive that I had looked at his ride in the Albi time trial and thought there had to be something wrong. But you can't voice those suspicions with no evidence. You can only see that it adds up if the rider eventually gets caught. At the time I had a chip on my shoulder as a result of that; I wasn't shy of saying what I thought about doping because it directly affected my livelihood and through that the lives of my family.

After 2006 and 2007, the drugs tests began to work more efficiently, more guys were getting caught, the blood passport came in, and it got harder for people to dope. I'm not claiming cycling is out of the woods, but doping in the sport became less of a worry to me personally. That eventually coincided with my making a serious attempt to forge a career on the road, finally putting my mind completely to that side of it after all those years on the track. Once I started getting successful, the doping question was less important to me, because I was no longer getting beaten by people who would then go on and test positive, or who I would be wondering about. If there is a difference in my attitude now compared to back then, it's that I'm more focused on what I am doing personally. I pay less attention to what's going on outside my bubble because I'm not coming second to riders who dope. I worry about it less.

The important thing is that nothing has changed in where I stand morally. Nothing has changed about the reasons why I would never dope. In fact, the reasons why I would never use drugs have become far more important. It comes down to my family, and the life I have built for myself and how I would feel about living with the possibility of getting caught. I wrote it all in my last book back in 2008, and I still feel the same now. It's just that I say it less. There is more attention on me, but that actually makes me more withdrawn, because I don't feel comfortable in a leader's role.

The question that needs to be asked is not why wouldn't I take drugs, but why would I? I know exactly why I wouldn't dope. To start with, I came to professional road racing from a different background to a lot of guys. The attitude to doping in the UK is different to on the Continent, where a rider like Richard Virenque can dope, be caught, be banned, come back and be a national hero. There is a different culture in British cycling. Britain is a country where doping is not morally acceptable. I grew up in the British environment, with the Olympic side of the sport as well as the Tour de France.

If I doped I would potentially stand to lose everything. It's a long list. My reputation, my livelihood, my marriage, my family, my house. Everything I have achieved, my Olympic medals, my world titles, the CBE I was given. I would have to take my children to the school gates in a small Lancashire village with everyone looking at me, knowing I had cheated, knowing I had, perhaps, won the Tour de France but then been caught. I remember in 2007 throwing that Cofidis kit in the bin at that small airport where no one knew me, because I didn't want any chance of being associated with doping. Then I imagine how it would be in a tiny community where everyone knows everyone.

It's not just about me. I've always lived in the UK. All my friends in cycling are here, and my extended family. Cycling isn't just about me and the Tour de France. My wife organises races in Lancashire. I have my own *sportif*, with people coming and paying £40 each to ride. If all that was built on sand, if I was deceiving all those people by doping, I would have to live with the knowledge it could all disappear just like that. Cath's family have been in cycling for fifty years, and I would bring shame and embarrassment on them: my father-in-law works at British Cycling, and would never be able to show his face there again. It's not just about me: if I doped it would jeopardise Sky – who sponsor the entire sport in the UK – Dave Brailsford and all he has done, and Tim Kerrison, my trainer. I would not want to end up sitting in a room with all that hanging on me, thinking, 'Shit, I don't want anyone to find out.' That is not something I wish to live with, so doping would simply not be worth it.

The problem with the accusations is that they begin that whole process of undermining what I have achieved. That's why I get angry about them.

This is only sport we are talking about. Sport does not mean more to me than all those other things I have. Winning the Tour de France at any cost is not worth the risk. That boils down to why I race a bike. I do it because I love it, and I love doing my best and working hard. I don't do it for a power trip. At the end of the day, I'm a shy bloke looking forward to taking my son rugby training after the Tour, perhaps bumping into my lad's hero Sam Tomkins. That thought in my head, what I would be able to do after the Tour, was what was keeping me going through those weeks. If I felt I had to take drugs, I would rather stop tomorrow, go and ride club ten-mile time trials, ride to the café on Sundays, and work in Tesco stacking shelves.

Another issue that came up during the Tour was that Geert Leinders, a doctor who had been working at Rabobank in 2007 when Michael Rasmussen was sacked for doping and Thomas Dekker failed a drugs test, had been employed by Sky for eighty days a year in 2011 and 2012. I'd rather have him with the team than a doctor fresh out of medical school who has come straight into it. I've had no sense of anything untoward with him. He is totally committed to what we believe in: a clean sport. He was there simply as a doctor for us because he's been around cycling a long time and he knows the sport from top to bottom.

It's vital that people like that are involved now because they have seen how it used to be and they can remind today's riders of how cycling was. He's seen the problems that were there in the past; he never agreed with what was going on, and was one of the sane people who were in the sport at that time. We need guys like Geert Leinders because on top of being a bloody good doctor with a heap of experience, guys like him can play a role, explaining to riders like Ben Swift, Luke Rowe and Peter Kennaugh – young lads who are determined to race clean – what it was like in the past and how lucky they are to be racing now.

It came out during the 2012 Vuelta that Lance Armstrong was being stripped of his titles and immediately there were people in touch with me wanting to know what I thought.

I haven't followed all the ins and outs of the Lance Armstrong case, but I know the broad lines: he's not contesting the doping charges against him (although he's still protesting his innocence); as it stands his Tour titles have been taken away from him; there is Tyler Hamilton's book, which is pretty damning; the USADA (United States Anti-Doping Agency) report on the US Postal case makes it clear that he was doping in a sophisticated way. Regardless of what I've said over the years I've always had my suspicions about him. When the news broke it was like when you're a kid and you find out Father Christmas doesn't exist. It's shocking still, but not a huge surprise. When he made his comeback in 2009 it became more relevant to me because I was actually racing against him, whereas during his earlier reign I think I only came up against him once, in the Critérium International in 2004.

By 2009 it had become clear that many of the top guys weren't clean at the time Lance was at his best – a lot of the guys who finished 2nd to him were subsequently caught, and quite a few of those who finished 3rd, 4th or 5th – but when he came back to the sport I quite liked him. He seemed much more relaxed, he seemed to be returning for reasons other than winning. He was quite gracious in defeat in some of those races; he was quite respectful, encouraging of what I was trying to do. I thought whatever had happened in the past had happened; it hadn't affected me in all those years. I wasn't surprised about him. I've heard stories from people, like my old boss and Lance's former US Postal teammate Jonathan Vaughters, who were there at the time about what they'd seen Lance do but it wasn't something I was going to go bleating about in the press.

In 2008 I gave an interview to Paul Kimmage in which he asked me why I thought it was good that Lance was coming back to the sport. It was difficult because when Paul interviews you, you are being scrutinised constantly. It's not a relaxed, informal chat; you feel very self-conscious, wary of each word you say and how it can be interpreted. I felt I was being set up a little bit as a voice for his beliefs – it was something I'd felt from doing interviews with him from 2006 onwards. I thought I was in danger of getting in a position with Paul where I was telling him what he wanted to hear, because he could be quite aggressive at times when you didn't say what he wanted you to. So I stuck to my line that Lance's return was a good thing for the sport.

I was also asked on Radio Five Live at the time what I thought about Armstrong coming back. I said you had to look at what he had done for the sport. Without Armstrong and the work he had done for cycling in America, American teams like the team I had just signed for, Garmin, probably wouldn't exist, and the financial backing that has come in from guys like Doug Ellis, who backs Garmin, wouldn't be available. Without Lance's achievement in the Tour, Livestrong, his cancer charity, wouldn't have such a high profile and perhaps wouldn't be able to do the work it does. Without Lance, cycling mightn't be as popular – he made it cool in a way. I said the fact alone that he was coming back to the sport had raised cycling's profile; he announced his comeback on the cover of *Vanity Fair*, not a cycling magazine, which shows how he had given the sport its current broad appeal. That was where I was coming from; that was why I said it was good for the sport.

I didn't know of course that eight or nine months down the line I was going to go toe-to-toe with him for a place on the podium in the Tour de France. With hindsight, I'm glad I never criticised him. I had to go and race with the guy and everyone around him. I know what Lance is like if you make an enemy of him. We've seen it in the past. He could have made my life very difficult.

But if it were confirmed that he was doping in 2009–10 then he can get fucked, completely. Before, he wouldn't have been alone in what he was doing, but the sport has changed since he retired the first time. After 2009, what Lance was or was not doing directly affected everybody, because the sport was making a real effort; Garmin and other teams were being pretty vocal about riding clean. At the time Lance was saying things about his coming back to prove a point, that he would publish his blood profiles: but if he was doping after 2009, he was treating us all like idiots. Ultimately I finished 4th in the Tour that year, by 38sec to Armstrong who was in 3rd place; getting on the podium of the Tour would have been something I would have had for the rest of my life. It might have been my only chance.

On a personal level, the way I look at it now is that, as the yellow jersey, the pressure is on me to answer all the questions about doping – even though I've never doped. I was asked the questions in the Tour and I gave the answers I did. I don't like talking about doping, but during the Tour, as the race leader, I had no choice. So I'm pissed off that Lance has done what he did; it feels as if he's disappeared and I have to answer all the questions. That really, really annoys me. And where is he? Halfway around the world, doing this that and the other. But we are the ones in this sport today who have got to answer all the questions.

It feels like Lance has dumped on the sport and we've got to clean it up because he's not around any more: he's not managing a team, he's not at the races like other riders from the past – Sean Kelly, Eddy Merckx – he's out there carrying on as he was before. He's still giving statements saying he's standing by this, it's a vendetta, everything that's been said out there is all rubbish. But as things stand today, I've won more Tours de France than he has.

If I'm asked what I feel about it, there is a lot of anger. We are the ones here, in this sport, right now, who have to pick up the pieces. We are the ones trying to race our bikes, the ones sitting there in front of the press trying to convince them of our innocence, continuing to do things in the right way; they've trashed the office and left; we're the ones trying to tidy it all up. I'm doing what I do. I just hope that by conducting myself as I have done this year, by winning the races I have and doing what we're doing clean, we're creating a legacy for the next lot of riders who come along.

CHAPTER 13

THE OTHER TEAM

The morning of the time trial in Besançon was exactly the same as for any other time trial I've ever ridden. I was in the old, familiar routine, which I relish so much. But one thing sticks out.

I finished my warm-up and was getting on the bus and putting all my kit on, when Tim asked me, 'How do you feel?'

'Amazing, Tim. I feel great.'

He just smiled at me. I got on my bike and followed the *soigneur* through the crowd to the start. When we got there, I sat on the chair by the ramp and all the cameras came in front of me: flash, flash, flash. At that point I've got my eyes shut; I don't look at them. I just sit like that with my eyes closed under the visor but I can still see all those flashing things through my eyelids.

I remember thinking, 'I wish they'd stop doing that', so I made a conscious mental note about it: when I got to Chartres eleven days later, and I went to the start, I would turn my chair around so that I could sit with my back to all the cameras. It wasn't a distraction, it was just that I was in such control of my emotions that I could take note of it and think, 'I don't like that, I'm going to change that next time.' I shifted it to a different part of my head, whereas when I was younger I'd have thought, 'For Pete's sake, get out of my flipping way', or something like that.

As the announcer introduced Cadel Evans, who was lying 2nd overall and was the second-last rider off, three minutes in front of me, my mind went back to waiting on the bus before the race. I was sitting there at the start, listening to the voice saying, 'This is Cadel Evans, the winner of last year's Tour de France; he's second overall only ten seconds behind Bradley Wiggins,' but in my mind I had gone back two and a half or three hours before. As usual, I was waiting for my warm-up time, doing my stretching. When I was lying in the back of the bus being taped up, they had the television on – that's where Dave sits and watches the race – and it was showing British Eurosport. I remember Tony Gibb saying some stuff; that the time trials I'd won this year were all uphill on a road bike with triathlon bars – skis as we call them – attached, and because of that it would be interesting to see how I would go in a long flat time trial today. He said that all the work I'd done in training was for the mountains, and so it would be interesting to see if my time trials on the flat suffered.

In actual fact, I was undefeated in longer time trials in 2012 – as opposed to the short prologues where I'd tended to come 2nd – and in the Dauphiné a few weeks earlier I'd won the long flat time trial by a street. So I was a bit annoyed about that.

Then they interviewed Alexander Vinokourov, who'd just finished the stage: 'How do you see it going today?'

'It's quite tough out there.'

'What do you think about Wiggins's and Evans's battle? Who do you think will be the faster of the two?'

'I think Wiggins will get the better of Cadel, but I don't see him taking a lot of time. I only see him taking ten, twenty seconds maximum on Cadel today, but as Wiggins has proved he's good on all types of course this year.'

I remember sitting there thinking, 'You've got a cheek – twenty seconds!' It really wound me up. 'Twenty seconds my arse!'

I fuel off those little things.

Back at the start, the announcer was talking about Cadel, and the crowd was getting hyped up, really hyped up, and eventually he came down the ramp. There was that massive crowd noise you hear when a rider starts, and that noise was following him up the road. I was wearing a thin little jersey over my skinsuit; the second he started I unzipped it, took it off and threw it on the floor to show I was really ready. I slapped my hands together and went to the ramp.

Usually, when you have that long to wait before a time trial, you sit down below in the chair for two minutes then go up on to the start ramp; here, I was desperate to get into the start house on top of the ramp so that I could watch him. In that time trial there was about a 3km straight from the start before a left-hand bend; I went up the ramp at once, sideways on with my bike, and then I stood in the entrance to the start house, watching his car going down that straight. I rested my arms on my skis and I was just watching the car going further and further away. I was talking to myself: 'I'm coming after you. I'm coming after you.'

Then they said, 'One minute to go', so I rolled up, clicked into the pedals, got myself ready, watching Cadel's car all the time. It was still in sight, like a pinprick in the distance and then it was suddenly gone. Then I heard the thirty seconds to go call, and the announcer said, 'Bradley Wiggins, winner of the Dauphiné Libéré, Paris–Nice, Tour of Romandie, this that and the other'. Ten seconds to go, the crowd were making a huge noise, and I could hear that count: five, four, three . . . I pushed back, and straight away I was out hard for the first ten or twelve seconds, then down on to the saddle and into my pace.

Sean started the dialogue: 'OK, Brad, you know what you've got to do today, you've got three kilometres straight here, then you've got a left-hander do what you do best.' So I settled down into my 460 watts. It felt really good, really strong, around a left-hander, then there was the first drag. I was sitting at 500 watts up that one, and Sean said to me, 'Looking good, Brad, this is good, you come to a little village here. Descend hard left-hander then you're away, you're on open road.'

We got out of that first 5km, then it was out on to a bigger, wider road that dragged up for about 1.5–2km. I remember Sean saying, 'You're twenty seconds ahead of Cadel.' It was after about 5km and I thought, 'What?' I hadn't even started pushing on at that point. On the GPS on the television they had me twenty seconds ahead. *Fucking hell.*

We went into a super-fast section, speeding round the sweeping bends, doing about 65km per hour. I put my head down and the visor flew off my helmet. It hadn't been stuck on properly; the magnet on the right-hand side had come undone, so it just whizzed off. And I had to deal with it. My eyes had got used to having the visor in front of them, so they started watering a lot in the wind; that's always the way when you take your glasses off on a bike: to begin with your eyes fill with water and then you get used to it. I was blinking continually at first but my eyes adapted. All that time the gap kept going up. All the checks until close to the end had been on Cadel; I remember getting to the last one, at 10km to go, and Sean said: 'You've got one-nineteen on Cadel, and you're sixteen seconds ahead of Froomie; he's got the best time.' I had been just thinking about Cadel the whole time until then, but I suddenly thought, 'Wow, Froomie, sixteen seconds, that's quite a good ride from him.'

Towards the end, the course was flat for about 6km, then there was a left-hander, up a climb and Sean said, 'This is where you're going to make the difference, this is all for you, Brad, this is like the track days.' I remember thinking, 'Forget Cadel, this is where I win the stage and I need to put a bit more time into Froomie.' I was motoring. I remember taking the effort up another level through the flat section; I didn't drop below 470 watts the whole way, and then I had to empty it on the last climb.

In the end I took 1min43sec on Cadel but the thing that struck me most when I finished was that I'd won a stage in the Tour de France. A couple of days before I had been thinking, 'I've taken the yellow jersey in the Tour de France', now I had won a stage. I just kept thinking back to when I was a kid when winning a stage seemed really something: 'You took the yellow jersey and now you've won a stage in the Tour de France.' That evening I was given the little glass bottle that you get for a stage win.

I remember talking to the press after that; the question they were all asking was: 'Is the Tour over now?' It felt strange to be asked that. I'd won a stage in the Tour and no one said, 'You're the stage winner, how does it feel?' They just kept asking if I'd won the Tour. What didn't really get through to me was that I had 1min53sec overall lead on Cadel and 2min05sec on Froomie. What was in my mind was that I had won a stage in the Tour and I had beaten Fabian Cancellara, Tony Martin and the other top time triallists.

That felt like a major achievement in itself so I hadn't had time to think of the bigger picture: at the start of the Tour, all I had told myself I needed was to be within thirty seconds of Cadel going into the last time trial at Chartres. After Besançon, nine days in, I had got the best part of two minutes lead on him.

On the Tour you become institutionalised. You do the same thing day in, day out, as a matter of routine for the best part of four weeks – the race is three weeks but you're there several days before it starts – and you only ever see the same people around you. Apart from the fans and the media who follow the race, you almost forget what's going on in the outside world. I don't know how it feels to be behind bars but seeing Cath on the rest day of the Tour de France always makes me wonder if this is what it's like getting a visitor when you're in prison.

I'm not sure Cath knew what to make of it either, being catapulted into the middle of the Tour for about twenty-four hours. From my point of view, it's just nice when you've been in the thick of it for two weeks to have someone come in from the outside to talk about some things other than cycling. It's a reality check. On the Tour you almost forget what's going on in the world, which is why it feels the way I imagine it must when you get a visitor in prison: you catch up on what the kids have been doing, how the Jubilee party in the village went. Here are the clean pants you wanted, and some clean socks, those yellow Adidas trainers you asked for – just little things like that. It's a rapid glance into the world back home, bits and pieces that were going on before you went to the Tour, that you've almost forgotten about: how's that thing with your mum? Oh, that's sorted now. Did you pay the bill for the council tax? And then she goes and that's it, the rest day is done, and you're left with the realisation that you've got another twelve days to go.

Cath's visit was brief; she was off home the next day. But seeing her was vital; throughout the whole of 2012 she was my most important influence. She's the constant one, the one who is always there, and she's been there for me for ten years.

We've known each other since I was about fifteen and we were on the junior national squad together. She's seen me through the good times, the bad times, the ups, the downs and the great times. Since we got together in 2002 we've been a team. The little things that she helps me with are as much a part of the big picture as the training and the planning I do with Shane and Tim. The difference is that Shane goes home every day, and Tim goes home every day, but Cath comes home every day with me. It's a very hard, very selfish life that I live, and Cath, Ben and Isabella are completely there with me.

Cath knows when I am on it, not on it, skiving, not skiving or when I'm making excuses. Because I've been through all those phases in my life with her, she knows me better than anyone. She'll always stand by me and support me. She gets on very well with Shane as well. If he is like a father to me, he's like a brother to her. And he's always calling her and they talk about things on the phone together that I'm not even aware of. He'll ring her up just to see that she's all right, so they have their own relationship. They fall out and make up. She is the keeper of everything for me, because she is the last point of protection. She is also my biggest fan, so even in that whole 2010 period she was always standing by me. She would just say, 'Forget it, they don't know, they haven't got a clue about all this.' In her eyes I can never do any wrong, but she will tell me pretty quick if I have done wrong in other people's.

I cannot say this often enough or loudly enough: when it comes to winning Olympic gold medals and yellow jerseys, there is as much sacrifice from my family, Cath and Isabella and Ben, as there is from me, if not more. I wasn't home much in 2012. I think it was five weeks between 1 January and 1 August. There were periods of that time when the family were with me, but I was in a training environment somewhere, usually Majorca. When we are doing that, I just go out on my bike for five or six hours a day and they go and do stuff, the best they can, but then I get back and I need to rest, so it's not as if we all go down the beach together.

In a way, in that environment, it can be harder than being at home. The kids just want to play with me when I get back from training. Two weeks before the Tour we were in Majorca, and I was training, obviously, four, five, six hours of the day. I'd have a split day – a time trial in the morning, time trial in the evening – and I'd come back in between and have food and a sleep. We'd nip down the beach with them at lunchtime and I'd have a coffee, but I'd have to sit in the shade. Cath and the kids would be outside; they'd all be on the beach and they'd run up and say, 'Come on, come in the sea with us, come on the lilo' and I would have to say, 'I can't, I've got to stay here, I've got to go out training again later.'

Where Cath and the kids have made a difference is in their willingness to give things up for me, enabling me to live the way you have to if you are riding for the overall in the Tour. It is a special lifestyle and everybody around you has to adapt to it. You have to live as much like a monk when you're at home as you would when you are actually racing in the Tour, but obviously when you are at home you are still going about your daily business in between training and resting. That's really hard to do but it's become almost like routine to me.

It's twelve months of the year. There is no question of taking two months off and then we'll see how we are and we'll start back on it. It's a constant thing. It involves everything you do on a daily basis in your life. You've got to do it.

For example, in 2012 I was ill only once or twice with minor colds, and I barely lost a day's training from it. That comes down to the way you live: it is just a matter of looking after myself, being healthy constantly, looking at the little things, never letting my hair down. So I'm always washing my hands.

It can seem extreme, but there's thinking behind everything I do. I try never to walk any further than I have to. It's OK if you have to walk a little bit, but when we go to Majorca for training, for example, and we go and eat at a restaurant which is a fifteen-minute walk away, I normally ride my bike to get there. I have a shopping bike that I use. It means that if I've got a session the next day my legs don't stiffen up.

A lot has been made of my diet. We don't have sugar, bread or biscuits in the house and neither do we have the usual no-nos like fizzy drinks. Shane is always on at me about it. 'Remember,' he'll say when I go home after a race, 'remember your eating this week. It's like owning a car. You don't need to put more fuel in it if you're not driving it.' He's always saying that to me. The dieting is like keeping a car on nearly empty all the time, and if you're going to drive that car to the supermarket – in other words, if you're using energy for training or something – you only put five-quid's-worth of fuel in it so that you can only just drive there and back. You don't ever put forty-quid's-worth in because you're not going to use the car for most of the week and the fuel would just sit there inside it. However, if you are going to drive to London – in other words, take part in a major race – you fill the car up, then fill the car up again to drive back. Once home, and the car is nearly empty again, you have to keep it like that, only putting in a little fuel when you have to go to the supermarket. I guess that's the best analogy to use. So the diet is just a constant daily thing. I fill up only as much as is absolutely necessary. That's the principle I live by.

It doesn't mean weighing my food. It's not quite as bad as that. You get to know what a portion contains. You have to be very careful you don't become extreme with it. I've learned over the years to accept that you have to have some moderation in your life. It's a bit like when Shane told me to have that weekend off before the Dauphiné. It's not just to go out on your bike and ride steady: 'Let's just go and turn the legs for two hours.' The weekend off is not a physical thing, it's more for your mind. You go and spend the time with your family. Some athletes couldn't envisage having a weekend off the week before a big event. So it's someone's birthday, it's April, you've got three months to the Tour, you'll have a glass of wine. That is not going to lose you the Tour de France. You have to avoid getting into that obsessive stage where you're weighing your food and you're saying, 'Oh, I can't have a boiled sweet because that might affect me.' It's just realising the boundaries and staying sane. You have to keep that sanity and that's what I've managed really well in 2012. There is a bit of balance and a lot of common sense with everything.

Living the way I do involves a whole lot of little things, such as not putting your suitcase into the car when you go to the airport before a race, and not taking your suitcase out of the car coming back. Cath does all that. She won't let me pick stuff up. The thinking is this: it just seems funny how you do all this training, all this preparation, all this work, all the fine-tuning for a race, the Dauphiné or whatever, and then, with two days to go, you've got to lift a twenty-five-kilogramme suitcase in and out of the back of your car, lug it around an airport, take it off the conveyer belt and chuck it in the back of the taxi. You could do yourself an injury, and all that work would be for nothing. To me, not lifting the luggage is a part of the race. I almost take it for granted now. When I had finished at the Olympics and we were loading up the car to come back, I was waiting for Cath to put the cases in as usual and she said I could do it for myself now: 'Come on, you ain't got that excuse no more.' All those things make a difference and Cath accepts every bit of it without a second thought; other women might just say, 'You can pick that up yourself', or they simply would not put up with never having their husband around the house.

The problem is that when I am at home, the UK isn't ideal for specific training to win the Tour de France, so I only really go home to rest and ride my bike. Then there comes a point where I have to go away and train again. That's the biggest sacrifice with Cath, Isabella and Ben: being out of their lives, missing their birthdays. But they all realise why I'm doing it, and the reward for doing something like this is worth the sacrifice. I always look at it this way: I could be doing other things in my life that mean a sacrifice. I could be in the army in Afghanistan, be there for years on end and never know when or if I was coming home. At least I get to go home. And I'm doing all this by choice.

Cath and I are both in it together, that's how I've always viewed it. That's how we deal with it as a family. It's not a matter of, 'I'm doing this, you're going to have to get on with it.' I've always said to her, 'So long as you're happy for me to do this, I'll carry on.' It's teamwork and she has been happy for me to do it, for ten years. It's hard, though, getting some of the phone calls when things are tough at home. I feel massively guilty. I feel like a terrible father to my children, that I'm not there for them. I feel like a terrible husband at times, because I'm not there to support Cath in things that are going on in her life. But I'm not going to do it for ever. It's now or never.

CHAPTER 14

UNDER ATTACK

It was a really satisfying rest day in spite of the fatigue after the time trial the day before. I remember being really pleased at having a day off; we had a few moments to chill out and briefly savour the stage wins and the yellow jersey. It was as if the first part of the race was over.

You have to be careful when you have that break in the race that you don't make the classic mistake of forgetting the next day. You can't sit there and just think about what you've won already. As well as relaxing, there was also a sense of making sure I did all the little things right, paying attention to those details: 'OK what are we doing tomorrow? Ten o'clock on the bikes; plan the route, we want two hours – we're doing it because we've got to go up the Grand Colombier tomorrow.' Everyone's attention is already turning to the following stage – what wheels to use, the gearing – and there's very little time to stop and think, 'Oh, wasn't it great yesterday?' That's how the Tour functions; you have to constantly look ahead. That's why you forget very quickly what you've done before, and it's only some time afterwards that you can look back and reflect on how you felt at the time.

The next obstacle was made up of a pair of Alpine stages. The first, to Bellegarde-sur-Valserine, took us over the Col du Grand Colombier, super-steep in places but, as it turned out, a climb where the problem was less the ascent than the descent. This was where Vincenzo Nibali attacked in what seemed to be a pre-planned move, with Peter Sagan further up the road waiting to help him a bit. His margin was never that threatening – only a minute at the foot of the climb – and we reeled him in well before the finish. The only GC contender to gain anything on me was Jurgen Van Den Broeck, who attacked before Nibali; I could afford to drop 32sec to him, as he was well down the order after his problems at La Planche des Belles Filles.

The following day, over the Col de la Madeleine and the Glandon/Croix de Fer en route to La Toussuire, the race took a more worrying turn, with Cadel making his most serious attack of the whole three weeks. It was a long-range move, and clearly had been planned; BMC had sent Tejay van Garderen up the road earlier on, the idea being, I imagine, that he and Cadel could link up and put us under pressure. So Cadel went for it on the Glandon with 75km to go, maybe 10km from the top, on quite a steep section before you turn on to the Col du Croix de Fer. It looked as if he'd attacked from quite a long way back in the group because when he came past us he wasn't accelerating, he was in full flight, as if he was sprinting for a finish line 400m away.

We had felt in control for most of the stage already, with Eddie doing a fantastic job over the Madeleine, and when Cadel put his foot down we were setting quite a decent tempo: 400 watts on the SRM screen. Our road captain Mick Rogers took it straight up to 450 and sat at that. So the feeling was: this is getting hard, we're on a really solid tempo here. Cadel pulled out to maybe 300 or 400m ahead straight away, and then he just hovered there. We were determined not to panic, but just kept riding at our own tempo. When you are riding at that kind of rhythm, not far off the limit, if someone is going to attack on a mountain and sustain it to the summit, they have to be extremely good to get away, let alone to open a decent gap. We were conscious that there was still a long way to go: down the Croix de Fer, up another ramp to the Col du Mollard, a second category climb, another descent to Saint-Jean-de-Maurienne, then the 17km climb to the finish.

So we slowly reeled in Cadel about a couple of kilometres before the summit of the Croix de Fer; you could see he was struggling. At that point, if we'd just turned it up a notch he would have gone, but I knew then that was it, he was finished. Any doubt had been removed. There was no need to worry about Cadel any more; I knew he would not be able to back it up on La Toussuire when we got up there. That was exactly what happened: he dropped almost 90sec and slipped to 4th overall. Later that day, when Tejay and I were behind the podium – Tejay was waiting to receive the white jersey for best young rider while I was being given yellow – he said to me, 'Hats off to you guys today.' BMC had done all that in an attempt to get us to panic, but it hadn't worked. The Glandon was the point in the race when I saw Cadel had laid himself open. There was no need for him to do a long-range attack of that kind.

That morning someone had said to me, 'I think Cadel's going to attack today', and I had thought, 'I can't see it. If I was him why would I attack?' We'd had the time trial by then, so he was nearly two minutes behind me in the Alps. I thought it would be a big gamble; he was 2nd overall in the Tour with the best part of ten days to go, which wasn't a bad defence of his Tour title this far. I thought he'd be a bit crazy to throw it all against the wall in a big Alpine attack to try and get two minutes back. I thought he would just stay with us; if he was going to try anything he would do it in the Pyrenees, when we would all be that much more fatigued. So my first thought was, 'What on earth are you doing?' It was bizarre. Straight away, I thought it was a sign of weakness.

Most of the stage to La Toussuire was a simple matter of attack and defence. Cadel threw down the gauntlet; we picked it up and threw it back. The rest wasn't so straight-forward: by that evening I wanted to go home. I simply felt the Tour involved too much stress for me.

We had a plan: control the race all day, then make the pace and do the peel-offs on the last climb in the same way that we had done at La Planche des Belles Filles. The idea was to put the opposition on the back foot and keep them there. Mick did an incredible job that day; he had already worked a fair bit on the Glandon when Cadel made his move, but when he hit the foot of La Toussuire he rode for the first kilometre and a half; then he was done for the day. Next Richie took over; he did 5km or so, he peeled off, and then Nibali attacked. Because Richie was done there was only one rider left to take over and that was Froomie, so he took up the job of setting the pace. He brought back Nibali's first attack and then once he'd got him back he stopped riding.

I assumed that he was finished, that the effort had taken its toll on him, but he kept pressing on for a little bit more and then Nibali attacked again, over the top of him, with Van Den Broeck taking it up with him. At this point Froomie seemed to dither a bit; I thought, 'He hasn't got enough in the tank to bring it back a second time.' Chris really slowed down, so I took it up. We had less than 10km to go, and I thought, 'Right, now I'm really going to have to pace this if I'm going to ride all the way to the summit on my own.' I was ready to calculate my effort: I would have to ride what amounted to a time trial so that when I hit the finish line I'd have got everything out. I knew Cadel was behind me and I didn't look back; I just assumed Froomie had gone. I thought, 'I'm on my own now; this is where I take responsibility for the Tour.'

I heard almost nothing through the radio earpiece. All I was getting was bits and bobs, because of the crowd making so much noise around us. I think I heard Sean saying, 'Pace your effort, Brad, you're the only one left, it's all down to you now, Brad,' or something like that. So I started riding hard, in time-trial mode; I'd been on the front for about 2km, then we went up again as the road steepened coming into the village of Toussuire, just on the outskirts. At that point, Chris came hurtling past me, using the speed from going into the dip; he went straight to the front and said, 'Come on, let's go.' I jumped on his wheel; he lifted the tempo quite a bit. I'd already been pushing hard for 2km, so his initial acceleration put me in the red slightly. I hung on to him, hung on to him and shouted at him to back off: 'Whoa, Chris, whoa.'

I could now hear Sean on the radio, saying 'Cadel's swinging, Cadel's swinging, he's going to go, you've got him, you've got him, he's gone.' Because of that, Froomie began pushing on a bit more, and by that point we'd closed in on Nibali and Van Den Broeck quite considerably, along with Janez Brajkovic, who had jumped away at the foot of the climb. Through another couple of hairpins, we'd got rid of Cadel but I was shouting to Froomie to slow down.

'You've got to let me recover a little bit.'

'No, I want to go again, I want to go again, I want to get rid of Nibali.'

So then we got on to the back of the Nibali group, and Froomie attacked again and I just thought, 'I'm not going to put myself even more in the red so I'll just ride at my own tempo.' Chris was doing his own thing; I let him go and he attacked through the group. I'd got on to Van Den Broeck and the others, and that's when Sean said on the radio, 'What are you doing?' We were right in among all the crowds so I couldn't really hear. There was a lot of confusion at that time. I was thinking, 'What on earth's he doing? I'm leading this race by two minutes.' So he stopped, we got back to him and then we rode the tempo that we'd planned to ride all day, up to the finish.

It was a really confusing episode. I remember thinking at the finish, 'What the hell was all that about?' My initial reaction was that I felt as if I'd been flicked, although I changed my mind when I stopped and thought about it. It was a little bit like having a battle plan going into a war, all being in a trench together, firing your guns at the enemy, and then one of your troops going off and doing his own thing somewhere else in another trench, completely unprompted, unplanned, and contrary to your original plan.

The point was that we had the yellow jersey. In normal circumstances after Richie did his stint at the end, Froomie should have taken the reins as last man, which he did when Nibali made his first attack. What had taken me by surprise was that he'd come back and attacked over the top of me; at that point I was in the yellow jersey and the hierarchy in the team – the GC order in other words – dictates that you have to put your aspirations aside to defend the jersey. That's how it works.

From that point on it felt as if we were defending both positions, and if it ever came down to it, if we got exposed, if we were attacked left, right and centre, it would be every man for himself. I never liked being in that position. I felt I was as much under attack from my own teammate as from anybody else.

It comes down to a decision for the *directeurs sportifs*; they have to step in and say, 'This is how it is.' I remember at the Vuelta the year before when it became apparent that Chris was stronger than me and that I didn't have it, well before the Angliru, after the time trial where he beat me, I said at the time, 'It's clear we should concentrate on Froomie now, he was better than me in the time trial.' The answer was, 'No, no, no. We don't have faith in him, we don't know what he's going to do. We don't know if he can last the three weeks, so we stay with you as leader.' I said, 'Well, as long as you're sure of that.' And that was how it stayed.

The Vuelta was a hard call, because whatever happened the management could be sure that I wasn't going to get a lot worse by the end of the race, while they simply didn't know what Froomie was going to achieve, although on that day he had performed better than me. I actually think we lost the Vuelta the year before through those decisions; we ended up finishing 2nd and 3rd, where in actual fact we should have won it, not necessarily with me, but maybe with Froomie. The day after we said all that, I took the jersey on a climb; Froomie lost 30secs and in the end he only lost the Vuelta by 13secs.

After La Toussuire I wanted to come home. I thought, 'Fuck this, I'm not doing another two weeks of this, not knowing what to expect.' But it wasn't the only instance of something getting blown out of proportion because of the hothouse atmosphere of the Tour; the debate over the insinuations on Twitter had showed that. I had a chat with Cav about it. I remember he said I was still in the jersey, still in the same position I had been in in the morning and I shouldn't be worried about it. I spoke to Shane and Sean, but it was Dave who told me I was being ridiculous.

At the time I was deadly serious: 'That's it, I'm going.' I don't like uncertainty. I don't like to wonder: are we doing it for him? What's the decision here? It needs to be one tactic or the other, not this matter of, 'Oh well, you're free to do it and see what happens.' And I had said that we could ride for Froomie if that was the case, just let me know either way. I said we needed to make up our minds. That was what I was most angry about: are we chasing 1st and 2nd here or are we trying just to win the Tour at the expense of everything else? I felt at times we were getting a bit greedy; we had done that at the Vuelta the previous year and it had ended up costing us the race.

In pretty much everything I do, I like to have a plan, a tactic. It's like when I start training: what's the plan going to be? It's very structured. Dave is always talking about clarity. We use all these overhead displays and projectors in the team bus in the morning, everyone has their role, so we leave the bus clear about what we're doing. Everyone likes clarity; Dave says that a lot. We implement this battle plan: Edvald's done the whole Madeleine, got dropped; Christian's done his bit and got dropped; Mick was 6th overall, he's done the start of the climb and got dropped; Richie's the same; we're down to 5km to go, Cadel's been left behind. I'm leading by two minutes – and all of a sudden my own teammate's attacking: he's attacking not necessarily to get ahead of me but to put time into Nibali so he can move into 2nd. That shouldn't be at the detriment of the job we're trying to do for me. I didn't like the fact that we had been going for one thing, I had been carrying the plan out in front of the entire world, when all of a sudden something else happened that I wasn't expecting.

If Nibali attacks, you're expecting that, that's not a surprise; Nibali and the rest are your rivals, so you know it's going to happen. It's a team sport and we're going into war as a team, so when someone does something unexpected it takes you aback. You think, 'I thought we'd all agreed that we were doing this.' That morning Froomie had said in the bus that he wanted to attack at the finish; he wanted more time on Cadel because he didn't think he would take it out of him in the time trials. I said, 'All right, but the priority is the yellow jersey that we have, and I don't think you should do that today.' He was confident that he could do it, which was fair enough; Dave had a word with him, Sean had a word as well, saying, 'Don't go off on one here, you're going well, but the priority is Brad and the yellow jersey.' What they didn't want was for him to attack, drag Nibali away and all of a sudden we were in a position where the yellow jersey was threatened. He said he was fine with that; then he did it anyway.

I don't think he had the idea in his head that he was going to flick me, far from it. I think he got carried away in the heat of the moment. He was moving into 2nd overall in the Tour de France; he was probably the best climber in the race. But I was the stronger time triallist; I took time out of him in all the time trials, and I ended up winning the Tour by three and a half minutes. I'd put my head on the block from the start of the season, answering all the questions, saying I wanted to win the Tour de France. It was there; I was doing it. And we had set off with the plan in Liège: 'Brad's a dead cert for this race, he's proven it, you guys are all here to support him, but if Brad crashes out, Froomie you're there as back-up.' Everyone agreed to that. Everyone had signed up to that. When I'm in 1st position with two minutes' lead, with the last time trial to come, where I would perhaps further my lead, you can't suddenly change it. The Tour was about the team winning, and I was in the position to win at that time.

One thing is certain: Chris is a better climber than me, that's for sure. He's a more natural climber than I am and he's lighter than me, but on both those mountaintop finishes, I was leading the race by two minutes, so why risk all that? It just seemed strange. There's no doubt that if we all wanted to support Chris he could potentially win the Tour, but at that time the simple question was: why jeopardise the race lead? That was what I couldn't get my head round.

The problem was that, from that moment on, through the rest of the Tour, I didn't quite know what to expect from Chris when it got into the heat of battle. When you're in that situation you need cool heads all around you. I felt that at any moment he might go off on a tangent to what we had planned earlier in the day; I became very wary.

Something similar did happen on the last mountaintop finish a week later, at Peyragudes in the Pyrenees. We'd gone over the Col de Peyresourde, the last big mountain pass of the Tour, which meant we'd done it: we'd won the race.

Chris said: 'I want to attack,' and we began talking on the descent.

'What for?'

'I want to attack.'

'What for? I've won the Tour, you don't need to.'

'I want to put more time into Nibali.'

'What for?' I asked yet again.

'Security for the time trial.'

'You're going to pump him.'

'Yeah, but you never know, you never know.'

We got to the last climb, and I said, 'Don't do it, don't attack, you don't need to.'

We went down; then the road rears up and you're into the last 3km, so I went on to the front and just rode at a good strong tempo. That got rid of Van Den Broeck and most of the others, then Froomie came over the top of me and started going, then waiting for me, telling me to go and I was saying, 'I'm not coming, I'm staying here, I'm riding this, we don't need to attack.' Then he kept going ahead, waiting, going again, gesturing at me to come on. It left me a bit confused.

Being on the Tour is a bit like being in the *Big Brother* house; you forget after a while that the cameras are watching you. For those three and a half weeks, everything you do when the live television coverage is on is analysed; everything you say before and after the stage is examined. Everyone who follows the race is interpreting whatever you say in a good way or a bad way.

After both episodes, because I was the one who had the yellow jersey and had to go into the mixed zone and face the microphones, it came down to me to answer all the questions at the finish: what was Chris Froome doing today? Why didn't you let him go for the stage because you're leading the Tour by two minutes? Why did you need to hold him back? Is he stronger than you? It felt as if Chris was doing his own thing but I had to deal with it because as the race leader I was the one who was up for scrutiny in front of the press and television every day.

The questions I was asking myself about Froomie, and the questions I was being asked each day after the stage finished, certainly didn't make the Tour enjoyable. On top of the constant pressure to remain focused at every minute of every day, those external things made it much more stressful than it could have been or should have been. It was only at the very end that the race became something to treasure, and going into Paris with my teammates made that last weekend incredibly enjoyable. But looking back at the rest of the race, I didn't really enjoy a lot of it. It wasn't a pleasant experience.

CHAPTER 15

LIFE IN YELLOW

Every day when you lead the Tour you are given several *maillots jaunes*. There's a presentation one, which you receive on the podium in the evening, which is long-sleeved, with a zip up the back. The next morning you are issued a bag containing the yellow kit for the race; one short-sleeved, one long-sleeved, one rain jacket and one gilet. Every day from La Planche des Belles Filles onwards, I folded up the ones from the podium and put them into my suitcase; the race jerseys might end up a bit shredded and dirty and would get washed; at the end of the race I signed a lot of them and gave them to the mechanics and *soigneurs* who'd helped me win them. I took one off at the finish at Luchon and gave it to a little British kid I saw. It still had the numbers on it; I said, 'Sorry about the smell, but if you still want it . . .' and threw it over to him.

All the gilets and so on got put in a black bin bag and are in a Sky team truck somewhere. I gave most of the others away: the only ones I've kept are the short-sleeved yellow jersey I wore on my first day in yellow, with the numbers on – I put it in a plastic bag and it's hanging in my spare bedroom – the yellow jersey from Paris with the number on and the presentation one from Paris. Those are the ones that mean the most.

It felt a bit bizarre the first day I was presented with the yellow jersey because it is something that you are so used to watching on the television; that famous ASO music, the tune they always use for the podium. And the podium itself is like no other, a huge, huge thing. You go up there; Daniel Mangeas – the speaker who announces all the riders – is presenting you. Bernard Hinault zips up the jersey as you pull it on, which is strange – shaking the hand of one of the all-time greats, a five-time winner of the Tour, a rider who's done the Giro-Tour double and won the World's and all those Classics.

I've seen Bernard a lot this year, what with winning Paris–Nice and the Dauphiné which are organised by ASO, the same company that runs the Tour. Each time you are on the podium with him he says something different. I always felt he had a bit of respect for me, because I won Paris–Nice and the Dauphiné and I value those races. He'd say things like, 'You are in good company', 'Not far now', and so on. The funniest memory I have of Bernard comes from the Dauphiné this year, before one of the stage starts, when he was feeling my tyres and moaning about how hard the ones we use today are, how hard they are pumped up: 'Too much air,' he was saying, 'too much.' Bernard Thévenet – who won the Tour twice before Hinault began his reign in 1978 – was there and he was saying, 'Ah, shut up, Bernard, you're always moaning about something.' Then someone asked for a photo of the three of us and said, 'If you win this tomorrow, there's not many people who've won this race twice – how many times have you won it, Bernard?' Hinault said something like three, then asked the other Bernard, who'd won it twice maybe, and we were discussing how many we'd won. As a fan and a cycling historian I know all about who they are, what they've achieved, so it was quite a nice moment.

On the road, being in yellow meant that overnight the race took on a hierarchy, a structure. As the team with the jersey, suddenly Sky had the right to ride on the front of the race, which meant that a lot of the fighting within the peloton would fall by the wayside; immediately, the racing became more controlled. We began to get respect in the peloton. Other riders began coming up to us, saying things like, 'Well done, good, this is it.' Overnight I had become the *patron* of the bunch, the more so because I had started the race as the favourite. There was no sense that I was just keeping the *maillot jaune* warm for someone else to take it later on in the race. I was the person everyone expected to be in that position. From that point onwards I had an open road.

That left us all in a completely different world compared to the chaos of the first week. Everything had changed. Sky were being shown respect on run-ins to bunch sprints; everyone was giving us that extra little bit of space on the road. If I stopped for a piss the whole race would seem to stop as well, because every rider knows there is no way anyone is going to attack when the *maillot jaune* has stopped; that's one of the unwritten rules of the peloton. If I went back to the car because I wanted to talk to Sean, everyone would think I'd got a mechanical, and again, no one would attack. In chaotic phases of the race, at the start of a stage – the bit few fans or media tend to see because it's rarely on live television – when the break was trying to get established, there would be riders coming to us and saying, 'OK, shut the race down now, that's enough attacking.' Holding the yellow jersey from nearly two weeks out from the finish in Paris was something that no cyclist had managed since Bernard Hinault in 1981. It would be a mammoth task and it would throw up situations that I had hardly expected.

On the stages that took the Tour from the Alps towards the Pyrenees, at Sky we moved into a daily routine that would look familiar to anyone who watches the big Tours. Firstly, a break would establish itself early in the stage, and Sean, Mick and I would decide how much of a margin it should be given. Sometimes there would be a long, intense period of attacking as one team or another tried to get riders in the move of the day, to get their sponsors time on live television and perhaps have a crack at the stage win; sometimes the move would go in the twinkling of an eye. Once the break had gone there would be a brief interlude while they pulled away, at which point I would usually stop for a piss; most of the peloton would stop with me, and then our workhorses – Bernie, Christian, Edvald – would go back to the front. They put in the daily chore of pulling the field along to keep the break at a reasonable distance, until the point when one of the sprinters' teams – usually Lotto on behalf of André Greipel – would begin setting the pace into the finish.

For those who wonder when they see me or another team leader sitting in the line behind their teammates, it's easier there, but not that easy. It's harder than sitting fifty or sixty back in the bunch, because you get more shelter when you are hidden deep in the peloton, but what Tim says is that you can't account for the mental stress of being back there, and the mental strain adds to the physical demands. What you can't calculate is the stress of leading a bike race. I remember that when I led the Dauphiné for just five days in 2011 I was mentally exhausted at the end because it was a new thing for me and it was a massive deal. In 2012 leading races like Paris–Nice, Romandie and the Dauphiné felt like second nature, but the Tour was different. I'm glad I came to it with all those days leading smaller events behind me; everything at the Tour is on such a huge scale that if I'd led it for two weeks in 2011 I don't think I would have coped.

David Millar won the stage out of the Alps to Annonay, and the next day, coming into Cap d'Agde, I did my best to lead out Eddie for what could have been a stage win in the bunch sprint. I didn't have to do it, indeed it's not normal for the yellow jersey to do that kind of job, but I felt I owed it to him on a finish where he might have won.

The biggest drama in the Pyrenees came on what had looked to be a relatively quiet stage into the little town of Foix, on what is now infamous as 'the day of the tacks', when someone – we still don't know who – tried to sabotage the race. There was one major climb on that stage, the Mur de Péguère, a steep, narrow one, ranked first category, but I remember feeling really good going up there; looking around me I could see that Van Den Broeck was struggling along with a few others. I figured that no one was feeling that great, because if anyone had been good there, they would have attacked. Close to the top, I went to the front of the group because it was getting quite narrow among all the spectators, and Sean told us to get bottles from the helpers the team had sent to wait at the top, because the cars were a fair way behind. I saw Rod standing by the road with a bottle, and swung over to the right-hand side to grab it; the other Sky riders did the same, and by all accounts most of the tacks had been dropped on the left, so we all missed them. We went over the top and thought, 'It's downhill all the way to the finish so that's the stage done now.'

But the next thing I heard was Sean saying over the radio that a lot of guys seemed to have punctured. What followed was just chaos. I had been having problems with my gears as well on that climb, so I told Sean that I needed to change my bike. He said, 'We're miles behind, we're miles behind, we'll tell you when we're there.' Eventually he caught the bunch up and I changed bikes; just after that, people started coming up to me, saying, 'Something's wrong, about fifteen guys have punctured all at once: Cadel, Frank Schleck, all these guys.' I knew something had happened. So I went to the front and told our boys to stop and shut it down; there was no point racing if everyone had punctured. We'd got over that climb and nothing had happened so slowing everyone down to wait for the guys who'd punctured seemed the right thing to do. The stage win had gone in any case as the break was fifteen minutes clear. There was a crash or two, the worst one involving Levi Leipheimer and Robert Kiserlovski of Astana; I still didn't quite understand what was happening.

As we tried to figure it out, Pierre Rolland of Europcar attacked and I remember trying to go after him. I thought, 'Hold on, what are you trying to gain here?' There's no point in trying to gain time from someone else's misfortune; that's why I was annoyed at him. I thought: if he'd gone on the climb, and was away before it all happened then that would be fair enough, but to do it knowing everyone's punctured just seems ridiculous. Someone came up to me, Richie perhaps, and said, 'Let him go, let him go', so we stopped again. Then Liquigas started riding – they said, 'Right, we're not waiting any more' – and Lotto joined in, so we ended up going full gas; because Cadel was still coming back we did about 10km full on. Eventually they stopped, Cadel came back and then BMC were pissed off because Lotto and Liquigas hadn't shown them respect. The race was all over the place.

People read quite a lot into the way I acted. It was said that stopping the field at a time like that showed that I was behaving like the new *patron* of the peloton. It's not quite that simple. I could never become a *patron* in the Bernard Hinault sense, a dominant senior figure telling the bunch how to race when it suited him. Sean Yates has told me about how in Hinault's Tours, he was always super-aggressive; they would be scared to attack when he was on the front. He'd ride on the front of the peloton and if you went past him he'd just flip; he ruled by fear. I did end up becoming a bit of a leader for the peloton on that day through my actions, not through being vocal.

At the time I wasn't aware of what was going on. A lot of the support cars had disappeared, stuck behind us on the climb, stopped to change wheels, or having punctured themselves. There were no motorbikes or anything; you're going down this hill with all the other bike riders you race with all year round, so you don't realise you're being watched by the world. You don't do things for show, you just do what you do instinctively at the time. And then you get to the finish and find that all of a sudden your actions have kind of taken on a life of their own. It reminded me of the whole thing in 2010 between Alberto Contador and Andy Schleck – the attack Contador made when Schleck's chain came off. So much was made of that.

There was one little event to savour when we reached the final rest day in Pau, with only three more days of racing before that final time trial. I had mentioned in an interview on the day I took the yellow jersey that I remembered watching the Tour as a kid and had never envisaged that one day I'd be taking the jersey; I said in that interview that my childhood hero in the Tour de France was Miguel Indurain, because he won every Tour from when I was eleven to the age of fifteen. It was the most influential period of my teenage years, and Indurain was the mainstay.

It must have got back to him somehow, and so on the rest day in Pau, Spanish television came to us and said, 'We want to do a piece with Brad, we've got something quite special for him.' They said it was from Indurain and that is how they got me to do the interview, otherwise I would have said no. It was a message from him, on the television screen; they translated it to me and it was basically him saying, 'Hello, Brad, I heard that you were a fan of mine, I think you're strong in the time trials like me' and various other things. I was honoured just to think that he knew who I was; they said, 'He's also sent you this.' They gave me an envelope with a red scarf in it, one of the ones that they wear during the bull run in Pamplona. This particular one was a very sacred thing, with his family emblem on it. They explained: you can't buy it in the shops and it's a massive honour that he's given it to you. He'd signed it 'To my friend Bradley.' It was recognition from someone who had been my childhood idol, something that I simply hadn't expected, and it meant all the more for that.

All through this, my philosophy was to take it day by day. There's enough stress on the Tour without wondering how the other guys are doing, and worrying about who might do what, when and where. Because of that I never think too much about any one rider in a race. Initially you just worry about yourself. You never assume anything. You never really expect anything because then it doesn't come as a surprise. People would ask me, for example, how worried I was about Cadel, how did I think he felt on the stage, would I be looking at him tomorrow? Whereas in fact he might not be the person I had to worry about. You never anticipate that a rider might do this, or you might do that, or think, 'Cadel looks good today.' In fact, he might be suffering. You just don't know.

With me, some of this inward focus comes from the track. There are times when you sit in the track centre and watch another heat going on – during qualifying for example – or you might be there on a training day when you can't help looking at the other riders. You'll be sitting waiting until it's time for your effort, and a rider like Brad McGee – the Australian who was my big rival for the pursuit at the Athens Olympics – might be floating effortlessly around the track. That might begin to get to you, but someone in the team will have a stopwatch on him and they'll take his times and say, 'He's only doing 61 [seconds per kilometre] laps', although to you he looks as if he's going faster. You end up realising that people are very quick to make assumptions about how a rider looks on any given day, and those assumptions can be totally wrong.

There was a classic case of this with Vincenzo Nibali in 2012 on the run in to Luchon, a long, brutal stage through the Pyrenees over four big *cols*: Aubisque, Tourmalet, Aspin and Peyresourde. He was obviously trying to put us under pressure on that stage; it was hard and we got him back. We came into Luchon, finished the stage, and the next day we assumed, 'Bloody hell, he's going to try that again for sure, because that was tough yesterday.'

On the next stage, the last one in the Pyrenees, Nibali put his boys on the front on the first big climb, Port de Balès; they made it hard there and lost some riders. So I sat behind Nibali the whole way up the climb and, towards the top of it, I got a sense of his body language, the way he was pedalling. That gave me the notion that actually he might be struggling a little bit. I always watch people's pedalling action and I've learned that Nibali drops his heels when he's suffering. He doesn't give a lot away when you ride beside him. He's very good at bluffing, he's conscious of that all the time, but he does have some tells. You're on a descent and he'll get out of the saddle and stretch his neck, little things like that that you do if you're conscious that someone's watching you and you want to make them think.

Nibali started dropping his heels towards the top of the Port de Balès. His pedal stroke made it look as if he might be a bit over-geared. His teammate Ivan Basso, the Giro winner back in 2005, hit the front towards the summit, set quite a strong tempo and we descended off Port de Balès to climb the Peyresourde, the last major ascent of the whole Tour, with the finish at the top at the Peyragudes ski station. Again Basso went to the front, again he set a really strong tempo, but about a kilometre and a half from the summit, the other riders started attacking and Nibali just couldn't respond. Straight away we realised he was actually on a bad day. He just hadn't backed up the efforts he'd made the day before. That was a classic case of concentrating on someone, expecting them to do something because of how they looked the day before, when in actual fact they haven't got the legs for it.

When you are leading the Tour, there are hard decisions to be made. It's not always a nice business and during that Tour I couldn't help feeling at times that Mark Cavendish deserved better than he got. Right from when he and Bernie had been selected for the Tour in June, I think he had been very conscious of what people thought. From day one in Liège he had said in team meetings that he recognised that we were going for yellow and that he was determined to be part of it in the same way that I had been part of the picture at the World's the September before.

His line was: 'I don't want to miss out on the opportunity to be in a British team going for the yellow jersey even if that means I'm not going to get a full lead out in the sprint.' It was difficult listening to him say that, because the nice part of me wanted to stand up and say, 'Sod it, Cav, we'll lead you out at those stage finishes. I'll try and ride for the yellow as well as support you when it comes down to a sprint.' But the coward in me had to say, 'Well, you know how this is, we can't ride for the sprint every day; we had a goal at the start of the Tour and that has to be the priority.'

Throughout the Tour, Cav was keen to feel that he had played his part in trying to have a British Tour winner for the first time. I got the sense that he was feeling a bit self-conscious, that he felt we might all be thinking we could have had someone else in the team instead of him. That's why he was coming back for bottles on the stages when it wasn't going to be a sprint, and that's why on the first day in the Pyrenees he rode on the front most of the way up the climb of the Mur de Péguère – the day of the tacks and the punctures. There was only so much of a role he could play, because he's restricted in his climbing, but a lot of the time his presence was enough to make a difference. Cav is a larger-than-life character, and sometimes in a team the things someone says and does are enough. All through the three and a half weeks, just having him around was a boost: he was brilliant, good at the dinner table, good with the other riders.

There were various flatter stages that Cav had picked out as ones he wanted to win. Bernie was his main helper on those days and Eddie was going to join in; the plan was that between them they were going to try to work off the other teams a bit so that Sky didn't have to take control for too long and use up too much energy.

Cav understood why we were in that position but that can't have made it any easier for him. There were some days where it was quite clear he could win the stage but in the team meeting Sean would say, 'Look, it's a bit of a day off for us all today; sit there and look after Brad.' I could see Cav thinking, 'We just need two guys to ride on the front and we could win this.' So there were stages when we had to let groups get ahead to contest the victory where Cav might have won it if it had come down to a bunch sprint.

When I felt the most guilty about Cav was the day after he put that work in up Péguère; stage 15 into Pau. At just under 160km it was a short run and it was basically flat, but the break took 60km to get established. Until we let it go, we had some of the hardest racing of the whole Tour; constantly flat-out in one long line, with everyone's legs screaming. When the break did eventually get away, there was a feeling in the team that we should ride for Cav, out of respect for him and for the rainbow jersey. So we decided to put two guys on the front and start chasing a little; later other teams would be likely to join in, most probably Lotto, who would want a bunch sprint for André Greipel. Our two guys had to push quite hard because the gap was five minutes and there were some strong lads in front: Thomas Voeckler, Nicki Sørensen, Christian Vande Velde – my old team leader at Garmin – and Pierrick Fédrigo, who won the stage.

As soon as Christian and Bernie had gone to the front, Mick Rogers came to me straight away and said, 'This is wrong, I don't agree with it, we shouldn't be doing this.' Mick's thinking was that we'd been racing full-pelt for nearly an hour and a half and we didn't need to put our guys on the front. They'd already had some hard days in the mountains, and we had two big stages in the Pyrenees still to come. Something had to give. We couldn't chase everything, we couldn't treat our bodies as if they were indestructible; we could either roll along for the last 100km and get through the stage, or we could potentially ride our backsides off to bring this back for the sprint.

Mick was saying this for about 5km, and then he got really annoyed. Eventually he said, 'This is fucking wrong, I am not happy about this.' So he went back to the car, and said to Sean: 'Look, this is the wrong decision, here, now.' He truly put his balls on the line, Mick did, because potentially he was risking the wrath of Cav. So the decision was made and Sean put the word out: 'OK, we're not going to ride. Stop riding, boys, that's it, Mick's right.' And that was that.

I remember talking to Cav on the road at the time; I could only say, 'Sorry, mate.' He was gutted that day because he really felt that he could win, but that was one of those situations where you have to play it safe. We may have won the Tour that day because we saved two pairs of legs: Christian's for sure, and probably Bernie's. When we got into the Pyrenees after the rest day, it was Bernie who made the pace all the way up the Aubisque and along the valley, and Christian was able to ride a fair bit of the way up the Tourmalet. I take my hat off to Mick because it takes a rider of huge experience and courage to make the call he did when he did, and particularly when you've got a sprinter of the quality of Mark Cavendish in the team. I wanted Mark to win but we had to be brutal at times and Mick took that decision. Although I was thinking the same thing, I didn't really have the guts to say it.

In our attempt to win the yellow jersey, Mark was the rider within Sky who lost out the most. So that helps to explain what happened coming into Brive on the last Friday of the Tour. It was a long stage, 230km, up and down; the break went early and the peloton never seemed to be happy with it. It was the last chance for a lot of riders to win a stage so people kept chasing; the break would come back, another one would go, someone wouldn't like it and they'd pull it back. Eventually twenty-odd riders went away and a few teams rode behind all day. It was a tough day for everybody and when it became clear that a bunch kick was on the cards, I gave it everything in the final kilometre and a half to get Cav within reach of those last few breakaways.

I like the satisfaction you get from being part of a lead-out train, having that open road in front of you, doing your job, swinging off, watching someone like Cav win. It's a better feeling sometimes than winning yourself. But the time leading up to when you get in the position to do the lead out is the tough one; it's not something I enjoy doing. As I've got older I've wanted to take fewer risks.

I knew that the following day I would have to go all out in the time trial and finish off the job of winning the Tour. But I had always wanted to be in yellow leading out the rainbow jersey for the sprint; it had been something I had thought about since the start of the Tour, and finally I got the chance to do it. I used the speed that I'd built up from that training on my core muscles, the little extra kick that had come through from the track, and pulled Cav until the final metres, when he produced one of the best sprints of his life to go past Luis León Sánchez and Nicolas Roche as if they were standing still. That was four stage wins in the bag for Sky. And two more stages to go.

CHAPTER 16

OPEN ROAD: II

Saturday 21 July, 16:36 European Summer Time
Avenue Jean Mermoz, Chartres
Stage 19, 2012 Tour de France

It was nine months since the 2012 route had been confirmed with the long time trial on the last Saturday; in all that time I would never have imagined, or perhaps only in my wildest dreams, that I would go into that stage with a two-minute lead on my rivals. I had my mind set on that day from long before the Tour started, but the ideal scenario had always looked quite different. It had seemed that if I could be within thirty or forty seconds of someone like Cadel Evans going into that last time trial I would be capable of taking the yellow jersey off him and winning the Tour.

Looking at the way the 2012 Tour was structured, we had always worked on the assumption that if I could avoid dropping too much time on the climbs to Cadel Evans and the others, I might be able to take the jersey on that day. I've never considered myself that good in the mountains at the Tour but I knew I could limit my losses on the best climbers at the summit finishes. The strategy we had worked on in the previous couple of years was simple: empty myself to the summit on every mountain stage of the Tour, but never with a view of winning up there or leading the race, just concentrate on losing as little time as possible. The improvements we made in climbing in 2012 had meant that I was always riding with the lead groups on the summit finishes in races such as Paris–Nice and the Dauphiné, so that made it a lot easier; in those races I was able to stretch my lead in the time trials. The Tour had ended up being exactly the same.

It was during the stage before, the stage into Brive, that I started thinking about that time trial. We had got the last two Pyrenean stages out of the way without any great damage, so then my thoughts immediately turned to Bonneval. About then, I began thinking, 'What if you can win the stage to seal the Tour?' That was the main thing. The stage to Brive was a long one; it turned out to be actually quite a tough stage, we came into the finish and obviously we had a job to do for Cav. At that point there were no thoughts about the day after; it was just, 'Let's do this for Mark.' But once he'd won, my thoughts turned to the time trial. I didn't do the press conference after the stage, because I wanted to go back to the team bus to warm down properly and then we – the lead riders in the standings – had to get in helicopters to fly north for the time trial. Leading the race clearly took the pressure off. I wasn't trying to take the yellow jersey off Cadel, I was defending it, but it wasn't a done deal, because any serious mechanical problem, or something else like a crash could have meant the race was over.

At the start of a time trial in a professional race a lot of the riders roll out of the gate in a very relaxed way, as if they're going out on the Sunday club run. But I always do the same thing: I bounce back on the bike when the starter does the final countdown, 'Five, four . . .' and then I push back on to the guy holding the back of the bike as if my back wheel is locked into a start gate on the track. I do it even in a one-hour time trial on the road; it's a habit I've maintained from going through that process on the boards so many times. Then I hit that first couple of hundred metres as if it was a pursuit: flat out. I always do it. At that point it's so difficult to keep calm. You've been working yourself up into this mental state for the last forty minutes and you're so hyped, so pumped. I have to control myself; I have to say, 'Come on, Bradley, you've still got an hour and five minutes to go here.'

So now, I've come down the ramp in Bonneval, made my massive start effort, and then it's time to get a grip. I really back off the pressure, as I always do after that initial big push down the ramp and into the first few hundred metres, and that's where I start to use my power output on the little screen on the handlebars as a guide to keep myself under control. I'm under way so I just settle down into the rhythm of whatever power I've chosen. At Bonneval, the stage started uphill, so naturally you're pushing a lot more power. For the first 600 or 700m I'm just trying not to go too much over 600 watts, get over the top, then I really settle down and that's where Sean starts talking to me: 'Right, come on, Brad, this is it, this is your area, this is your domain, this is what you do best. Let's settle in.' The power I've chosen is over 450 watts so on the flat sections I'm looking at holding 450–460 watts, and whenever the road ramps up slightly I'm taking it up to about 470, 480, 490, but again trying not to go over 500 watts, and likewise then, when it was slightly downhill, I'm coming back down to 430.

I can sustain 450 watts for an hour, so obviously the first twenty minutes of that is not difficult. It's a bit like being a 400m runner: running the first 100m should feel relatively easy. In a time trial, the first twenty minutes you're just out there, cruising along; you're trying not to go too hard, to hold back the emotion, not to get too much adrenaline from all the crowds along the way and all the British flags, to resist that urge to go that little bit harder, because that's where the danger is.

You can think, 'Let's go out hard early, kill the race.' I made that mistake in the 2011 Vuelta in the time trial, went off way too fast for the condition I had at the time and paid for it at the end. Here I know that I'm in the best shape of my life, so it's about keeping in that controlled state. That's what time trialling is all about, especially over those distances. It's being able to ride that fine line, and keep the concentration, keep the composure. That's the key; that's what makes some people better time triallists than others. So at that stage, you're concentrating, but you're still very aware of everything around you; it's not like a pursuit where you perform so intensely and you're unaware of everything else, the crowd for example. So

I'm riding along, I'm seeing British cycling fans at the roadside, Union Jacks, posters and things, and every now and again I might think, 'Oh yeah, I'm at 460 watts; that's fine.'

The first reference point in my head is seventeen or eighteen minutes into the stage, because that's when I take a gel. I'm thinking, 'Right, ten minutes gone, ride along a few more minutes; fifteen minutes gone, I've got three minutes until I have to take this gel; so it's eighteen minutes: right, gel, big gel, swig a drink, down, OK, on to phase two.' I use these little markers for myself as well as the time checks out on the course.

By then I've had the first time check which is at 14km; I'm 12secs up on Chris Froome: 'Brilliant, perfect, it's all going to plan, that's confirmation of what I'm feeling; I haven't really started pushing on yet and I'm getting twelve seconds already on him . . .' At that point I'm thinking, 'Right, you've got forty-five minutes to go, Brad, you're twelve seconds up, your lead is intact, you're going to win the Tour, let's keep concentrating, you've got forty-five minutes left of everything you've worked for this year; this is it.' I'm really positive, thinking that everything here is confirmation of what I've been doing: 'You deserve this, Brad, this is what you've worked towards . . .'

Sean is talking to me in the earphone all the time, but I'm not always listening to him. He's saying, 'This is great, Brad, you're flowing, you're eating up the kilometres, you're twelve seconds up on Froome, the rest are nowhere.' But he's actually giving me very important information, for example, 'You're coming into a little village now, Brad, there's a slow, sweeping right, it's full.' When he says 'It's full', that means I can stay in the skis – stretched out on the time trial handlebars – 'No worries, you're coming up now, round this corner there's a sharp left. Back off slightly, take care, you don't need to risk it at this point, hard right, then you're away, then you can get back down to it.' That means I know coming into this village I'm going to be sweeping left, hard right, accelerating out, then I get back on to my rhythm. He's seen the course at least three or four times. He's ridden the course with me in March, he's driven the course the day before, he's driven it in the morning behind one of the other riders, so he's got everything written out in the car next to him. He's constantly giving me that info like a co-driver in a rally.

Sean is feeding that information into my earpiece constantly throughout the stage, then little bits of encouragement here and there, and the encouragement becomes stronger and stronger towards the end. One thing I like about him is that he's very controlled. He never gets too carried away. You see some *directeurs sportifs* hanging out of windows, it's just ridiculous. Sean is a bit like a boxer's trainer in the corner, with that calm voice: 'Come on, Brad, this is fantastic what you're doing now, just keep on what you're doing now.' He is constantly bringing me back under control, because as a bike rider your urge is always to go harder in time trials. Sean is the guide, the cool head. So he's saying, 'This is great, Brad, keep at what you're doing, you're fantastic, you're eating up the kilometres, you look fantastic, you're flowing' and all that sort of stuff.

That time trial's superb for me because it's all long, straight, flat roads – just what I like. As I progress I start to see Froomie's helicopter – the one up above him taking pictures for the television – so I know exactly where he is. The helicopter is getting closer to me all the way through so I know I'm gaining on him. When you aren't getting time checks it's just a little way of seeing where he is.

A lot of the time you don't remember the whole ride afterwards, just little clips of it. I remember, distinctly, one section after about forty minutes, with about twenty-five minutes left of the race. I'd pushed the pace a little bit above what I was aiming to go at. If I aim for 450 or 460 watts, I'll always push the top part of that, so I was trying to hold 460; and after forty-odd minutes I'd been sustaining this, I knew I was floating; I was on a good one. We were just going up this small incline, maybe 2 per cent, for a long, long time, and I was motoring up it, and I remember holding 490 odd watts up this rise for a couple of minutes, and then just over the top Sean saying to me, 'You're absolutely flying, Brad, you're eating up the kilometres, I tell you this is impressive.' I know James Murdoch (who had been crucial in securing Sky's sponsorship) is in the passenger seat, and I wonder what he thinks of all this. I allow myself to have that thought for a second and then I get back down to it.

The further we go into the race, the more I'm beginning to realise: 'This is it, I've won the Tour, I've done it.' With each kilometre going by, I'm a little more inspired by that thought and that makes me push even more; there is a sort of aggression, a hunger within me, an urge to keep gaining as much time as possible. I want to win this race. There is no sense of,

'Oh, you've done it now, you can back off slightly.' No: I want more, more, more.

So then we come off the big wide main roads on to smaller roads in the last 10km and it's at that point that it's starting to get painful at this pace. The physical effort is beginning to take its toll: the first twenty minutes are almost easy, the next twenty minutes you're having to concentrate more, but the last twenty minutes is where the pain starts kicking in. In that first forty minutes you feel, 'Yeah, I can sustain this power, at any stage I could take it up twenty, thirty watts.' In the last 10km that's gone and you're thinking, 'I'm actually struggling to hold this now.' But in spite of the pain, I'm still able to lift it up. And at about 5km to go we turn left on to this little road and then the gradient starts ramping up, and I'm still pushing and it's really hurting and with every kilometre that's going past, once we're within 5km to go, I'm beginning to think of a lot of other things, and that is inspiring me to push on even harder.

The thoughts come, but not to the detriment of the effort. I'm not wavering and losing concentration or slowing down. I'm going just as hard, and what's going through my head is inspiring me more and more. Sean says, 'You've got 5k to go, Brad, you've got eight minutes left of this Tour de France, eight minutes and you've won the Tour, 4k to go, Brad, six minutes to go and you've won the Tour de France, six minutes left and it's all over.' With those little things that Sean is saying to me I'm thinking, 'This is it, six more minutes', and my mind starts going back . . .

I'd be going out in December, I'd be in the gym at 6 a.m. doing my core work, then getting out on the bike early doors;

four hours, five hours; I'd be riding all round Pendle, out on Waddington Fell in a hailstorm, thinking, 'Oh shit, I'm two hours from home now, this is ridiculous, I'm two hours out, how am I going to get home?' I'd get back and my fingers wouldn't bend from the cold, so Cath would have to take the gloves off my hands, but I'd think, 'This is what is going to win the Tour.' It had said four hours on the programme; it was three degrees outside and it was hailing up there in the hills, but I just had to go and do that four hours because that might make the difference; Cadel Evans might not go out, might not do anything that day.

Sean is saying, 'Brad, 3k to go, and it's all over, this is it, Brad, this is where all the training's come in, just think of all those rides we were doing in Tenerife, you know all those little things . . .'

I'm back in Tenerife on a day when we've done four and a half, five, six hours; we've done five or six efforts throughout the day and a couple of the guys are stuck to the floor. Tim is saying, 'OK, guys, there's an option of a last effort here, I know a few of you are a bit nailed now so you can just roll up if you want, but if you feel you can do this last one, go for it.' I'm going over those summits in Tenerife, with Shane telling me, 'Come on, Brad, this is where the Tour's won, you know.' That was where I'd hit it: it's like not everyone is going to do that last effort. That was the one which would push me over the edge, but that's what I've always done with the training. It was all for the Tour de France . . .

And here I am with six minutes left of it. *This is what it was for . . .*

I'm on the phone to Cath when I was in Tenerife training at Easter; the kids were off school, and she was saying 'God, they're being a nightmare, running riot, I wish you were here.' It was Ben's birthday, 'Why are you not here?' he and Bella ask; I tell them and they sort of understand why. I say to Cath on the phone, 'Come on, it will be all right, love, this will all be worth it, you know, we're not going to do this for ever . . .'

This is what it's been all about; Cath and the kids, all the sacrifices they've made to get me here . . .

We're getting into those last kilometres and I'm thinking of those things, thinking of my childhood, when I started dreaming about the Tour, how I started cycling when I was twelve. I'm about to win the Tour de France, and I'm taking my mind back to riding my bike as a kid going to my grandparents', thinking of everything I've gone through to be at this point now.

There is a lot of pride at what I've achieved and what I've been through to achieve it. I can hear what people were saying when I signed for Sky – 'He's never going to win the Tour, they're mad, he's overpaid, it was a fluke, a one-off when he got that 4th place in 2009.' There have been all the questions, not only for the last three weeks but from the moment I won that first time trial in Algarve: 'Do you really think you can win the Tour? Is this all a little bit too soon? Have you peaked too early? Is being the favourite a problem for you?' All those things, all the questions, all the doping stuff, all the suspicion, sitting at the press conferences every day.

I've led the Tour for two weeks: I look back and think, 'Bloody hell, two weeks. There have been only two leaders of

Top: Slogging it out on a training ride in Majorca

Bottom: On my way to winning the 2012 Paris–Nice. It was that kind of year, where everything just seemed to go right.

Previous Page: The punch in the air as I seal the Tour at Chartres

Above: Celebrating with the Sky lads on the final Sunday's brief run into Paris

Right: When I crossed the line on the Champs Elysées my first thought, as ever, was to seek out my wife Cath

Previous Page: Proud moments in London: leading the road race up Box Hill with Froomie, David Millar, Ian Stannard and Cav on my wheel; contemplating my fate at the time trial start

Above: Thanking the incredible support after one of the greatest days of my life

this year's Tour de France.' Bernard Hinault managed two weeks in the jersey once, in 1981; Lance Armstrong never managed it; Eddy Merckx led for longer, but he was the greatest ever.

The closer I'm getting to the line, Sean starts saying to me, 'Come on, Brad, just empty it, 1k to go, 600 metres to go and the Tour's over.' It's always in that way: it's never Sean saying to me, '2k to go, that's it, you've won the Tour', it's always, 'Come on, Brad, one minute and it's over.'

So I am emptying it to the line as if it is a training effort in Tenerife and I have to get out every last little bit. And that's where the punch in the air happens as I cross the line. It comes from all that emotion I was going through in that last couple of kilometres, for all that hour, for all that morning, for all the days before that time trial. It all comes out in that punch in the air as I go across the line. That's the defining image of the Tour for me: crossing the line and the punch. It is an incredible, incredible feeling.

Afterwards, my first stop was the team bus to say thanks to my teammates. The job was truly done now: the moment had to be shared with them. At the hotel later on, after giving the winner's press conference – at the Tour they always do this on the Saturday night because there is so much going on at the Champs-Elysées on the Sunday – I bumped into Sean just round the back of our accommodation, the Campanile, which is a curious kind of hotel where you have to go outside to get to all the bedrooms.

Sean had that massive, creased smile on his face; he

laughed a Dick Dastardly laugh, put one arm round me and hugged me. I said, 'Fuck me!' and he replied in a funny accent, 'Tell me about it . . . I'm just so happy for you.' The most amazing thing was seeing what it meant to people like him, who had known me for years. It's a nice feeling, that you can have that kind of impact on other people. He wasn't the only one: Scott, the photographer who has been working with me for a couple of years, broke down, and one of the mechanics was in tears as well. It's at that point you realise, hell, it's not just me who's gone through this: everyone else around me has lived it too.

Part Three

My Time

CHAPTER 17

AN ENGLISHMAN IN PARIS

There is an iconic image of the final stage of the Tour de France that every cycling fan knows. It shows the peloton lined out along the banks of the Seine when the race is going into the centre of Paris, with the yellow jersey sitting behind his teammates at the front of the bunch, and the Eiffel Tower to the right. I remembered watching this on television as a kid: a team riding down the quays, most often with Miguel Indurain riding behind all his guys in the Banesto blue, red and white. It's a phenomenal moment for a cycling fan, truly legendary. And on the final Sunday of the 2012 Tour, as we rode along past the Eiffel Tower, there was a brief instant when I allowed myself to forget I had a job to do that day; suddenly I saw myself riding at the front of the bunch in the same way I had watched Indurain and company while sitting in our little flat in Kilburn all those years ago.

That wasn't the only moment from that Sunday afternoon that will always stay with me. We are on the front, all eight of us from Sky, with Cav sitting behind me at the back of the string as he is going for the sprint. We join the circuit, along the Rue de Rivoli, take a left down through the tunnel and out into the bright sunshine at the exit into the Place de la Concorde. I'm hearing the crowd for the first time, seeing the wall of British flags. It's phenomenal, absolutely phenomenal; as the noise hits us we start riding a decent tempo across the Place de la Concorde towards the Champs-Elysées.

I'm taken back to my first sight of the Tour. I'm standing on the railings just before the kilometre-to-go kite on the entrance to the square, with my mother and my brother, watching them all go past. It's 25 July 1993; I remember spotting Miguel Indurain in the yellow jersey, Gianni Bugno in the rainbow jersey of world champion. We'd come over from London for the weekend, gone up the Eiffel Tower on the Saturday, gone to see the Tour on the Sunday.

Nineteen years later, we pedal up the Champs-Elysées, bouncing on the cobbles, past the finish line, past the stands, up to the turn at the top in front of the Arc de Triomphe. I know my family is there in the stands on the right; Cath has told me, and that morning at the hotel in Chartres we made sure a pair of little yellow Pinarellos were ready for Bella and Ben to ride with me on the victory parade down the Champs. As we make the U-turn, the wall of sound from the Brits when I come into sight round the bend is unbelievable. It's quiet as the first seven riders from Sky take the bend and then when the Brits see me in the yellow jersey the noise comes up at me and wallops me in the face. Amazing. I'm getting goose pimples. And then of course the attacks start, I'm thrust back to reality, and that's it. Time to start concentrating: we have got a job to do for Cav.

I'd finished the Tour on the Champs-Elysées three times, and I'd always ridden that stage watching the person who's won the Tour, imagining the delight he must be feeling: Floyd Landis in 2006, Alberto Contador in 2009 and 2010. I remember sitting at home in 2011 looking at the television and seeing Cadel doing it, thinking, 'God, that must be incredible, knowing the whole race is finished and you've won it.' It is quite ceremonial, the whole parade from the start to the suburbs of Paris, with other riders coming up and congratulating you as you ride along. We got all the Sky guys riding abreast across the road for photographs; I posed on the front of the bunch with Peter Sagan, who had won the points jersey and Thomas Voeckler, who was King of the Mountains. As we were riding in, there were some guys – particularly the French lads – coming up to me and saying, 'Is it all right if I have my photo taken with you?' And they'd arranged it with one of the photographers on the motorbikes, so they would come up and take the photo. That felt like the ultimate accolade from your work colleagues: they respect you and what you've done so much that they actually want a photo taken to mark the occasion, perhaps so they can show their kids and tell them, 'One day I raced the 2012 Tour and made it to Paris with Bradley Wiggins; he's that bloke in the yellow jersey with the long sideburns.'

Every minute of that final stage was as sweet as I had expected, as good as it had always looked when I was watching it on television as a kid. There was a little moment on the outskirts of Paris when we went through Saint-Rémy-lès-Chevreuse, where the Paris–Nice prologue had finished; I remember thinking, 'Wow, I was back here in March when it all started, we went over all those roads, in the freezing cold, and now here we are in July, it's thirty degrees and it's completely different.' As we began riding through the suburbs of Paris, there was a lot of talk through the radio earpieces, with Mick calling the shots about when we were going to get to the front. It's a matter of protocol: if you are the Tour winner, your team leads the race into Paris, with you sitting behind them. We started riding and that was it, there I was sitting 8th wheel, doing what I'd seen all those other guys do.

The noise hit me as we turned by the Arc de Triomphe and from that moment on I expected it every lap. You go so fast around the eight laps up and down the Champs-Elysées that you wish it could last for ever, but at the same time you wish it wouldn't because it's quite hard. Relatively speaking, I had a straightforward ride being in yellow, with the other guys giving us a fair bit of road space and letting us get on with it. But even then you know the judges don't stop the clocks until you get to 3km to go – and 6km out there was a serious crash with Danilo Hondo in it. It could, in theory, still be all over at that point.

I'd always wanted to lead Cav out on the Champs-Elysées in the rainbow stripes; at times in the last three weeks it had crossed my mind I might end up doing it in the yellow jersey. I was just concentrating so hard the closer we got to the finish. I knew the job I had to do: after we came out of the first tunnel I had to take up the running and pull Eddie to about 800 or 700m to go so that he could unleash Cav. It was a phenomenal feeling; turning on the power, seeing Cav come past tucked in safely on Eddie's wheel, then pedalling up the Avenue next to Mick and Richie. I knew Cav would win; I knew I'd done the job.

I had been so focused on what I was doing for Cav that by the last lap I had forgotten that I had the yellow jersey on. There was no thinking, 'This is the last lap, I've done it, I've won the Tour.' It was, 'It's 3k to go, 2k to go – I'm going to hit the front; 1k – after this tunnel that's it, we're going.' That was the whole thought process for the last couple of laps; then peeling off after I'd done my job for Cav, I was thinking, 'I've done it, I've done what I needed to do for him', rolling across the Place de la Concorde, turning right up the Champs-Elysées and then I thought, 'Oh fuck, I've won the Tour de France.' It came on me very suddenly because I'd been thinking only about doing that job for Mark.

The finish was a mad rush. Being given the yellow jersey for the last time was strange; I got up on the podium to accept it, shook someone's hand, a young lad; next thing Bernard Hinault is flying across, and he's chucked this fella off the podium. It's six foot high, and he's just thrown him off the side. I'd shaken this guy's hand, thinking he was the president or somebody and it turned out he had just got in there; the police grabbed him.

With every race I won in 2012 I was thinking that if I never did anything else again, I would always be the winner of Paris–Nice, then the winner of Romandie, then the

Dauphiné, twice; then I'd taken the yellow jersey in the Tour, then I'd won a stage, then I'd won the Tour. There was an element of counting up the victories, trying to savour a little bit of the moment with each one, because this might be my last.

I was conscious of all the British fans being there, so on the podium I made a point of turning towards them. You can look up the Champs-Elysées and see a sea of Union Jacks waving right up to the Arc de Triomphe so that is where all the fans were. I guess they felt more important to me than the president of France, although at the time I didn't think about it.

It was bizarre. I don't have many memories of it. I just did what I had to do. At that point I was still feeling like a bit of a fraud. Part of me was thinking, 'I'm not supposed to win the Tour de France.' I never, ever considered myself in the same bracket as people like Hinault and Merckx, people like Miguel Indurain who I'd watched winning the Tour. Now I was standing up there as the winner. I suppose if I ever look at the video of me on the podium with the Arc de Triomphe in the background, the way I behave on the podium pretty much sums up how I felt. When Lesley Garrett sang 'God Save the Queen' it felt a bit embarrassing being up there – that's why I made a little crack about picking the raffle prizes, like I've done at dozens of British cycling club dinners over the years. Then I wished them a safe journey home, 'and don't get too drunk'. As a fan of the sport, part of me will always feel, 'Nah, I'm not supposed to win the Tour de France. I'm still only Brad, not Hinault or Indurain.'

Although I believe in myself as an athlete, that part of me that's a fan of the sport will never believe I'm comparable with them.

All that while, Cath and the kids and our families were down to the left of the podium; I did the media stuff, dope control, rode down the Champs with Ben on his little yellow Pinarello, with Isabella behind in the car. That was surreal again; I remember taking the yellow jersey off after the podium. That's when I jumped on the team car in my Sky kit. It was a bit weird because everyone was looking at me, and it was a bit quiet and I couldn't think what to do, so I jumped on top of the car. I didn't want to wear the yellow jersey on the lap of honour, but Dave and the others said you've got to. I didn't want to be singled out as the yellow jersey; I wanted to be with the team, as they were. There was an element of me going back a few years, feeling a little bit shy, not wanting to be seen as the leader, I'd rather be at the back of the group. I didn't really like it when they picked me up on their shoulders at the other end of the Champs; we'd done it together, I couldn't have done it without them, and I didn't want it to be just about me. That part of me will never change.

Then we were all whisked off to the Ritz to have a little reception, after which it was a mad rush. I think Dave Brailsford or James Murdoch made a short speech, but to be honest I was so hungry at that point I can't remember. We had to sprint off and get our bags together; it was a bit surreal being in the Ritz and then at home six hours later. It was all done.

*

It's curious thinking about the moment when Cath and I walked in through the front door of the house, having just won the Tour de France. It was emotional, and strange. It was the point when we had to start dealing with it, and we were both a little stressed out. I was simultaneously trying to come to terms with the fact I'd just won the Tour and trying to get myself organised with only five days before the Olympic road race. I had to start thinking of the Olympics the very next day. There were things to sort out: have I got a bike here yet? Where was the one that had been dropped off last week?

I'd won the Tour de France, but I felt as if I would be the last person to take it on board; it reminded me a little of how I felt when I won the Olympic pursuit for the first time in 2004. It's almost a kind of disbelief that this is happening; it's little things like seeing the front page of *l'Equipe*, with my picture on it in the yellow jersey. You don't realise it's you on there. It's strange. And there are messages like the one I had from Sir Chris Hoy, who said he thought the Tour win was the greatest achievement ever in British sport: it's humbling to hear praise of that kind. The biggest accolade is respect from your peers, people I look up to.

The build-up all through 2012 was not just about the Tour de France. We had been thinking about the Olympic road race and in particular the time trial from the moment we started planning, because the silver medal in the World's at Copenhagen had made it clear that I was in the ballpark. All the training from 1 November 2011 had been about backing up, being able to work hard day after day, back to back, being fit enough to sustain the workload to win the Tour. With that under my belt, if I stayed healthy, the one-hour Olympic time trial nine days after the Tour was going to be a doddle in comparison. The issue we identified was not actually getting fit for the time trial, but what we were going to do in the nine days between the Tour finishing on the Champs-Elysées and rolling down the ramp in Hampton Court. It boiled down to how you recover, but the Olympics are what Dave and his team do best so there was plenty of accumulated knowledge to tap into.

There was definitely no question of simply seeing what happened when we got to the end of the Tour. The plans for 22 July and afterwards were put in place well before the Dauphiné. We knew that if I did manage to win the Tour de France it would be hard to leave Paris on the Sunday night and forget about it; even so, I would have to be out of Paris quickly and I would probably go home. We had to take all that into account, because you very rarely ask the question of yourself: if you win what are you going to do? How are you going to handle the media and concentrate on winning the Olympics? We accounted for every scenario, even to the point of figuring out how it was going to work in terms of building up to the Olympics if I were to crash out of the Tour again, God forbid. We weren't taking anything for granted.

I'd insisted on going home. It was what I had wanted and had looked forward to throughout the Tour, but in spite of all the thought we'd put into it, being back in Lancashire wasn't quite what I expected. The very next day people started knocking on the door. That Monday morning, there were cars parked for half a mile down the road. We woke up to find a mass of press and other people outside, so it felt as if we were under siege. On my first day home, we went to Wigan. The photographers were all taking pictures of us as we drove out, which felt very strange: what were they all doing? What do they want? It was all bizarre, coming back four weeks later to what I'd left. All of a sudden a lot had changed. I'd under-estimated quite how big the whole thing would be. By the evening I was saying, 'I've got to go out on my bike for an hour', so I went for a quick spin, but at first I couldn't get through the mass of people, and I had to give the journalists a few minutes.

There was a line of cars following me as I rode, people taking photographs, people wanting me to sign things – some of them piles of pictures that they were going to sell on eBay I suspect – and the next day when I went out to the Co-op for a pint of milk and a loaf of bread I was mobbed. The same thing happened when I took Ben to a rugby-league training day; all the rugby people kept coming over, which you don't expect because cycling isn't their thing. We met Sam Tomkins, a Wigan hero, and there he was praising me.

Cycling is a sport that levels people out. When you go on a club run, if you puncture you repair it yourself. You don't get someone else to do it for you. I still wash my own bike when I'm at home and it gets covered in shit – I did that the Monday after the Tour. I spent several years getting laughed at and called names when I was a kid wearing Lycra, which wasn't the thing to do in the 1990s. As cyclists we become famous in our own little world, but we don't usually become celebrities. It all takes a bit of getting used to.

CHAPTER 18

LONDON CALLING

On the Thursday after the Tour finished, I was down in Surrey at the Great Britain team hotel. The GB squad is an environment that I love. Being with them feels like coming home. That's because there are people there who have been constant presences since I joined them in 1998, senior staff like Doug Dailey, a former top amateur rider who was the national team head all through the 1990s and was working for them as a logistics manager up to the end of 2012. He had been at every Games I had ridden: Sydney, Athens, Beijing, and now London. I only really see Doug every four years; every time I've progressed a little bit, and every time he says to me, 'You've done a bit better since I saw you last.' Seeing him again brought home that this was it: we were definitely at the Olympics.

I'd been a member of the British Cycling team since July 1998, when Peter Keen called me into his office in the Manchester velodrome and signed me up to what was initially

known as the World Class Performance Programme. Back
then, his vision was for Britain to be the number one cycling
nation, but it was all about the Olympics, rather than in
professional road cycling. You have to remember where the
Tour de France was in 1998. It was on its knees after the
Festina drug scandal. At that time could you ever have
envisaged a British Tour winner? But eleven years after that
I came 4th and now I've won it, fourteen years on from that
moment when Peter Keen had that vision of what he wanted
to do. We've had our successful London Olympics and I've
won the Tour de France and we've had a British world
champion on the road. Clearly we've achieved what he
foresaw; perhaps we've achieved even more. I sometimes
wonder what he makes of all that has happened in the last
four or five years.

Credit for the British Cycling team's recent success is
rightly given to Dave Brailsford, and it's an amusing thought
that he joined World Class at the same time as me. Since I
was eighteen and walked into the Manchester velodrome and
saw Dave for the first time, he's been a bit like a mischievous
older brother to me. If Cav is like my younger brother, Dave
is the one who is a lot older, not just a couple of years older,
but maybe a ten- or fifteen-year age gap. We've not always got
on; I sometimes think, 'Oh hell, Dave, honestly!', and I know
there are times when he thinks, 'Brad, I wish you wouldn't do
that.' But through our time together we've always been
successful and he's always been there.

Dave was in charge when I won in Athens and Beijing; he's
always been incredibly supportive. There are two things with

Dave. One is that he has always said, 'Whatever it takes, Brad, whatever you need', and he has given me whatever I've needed to succeed, be it bikes, coaching, racing. The other thing with Dave is that I've never had a bollocking face to face from him. He might have sent me a damning text here or there, or Shane might ring me and say, 'Dave's fuming about you', but then I'll see Dave and it's different.

I think what happens is that he gets het up about me when I'm not there, but when he sees me walk into his office he sees me as a person. I think he really likes me and he always has done, but he understands me as well. So at times when I'm a bit low, such as when I was in that vulnerable state at the end of 2010, he feels sorry for me. Because of that, instead of having a go at me, he'll think, 'Oh well, I want to help this lad.'

For example, towards the end of 2012, after the London Olympics, when a newspaper had printed photographs of me in Majorca sitting on a wall and smoking a cigarette, he rang me the very next day. I had a missed call from him, I was at Wigan Warriors training pitch, and I thought, 'Uh oh, Dave's called me, I bet it's about that. I wonder what he thinks.' I was fairly worried, so I rang him straight back: 'Are you all right, Dave?'

'Are *you* all right? I'm at the start of the Vuelta. I just wanted to see how you were finding it all since London.'

'Obviously it's been a bit hard, you know, I'm struggling with all the attention. You saw the papers yesterday. I can't really go out any more without someone taking a picture.'

'Yeah, I thought that. That's why I thought I'd ring you and see if you're all right, just so you know there are people here to help you. We've been in this position before but I just wanted to tell you that if you ever feel like that or anything else, just give Chris Hoy a ring because he went through exactly the same thing as you are now.' He was so supportive, he didn't give a monkey's about the photo because he's a man of the world. He doesn't claim to be perfect. He understands. He has a lot of empathy. He might slap you on the wrist and say, 'Come on, you know, people are expecting you to behave like this', but it always feels as if he's giving advice like an older brother.

If you look for the secret of his success, I think you have to remember that Dave is not a coach. He's raced a bike but never at a high level. He's a hard worker. He's a grafter. He'll sit in that velodrome for five, six, seven days and not see his own family for weeks on end. If you look at his man-management skills, I would describe him as being like a football team manager in the Alex Ferguson sense of the word. He runs British Cycling from top to bottom. He's in budget meetings, rider-selection meetings, equipment meetings and he's in the workshop deciding which mechanics they need to hire. He knows every in and out of it: who, where and what. He's not this chief executive figure that you never see, who's just there in the board meetings.

Dave's great strength is that he can walk into any environment, talk the back legs off a donkey, but still keep your attention. Dave can go into a meeting with all the chief executives at Sky, with James Murdoch and the others, and talk about financial forecasts and where they see their team in ten years' time. He can stand up in a suit talking about what kind of financial backing this or that is going to take, but a week later he could be in his Bermuda shorts and Great Britain T-shirt in a mechanics workshop discussing what tyres they're going to use next week.

He can give a presentation to five hundred people in a room with the chief executives of some of the biggest companies in the country and keep them enthralled for an hour about Steve Peters's chimp and computer – which is the model Steve uses when he's sorting our minds out – but he can also sit there and give the most motivational talk imaginable to eight of us at Sky before we go out to race a Pyrenean stage in the Tour de France. And finally, when it is all done, he's first to the bar with us, buying us all a drink and getting us drunk at the right time. That's where the big brother thing – in the nicest sense of the words – comes in. He's not the sort of manager that everyone is scared of within the team or who you never see. He has got that ability to adapt to whatever environment he's in, to give the right kind of talk or guidance.

Apart from Dave and Pete's contributions, it's hard for me to put my finger on what has made British Cycling so successful, because it's been part of my life for so long that it's difficult to see it from an objective viewpoint. What I have seen over the years is how the European pro teams do it. There's just no comparison. The difference is just incredible. One of the major things that British Cycling, or World Class as it was, has always had is a central base: the velodrome. Pro teams don't have one, although Garmin have tried to build something like that in Girona. Gradually, over the years, all the British Cycling team riders and staff started moving into the Manchester area so the velodrome became the daily training venue, whether you were meeting to go out on the road, putting the hours in on the track, going in to see a physio, or working out in the gyms. I think that makes a huge difference. It's a bit like a football team training at the same facility every day, whereas traditionally in cycling people had been spread out, and you only met when you turned up at one race or another. It's still like that in the pro scene.

I remember that when I was riding for the French teams from 2003 to 2007, they felt very old school in contrast to the Great Britain team. They were supposed to be the best in the sport, but GB were ahead of them. At a pro team, no one contacted you when you were at home; you were just handed your race programme and told: 'Turn up here on such and such day.' At the time there was no science behind anything in a French pro team: no sports scientists involved; no nutritionist. There was no attention to detail with the equipment and aerodynamics. It was just very much a question of 'Here is your bike, now crack on and race', even to the point where no one asked what length cranks you wanted on your road bike when they were sorting it out in January. You were given a bike and you just had to get on with it. I think a lot of the teams are very different now, but at the time it was a massive contrast.

The British Olympic team has snowballed since Jason Queally won that gold in Sydney; every year British Cycling have improved a bit on all fronts: a bit better planning; a bit more learning from mistakes; and there has been a constant ongoing attempt to find the fastest equipment. If I was asked to name one thing that has made them so successful, I'd say they may have great management, great athletes and are incredibly good at planning, but the biggest asset they have always had is common sense.

During the week before the Olympics, Dave rang me from the track team's holding camp in Newport and said, 'Look, they want you to ring the bell at the Olympic opening ceremony. It's massive, you know you can't say no to it.' I would, he told me, be on every television channel around the world. It was kept very, very quiet: no one else knew other than Dave and Shane. It was important that doing it wouldn't disrupt our preparation for the road race, which was the morning after, so I said to Dave, 'So long as you are happy for me to do it from a performance point of view, you organise it and I'll do it.'

Even now, looking back, I haven't quite figured out how big it was or the importance of it. That whole period was very surreal in some ways. It was one high after another; winning that time trial in Chartres, the next day the Champs-Elysées, drinking champagne in the Ritz, private-jetting home back to Lancashire, out on the bike the next morning overwhelmed by the amount of press at the end of the lane and the cars following me, then down to Surrey in a helicopter. We had a taste of how big it all was when we went out training as a team before the Olympic road race, with people who were just going about their daily business saying, 'Bloody hell, there go Great Britain.' The support was massive in the villages around the team hotel, and on Box Hill there were people everywhere looking for a glimpse of us and all the others. You could feel the buzz.

That Friday evening we drove across to east London; just being in the Olympic village was incredible. I love that atmosphere, the feeling you get from being in the village with all the other athletes; I wasn't going to get it at this Games, as we were staying in Surrey, so this was my only chance to experience it. The minute I got inside, there were people coming up to me, athletes asking to have their photo taken with me. Dave came with me; I'd arranged to meet Chris Hoy to have dinner in there, because I hadn't seen him for a while. I hugged Chris and we had our meal in the Olympic village together, with all kinds of people looking at us. Chris was carrying the flag that night for Great Britain in the opening ceremony parade, and after he went off to join the team, Dave and I walked over to the stadium. It was a matter of taking everything in my stride; 'Oh yeah, we're going to go to the opening ceremony . . .'

So I stood backstage, wearing the yellow jersey that they gave me, with these things going over my ears and into my earholes; I was wired up in the way that bands are on arena tours, so they can hear the backing tracks. It felt rather like wearing earplugs. Someone said, 'OK, Bradley, on in two seconds.' They opened the door: 'Go.' I walked to the front of the stage, stopped at the cross marked on the floor; waved to the crowd. All I saw was a wall of flashing lights because everyone was taking photos and I couldn't hear anything except the type of sound you have when you have earplugs in when you are going to sleep; all I could register was the sound of my breathing in my ears in the middle of this wall of flash lights: 'All right Bradley, turn around, go up to the bell, stand at the bell, and wait for your command to ring it.' I rang the bell, walked down the steps and out of the stadium.

Someone threw a jacket over me and I was whisked straight out; within two minutes I was in a private car with a police escort all round me, and we were going through the streets of London, uniformed motorcyclists stopping traffic all the way. I was on stage at two minutes past nine, and by half past I was back in the hotel at Hyde Park Corner with the Great Britain boys. As soon as I walked into the hotel, Rod – who is team manager for GB road teams as well as working at Sky – said to me, 'Right, we've got a meeting in ten minutes,' so in no time I was changed into team kit to talk through the next day and work out how we were going to do everything we could to win the Olympic road race for Cav. Then I had to go and shave my legs, pin my numbers on and go through all the pre-race routine for the next morning.

I simply couldn't dwell on anything. In the space of five days I'd gone from standing up talking to the whole of the Champs-Elysées to opening the Olympic Games. Stuff that would have seemed completely bizarre to me, that you can't even dream about, was becoming the norm and it was all happening in a blur. It was literally a matter of nipping in and out of the stadium to be the opener at the Greatest Show on Earth and driving back with an escort that made me feel as if I was the president of the United States. As you do. Right after that we were doing the road race, with the whole country expecting us to produce a gold medal in the first event of the Games. The minute that was done, my thoughts had to turn to the time trial, so among all that you forget about what you've just done in the stadium.

It's very hard to understand the significance of it all. Maybe in twenty years' time I'll look back and tell my grandchildren, 'Oh yeah, the Olympic Games in London, I was there, I did the thing with the bell.' It was fantastic to be asked. It was definitely special to play a part in some way. But I had no idea what public opinion was about what I'd done at the Tour. I hadn't been anywhere in public other than the Co-op in the village to get a pint of milk. I hadn't stood on a station platform, or been through an airport, or gone anywhere in the world outside the Tour, my home and the team hotel. I'd been helicoptered from my house down to Surrey, straight into the Foxhills resort where there were police on the gates so that we were completely shut away – which was a huge relief after the Tour – and I'd only been out of there on the bike with the lads. Apart from seeing the media at the GB hotel for a few hours, I'd been in a bubble.

That might explain what happened when I was waiting to go out into the stadium to ring the bell. When we got there, the volunteer at the entrance said, 'It's quite good in that stadium, you know.'

So I asked, 'I'm not going to get booed or something, am I?'

'Trust me,' he said. 'No, you won't get booed.'

CHAPTER 19

THE ROLLERCOASTER

Sitting in the minibus as we were driven to the start of the Olympic road race on The Mall, I could see Mark Cavendish's leg twitching. It's a little habit he has, almost a tic. Cav is quite a fidgety guy; he's always bouncing around, he has to be with people and hates rooming alone. I think it's a sprinter's thing. When he's sitting down, he's always twitching his legs, rocking his leg on the heel of his foot as if he's pumping up a camp bed with a footpump. He does it constantly: when we are on the bus in the morning, when he's eating; this time, I had a feeling I knew what was in his mind.

He looked at me, smiled, and said, 'I'm shitting myself.'

'You'll be all right, mate, you'll be fine. We'll take this thing on.'

In the days before, as we had pottered through the Surrey lanes on little training rides and hung around the Foxhills golf resort, Cav had seemed like a man with the weight of the nation on his shoulders. He was paying particular attention to every little detail: looking at his bike, making sure his overshoes were right, checking that his shoes were exactly what he wanted. It's not often that you see a rider as pumped for a single event as he was.

During the Tour, Cav had been extremely understanding about the situation we were in; that is why I wanted to ride for him at the Olympics until I had nothing left in my legs. All year, until we got to July, I had been thinking, 'Ah, the Olympic road race, I'm just going to do what I have to do and get out.' That was what Tony Martin did on the day; he stopped after about 100km to save his strength. That was what had been in my mind, but, after the way Mark had helped me out in the Tour, there was no way I could do that to him, I so desperately wanted him to win at the Olympics and he was only doing the one event. The very least I owed him was to give it everything. It wouldn't affect the time trial; I realised that at Chartres I had put in one of the best rides I've ever done against the watch, and I had done it after three weeks of hard bike racing, so there was no risk that the road race was going to tire me out for my other goal of the summer. When I told the media I thought that with three days to recover after the road race, it would be a doddle compared to the time trials in the Tour, I meant it.

The course started in the Mall and headed out through south-west London into Surrey for the nine laps of the circuit around Box Hill. Great Britain had to get on the case early. The four of us – David Millar, Froomie, Ian Stannard and I – started riding at the front of the peloton just 20km into the race. We didn't want to try and keep the whole thing together at that stage; the plan was to keep the peloton within reach of any lead groups that formed around the Box Hill circuits, so that the race would regroup coming back into London and then Cav could put his sprint to good use.

It was a long day: I'd been working at the head of the bunch for about 220km when I finally peeled off as we came back through Knightsbridge, with 4 or 5 km to go. I think I spent six of the nine laps on the front up Box Hill. We had experimented with the intensity that we needed to be riding at on the climb on one of the days when we were training there. First up, I tried it at 400 watts with Cav right behind me. That power had been too hard for him, so I expected to back off a little on the day. But it always feels a bit harder when you test yourself on a climb in training than it does when you are actually competing; as a result Cav was actually going far better in the race. The first lap, I went up it at 440 watts; the other guys were attacking up it after that so the next time I was at 450; again they were attacking over the top of that, but I was just holding them at 100m each time. A couple of times it got a bit lively up there so I was pushing it up to 460.

Box Hill itself takes only about five minutes in total, and we were just below the power outputs we had been sustaining at La Planche des Belles Filles for twenty minutes so it wasn't hard for me to do. The problem was not just the climb, but the rest of the circuit, where there was no let-up. On the first few laps up the big climb, Cav was saying to me that it was too hard and we needed to slow down; it wasn't really possible to back off that much as we needed to keep the break within reach but actually, as the race went on in the last laps, he felt better. Eventually, he could have gone with the last attacks on the hill, and got with the front group. He wishes now he had; by the last time up the hill, a little peloton of thirty-three had come together at the front. It was one of those things that you simply can't predict; we worked our utmost, but the group never came back. In a sense, we'd done our job; if someone had said to us in the morning that at the top of Box Hill for the last time, with 47km to go, we would have a group 51secs ahead of us, we'd have taken that. But it just didn't work out over those final miles. It needed another team or two to come to the front and work, but none of them wanted to help Cav get to the finish. Ironically, if a team with a sprinter had put some graft in, they'd have beaten him on The Mall, as he finished with a slow puncture and wasn't able to sprint properly.

As the gold medal was presented to Alexander Vinokourov of Kazakhstan – he of the blood-doping positive from 2007 – we sat in the tent in the pits for an hour after the finish with our skinsuits unzipped. We were too exhausted to get changed, and just too depressed. No one said a word. It was as if we'd all lost the race, all five of us, or as if we'd lost a man during war. I was empty and exhausted but television wanted us the minute we went across the line; I was gutted we hadn't won. I was also a bit angry because one of the other riders had really pissed me off; he said as we were riding in towards the finish, 'So what happened to your legs, couldn't bring the group back?' It felt as if some of our rivals were really pleased to see us fail rather than doing some work themselves, so that left us all a bit upset.

On the other hand, I think the press really did build Cav up a bit too much, and I don't think he'd fully appreciated how hard it is to win an Olympic road race with a small team. All the headlines that night were along the lines of, 'Cav fails to win Britain's first gold medal of the Olympic Games; the team let the gap get too big'. I actually saw one story that read, 'Even Bradley Wiggins was struggling to hold the pace at the end' with a picture of me being dropped at 5km to go, asking if our 'failure' might be due to fatigue from the Tour de France. You read that and you think, 'Are you serious, did you not see me riding on the front for over two hundred kilometres?'

The misunderstanding happened, I think, because from the outside the last two weeks of the Tour had looked pretty straightforward. There had been no massive dramas or nail-biting suspense once I got the yellow jersey – although obviously it's never like that when you are on the inside – and having watched that for fourteen days, most of the press just assumed that when it came to the Olympic road race Great Britain would carry on where Sky left off. The problem was that a one-day race on a hilly course with a five-man team is a completely different matter to a three-week Tour with nine men. There were some writers who tried to point out that we were taking on a huge challenge that might be beyond us, but they were a minority.

After the race, I was going back to the team hotel and Cav was heading straight off to do some criteriums in Belgium and France; he hugged me, and I said, 'I'll see you later.' He wouldn't let go, and it felt as if he was crying on my shoulder because of what I'd done for him. So we went our separate ways and he sent me a lovely text the next day, a long, long message saying that what I did meant more to him than winning, gentleman isn't enough and so on. He said he didn't want to say it at the time because it would have been over the top; he sent me another one before the time trial saying, 'Go and bash them all tomorrow', and I didn't see him again until the Tour of Britain.

That night I was completely out of it, totally on my knees, and the day after I was still absolutely knackered. But we had a good routine at Foxhills: recovering, sleeping, out on the bikes. The next day went easily, and the third day I started feeling really good again. The chances were, I needed that ride in the road race to open me up, having stopped after the Tour for a few days. I remember going through all the numbers with Tim, and the figures said the Olympic road race had been one of my hardest days of the year.

We looked closely at the TSS scores that are such an integral part of my training. Some days in the Tour register only 120 TSS, meaning that although you've been out there for six hours, it hasn't taken as much toll on your body as you might have thought. At Paris–Roubaix in 2011 I clocked up 450, so that was a huge day, and I remember the Olympic road race came in about 320, so that was quite a big outing too. But it was perfectly reasonable going into that time trial in the Games. If you look at the last three days before the *contre-la-montre* from Bonneval to Chartres in the Tour, there were the two Pyrenean stages at a TSS of 332 and 342, and the day into Brive where I led Cav out was about 290. So that had worked out at three really tough days. Tim said, 'You've just had that Olympic road race at 320, so now you've got three days' rest; don't worry, you're going to recover and you're going to be fine.'

During the Tour it had struck Tim, Shane and me that on each of the occasions when I had won a time trial all year Sean Yates had been there every step of the way. So I asked Sean if he wanted to be driving the car behind me in London, and he said, 'Bloody right, I'd love to do it, will I get a tracksuit?' So we sorted him out with a day's accreditation and he came along, drove the course the day before, and rode it; that meant he had all that information and we had the usual dialogue in the same way that I had had in every time trial I'd ridden all season.

The overriding thing with the time trial was that from the day before, going through that whole routine in the morning beforehand, it was the same process that I had been through at the Tour and every other time trial in recent years. So that put me in Hampton Court on the Wednesday morning knowing what I'd achieved in Chartres nine days before, feeling super-confident that I could win. I had no idea about the public out on the road at that point, because you go into a tented area at the start, and you concentrate on your warm-up. There was British support all around though, so I wasn't sitting there in a state, saying to myself, 'Oh God what are they all going to think?' I was thriving off it. All I had to do was go out and put my ride together.

That silver medal in Copenhagen had given Tim, Shane and me confidence in the approach we had taken to time trialling, where we had been looking to move closer to Fabian Cancellara in every way. It was similar to the approach Great Britain had adopted on the track. You analyse where you are and see where the rest of the world is, and you look at what they're doing. What we used to do with the team pursuit when we were trying to catch up with the Aussies was to look at their gearing, whether they were doing lap turns or more, where each rider was placed in the line, the kind of schedules they were riding. You look at everything.

It was the same with time trialling. The big thing we had flagged up with Fabian over the years was how much time he took out of the other riders just because he was better at cornering. That was always one area we were looking to improve in. In terms of flat speed we were very similar, but he'd always been renowned for taking a lot of risks on descents and corners. With Tony Martin after the 2011 World's, it was more about looking at his cadence. We looked in detail at how he had managed to take 1min20secs out of me at the World's. We worked out his average power and realised that for me to go 1min20secs faster, the power I would have had to produce would have been impossible. It would not have been human. So there must have been something else, aerodynamics maybe; there was certainly something in his cadence. I tended to spin a lower gear, partly because of my background as a track cyclist, where fast pedalling is a key element. He was turning the pedals a good 15 or 20rpm slower than me and it was something that he and another German, Bert Grabsch, tended to do. It's a bit like driving a car in a high gear, sixth maybe, for a long time down a motorway as opposed to trying to whizz along in third.

This was typical of how we built to 2012: not accepting how I was, but trying to change it a little bit. So we worked on torque all through the winter of 2011–12, simply putting more power into my pedalling but at lower revs. That meant riding at the same sort of power output I would have in any time trial, but doing it at 50rpm rather than the usual 90. We started with five-minute blocks and progressed through the winter – seven-and-a-half-minute blocks, fifteen-minute blocks – until before the Tour I was doing forty-minute climbs at threshold at 50rpm. So by the time we got to August, and the time trial in the London Olympic Games, I was 40secs ahead of Tony for a little bit more power, but I'd brought my cadence down by about 7rpm (Tim's figures are that in the 2011 World's I averaged 103rpm; at the Games, 96rpm); I was rolling along in a bigger gear rather than spinning a smaller one. I didn't have bigger ratios on but I was using higher gears than in the past – the 11- or 12-tooth sprocket, where in the past I would have been on the 13-tooth. The thing to remember is that we knew it was going to take me a long time to build up to that kind of time and torque. That was why we had had to start in November.

Back in Hampton Court in August 2012 I was very relaxed. I remember talking to my mechanic Diego beforehand, and him saying, 'Brad I've got something to tell you.'

'What is it, Diego?'

'On the way to the start we went round this round and your bike wasn't attached properly to the roof and it fell off and it smashed your handlebars.'

'What – my race bike? Oh fuck . . .'

'No, your spare bike.'

He had to put some other handlebars on the second bike, which weren't the same as the ones on the race bike, but there were no toys being thrown out of the pram instead I was sitting there laughing, 'Don't worry about that, Diego, I'm not going to need a spare bike today.'

That sums up the state of mind I was in at the time. In the Tour, and in the first few days after the Tour, I remember thinking that if I could just get a medal of any colour in London that would be fantastic. That depended on how I shaped up after the Tour, but the closer it got to the time trial, the more I knew that in terms of the power I could get out, I was going to be as good as I had been in Chartres; I'd been flying the day before in training. So on the day I was raring to go. I was thinking about the process: the walk up the ramp, launching myself out of the start house, not getting carried away too early on, and all the incremental steps through the ride, all the things going well, fuelling after seventeen minutes and so on. I knew I had it in the bag if I could avoid getting anything wrong.

The minute I turned up in the start area, I couldn't believe the roar I got. I remember sitting in the stage area next to the ramp and getting a buzz from the crowd. It wasn't the loudest thing I'd ever heard, not quite, but then I rolled down the ramp and the sound of the crowd really hit me.

I turned left out of the ticketed area, on to Hampton Court Bridge, and the noise was unbelievable. It was the same all the way around that course, but the bit I will always remember to the day I die was going through the last time check. It wasn't official, it was one that the team had set up – we just made sure someone was at a certain point with a stopwatch – and it was at 9km to go, just before Kingston. Sean had been telling me I was 29secs ahead of Tony Martin: knowing that there were about five miles to go and I wasn't dying off at that point, all I had to do was keep it together and I was going to win.

That was inspiring me to press on even harder, and I remember going through Kingston, not taking any super risks on the couple of little corners, through a shopping precinct; then the route went left out of the shopping precinct, over Kingston Bridge and down to a roundabout, where the Sigma Sport bike shop is, which you had to take on the opposite side rather than using the race line. So I had to slow down quite a bit, coming out of the roundabout, and because I'd pulled up, I was then accelerating away almost from a standing start. The road had narrowed down so the yells and screams from the crowd were actually deafening, to the point where I got ringing in my ears. I was thinking, 'Fuck me, the noise,' and then it was a matter of giving it everything I had all the way to the finish.

I turned into Bushy Park towards the end, and I could see Tony Martin's cars up the road, so I knew I'd beaten him. At that point you're emptying it, you're nailed, you're just trying to keep it together; I kept giving more than I had to, thinking, 'Empty it to the line'; I'd lift the pace quite a bit and then I'd bring it back down, because I knew I couldn't sustain it. I was already fifty minutes into the ride and thinking, 'No, no, you don't need to do that, Brad, just hold it, hold it, you don't need to push like that.' I was continually doing that in those last few kilometres, and coming out across the cobbled section towards Hampton Court Palace, Sean was saying, 'You're not taking it too hard, don't take any mad crazy risks.' Even at that point, when it was clear I'd got it in the bag, he never said, 'You've got this, you've got this, you've won it.' He was just concentrating on getting me to the end.

Coming round that last sweeping bend and up to the line, the crowd seemed to go dead silent. I was thinking, 'Uh oh.' Normally when you cross the line everyone cheers so I thought, 'Shit, I've lost it, I must have done something to have lost it.' Further up, towards Hampton Court Bridge, the crowd erupted. That had to be for me, with the best time, but I still wasn't certain. I was confused, so I turned around and went back to my *soigneur*; I stood there and he didn't say anything.

I kept saying to him, 'Have I got the fastest time?'

And he kept saying, 'Yeah, you got the fastest time.'

'Are you sure?'

'Yeah, yeah.'

'No, they are fucking lying to me.'

I was getting really irate and saying I can't exactly remember what. I was really confused; the fatigue was kicking in a bit. Fabian Cancellara was last off as the defending champion; he hadn't come in yet.

I remember saying something like, 'Are you sure? Fabian's not ahead of me on the road, is he?'

'No, no he isn't.' The exhaustion began hitting me; I had to sit down for a bit.

'Is Fabian in yet? Is Fabian in yet?'

'No, no.' But eventually Fabian came in and they said, 'That's it you've done it.'

So I stood up again, went up there into the finish area; people were cheering and I was trying to soak it all in. I was still a bit confused as to what was going on. I was just looking for Cath and the kids: Where are they? Where are they? I kept trying to look in the stands for them; they directed me to the throne which they had been putting each of the leaders on as they waited for their time to be beaten; I sat there for a second, which was bizarre. It's that picture that everyone printed; I always sit in a chair in that way, so as soon as I sat down I did a Winston Churchill victory sign.

I spotted Dave, and said 'Where's Cath? Where's Cath?'

'We'll go and find them, we'll go and find them.'

Down off the throne, and the chaperones started saying, 'Come behind now, we've got to get ready for the podium.'

'I want my wife and kids.' I had to find them.

So I got back on my bike, rode out and waved to the crowd for a bit – that's where all the public were, outside the finish area which was cordoned off inside the palace gates – turned around, came back down and then went up to the finish line looking for Cath and the kids. I turned back round, waved to the crowd again, rode up to Hampton Court Bridge, went back in, and finally found Cath and the kids at the end where the start was. We all went behind the podium, I got changed and then it was time to get the medal.

*

Some time later, when they were selling off the bits and pieces after the Games, I asked if I could have that throne as a memento. They wanted a hundred grand for it because there was so much interest in it, so I told them that perhaps they should find another customer. At that price! The cheek of it, you know! They did offer to do me a replica one for two grand or something but it's not quite the same.

CHAPTER 20

WHAT NEXT?

That time trial has to rate as my greatest Olympic moment, more than the pursuit final win against Brad McGee in Athens, and maybe even more than the team pursuit world record in the final in Beijing along with G, Ed Clancy and Paul Manning. To win that gold medal in that setting, in London, in front of Hampton Court, with all the history going back to Henry VIII; it was about as British as you can get. The time trial lasted an hour, whereas the track races I'd done in the previous Olympics had been only four minutes long. There was so much time to savour it.

Every athlete has a defining year during their career. Sir Chris Hoy's was Beijing when he won his three gold medals, and 2012 is probably mine. I remember when I was a kid Chris Boardman talking about his hour record in Manchester in 1996; he reckoned nothing would ever top the feeling of going round that track to the roar of the crowd for one whole hour. That may well have been the height of Chris's career; it was probably the best he ever got physically. For the best part of an hour that Wednesday in Surrey, I was able to savour that feeling, of being at my best, with a massive crowd deafening me with their support. It was phenomenal; I am never going to experience anything like that again in my sporting life. I am not saying it is the end of my career by any means, but nothing is ever going to top that. And that's a poignant feeling.

Ever since, I've been trying to take it all in, wondering whether that time trial was my greatest sporting moment. I don't know if it was better than the Tour de France. I still haven't come to terms with the fact that I've won the Tour, so at this stage I don't know. In my eyes, the Tour will always be phenomenal because of what the team did for me. In the last time trial from Bonneval to Chartres I had a fantastic day; I did the job, but the whole race, all twenty-two days of it, was about the team putting me in a position to win the Tour de France. After the Tour, I struggled to work out quite how to thank them. I didn't speak to any of the riders who helped me win the Tour, other than Cav, for a fair while, because I didn't know what to say to them. I didn't want to send them some cheesy email saying, 'Guys, I can't thank you enough', because I don't think that was quite what was needed. In the initial aftermath of the Tour it didn't seem to sum up what those guys did for me. It's got to come from the heart and not just in an email. What I do know is that I will never forget it.

Part of what drives me is the love and respect I feel for the sport and its history. That goes back to my childhood. I grew up with posters of Indurain, Museeuw and the rest on my bedroom walls, while other kids were into football: Lineker, Gascoigne and so on. In those days, a child's dream was to go and lift the FA Cup because that was what those great players had achieved. For me when I was a kid, the dream would be to lead a race like the Dauphiné, or even the Tour for one day. So a lot of my motivation comes from the fact that I realise what the great races mean, and how many people have won those races.

There haven't been many Tour winners in my lifetime, perhaps a dozen, so it's a very special list to be on. I never see myself as up there with people like Robert Millar and Tom Simpson because they were the big names when I was a child. You never imagine you will be better than them. Simpson was long gone when I was a kid but even though Millar and the others like Sean Kelly rarely raced in the UK, they were cult heroes. They lived in France, we didn't have the Internet, you could only see them in cycling magazines, which came out once a week. You never imagine you will be up there with those names: Hinault, Merckx and so on. You never imagine that not only will you be the winner of the Tour, but you'll also win Paris–Nice, Dauphiné and the Tour of Romandie in the same year, which is incredible.

I've always loved cycling because it's you against the machine. You apply yourself to something in your life, and then it's all about numbers, pace judgement, putting the ride together, having it all go to plan. You do the training, you get this power; it's very quantifiable. I love the sense of accomplishment. You come away and see if you can train harder, work harder and get a result at the end from it. It's nice to be recognised and get respect for being good at something, to see what your achievements mean to people. It's incredible that sport can do that, although it is just sport and you can't lose sight of that.

I think the difference between the Olympic gold medal and the Tour is that the time trial was all about me. It was all about my individual performance on the day, about what I could put together nine days after the Tour. As an individual feat it was probably the best sporting performance of my career. It will stick in my mind as my greatest ride, the peak of my physical condition. Shane has said a few times that we never saw the best Bradley Wiggins on the track but maybe we saw something of that kind there. Even if I go on to Rio and win the time trial there, or even if I had won the time trial in Beijing, nothing would ever be the same as winning it in London nine days after winning the Tour de France as well.

If I had to look at that day, getting 40secs on Tony, beating Fabian and all those guys, the margin of victory was significant, and to do it on those roads and in that atmosphere was incredible. It had been raining in the morning and it seemed as if the sun came out just for those few hours; it was a great, great occasion, it really was. I spoke to John Dower, the film-maker, and he said there was a bizarre sense of joy lasting long after I'd left with the other riders. The organisers had started taking all the barriers down, but, he said, people just hung around in the pubs and bars down there by the river, it felt almost as if a football team had won the Champions League or something and everyone was celebrating that.

There was this great atmosphere down there; it was a beautiful evening and it was as if people simply didn't want to go home, as if they wanted the day to go on for ever.

There's an interview we did at my house in December 2011, when I've got a beard because it's midwinter. John asked me, 'Can you imagine rolling down the Champs-Elysées and winning the Tour de France, then winning the Olympics the next week in London? Can you imagine what that is going to feel like? Would you take one over the other?' My answer was that I couldn't really choose, because I'm greedy and I wanted to do both. He told me that that interview is priceless now; when I said that to him back then, I didn't believe for one second that I was going to do both. And here we are now; it's happened.

Looking back to 2010, it was as if everything I did seemed to go wrong, no matter how I tried; in 2012 it was as if I could do no wrong. When you see pictures of Fabian Cancellara, defining pictures of his career, he's bouncing across the cobbles in Roubaix or winning a time trial. Contador is always coming across the line on a mountain stage making his firing gun gesture, whereas I've kind of got a bit of everything in there. It's nice to look back, for example, on winning that bunch sprint in the Tour of Romandie and having that picture in my mind. All the wins in 2012 were different; the Col d'Eze time trial, that bunch kick, climbing on the Joux Plane to win the Dauphiné, and then the defining images of the Tour. I'm proud of that as well. It's been as if everything I did seemed to turn to gold.

*

Shane has always said to me that we train to be successful for the performance side of things, but we don't train for success and what it brings. That's very true. So I don't know what the future holds. The London Games was always going to be a massive watershed. It's been the pinnacle ever since we knew it was going to take place. Beijing was amazing, but the minute it was finished, everyone's sights turned to London. Everyone's plans seemed to finish there. As for me, I never looked further than 1 August 2012 and that time trial.

I struggle with the idea that I may have turned into a role model overnight. People say to me, 'Are you ready now, do you realise you are a role model for so many people out there?' I was constantly saying that I can understand why in an inspirational sense for what I do on the bike, but please don't hold me up there as something to aspire to, because outside a sports environment I'm as normal as everyone else. I'm not perfect. I make mistakes. People seem to have illusions before they meet you; then they find out that you're not precisely what they would like you to be. It's the same with most celebrities in this country: porcelain gods that shatter when they fall. So I say that I've got a normal life like everyone else. I have a different job to everyone else, but I'm normal in some of the problems I face like any other person. I have a family, and it's not easier because of what you do or what you get paid.

Adapting to what 2012 has brought me may not be easy. Trying to be as good as I could be in the Tour, and if possible winning it, was something that Cath, Ben, Isabella and I bought into together. It was a complete lifestyle, twelve months of the year. It's not something you can stop and then go back to. So Cath got on with it, and I got on with it. It wasn't easy, but it raises a whole new set of issues when it's all over. Doing what I have done involves sacrifice for me, but most of all for the family; being away for my kids' birthdays, not being around at times when they need me. The justification was that I could win the Tour; when Daddy wins the Tour it will all be over, that is what you tell the kids, and that's what we have lived by for four years, and that's gone now. If I say it again the answer now might be, 'Well, you said that last year and you've done it now.' It was worth the sacrifice in 2012 to do it all once, but it's hard to say if it would be worth it to do it all again. And if I do it again, do I go and win a third? I suppose if you do that, it stops when you keep going back and doing it and finally you don't win. And it's the end of your reign. That's what happened to Miguel Indurain. I never want to do that.

In many ways, I don't want to go back to the Tour ever again. I don't need to: I'll always have winning it in 2012. I don't know if the desire is going to be there. It doesn't matter if it isn't. I could retire tomorrow and go and be totally happy with what I've achieved. If I were to go back to the Tour and my heart was not in it, or I hadn't done the work, I'd be in big trouble. What it boils down to is this: I watched Cadel Evans this year, coming back to defend his Tour title, struggling for 8th place, and that's not for me. If I can't do it 110 per cent to win, I'd rather not be there.

If I'm honest, I have other goals. I'm not going to be doing this for ever; I have said I'll do another two years at this level, so that means I don't have much time to win other events I feel are important such as the Giro d'Italia and Paris–Roubaix. After that I would like to go back on the track squad for two years, try and win the Olympic team pursuit, then I'm retiring. Returning to the track would be a different challenge, eight years after Beijing. It would be fresh again, and the Olympics is really where my career all started in Sydney in 2000. It would be difficult, but I think I know what it takes. I wouldn't underestimate it. I like the idea of a different type of commitment: to be a pure track rider, a pure endurance rider, go to the gym with the other guys every day.

There have been other things: visions, one dream more than anything else, and I couldn't justify doing it because I'd be silly to move from cycling now with the money I could earn, but I would love to try to be a rower at the next Olympics, in a lightweight four or something. It would be impossible to do: go down, lock, stock and barrel, live in Henley, train and try and be at the next Olympics in a rowing boat. It's never going to happen, but it would be a different challenge. Imagine that, going and winning the coxless lightweight four: Olympic gold in rowing, four years off. Unfortunately there is no way I could do it.

So I'm thinking of going through to 2014, riding the Commonwealth Games, then, from Glasgow onwards, becoming a track rider again, still racing on the road, but the road would only be to build my fitness for the track, in the way that G's done this year: Glasgow 2014, world championships 2015, track at the 2016 Olympics.

So that's that.

*

I've sometimes wondered what George would have thought of all that has happened to me and the family in the two years since we lost him. As my granddad, my father figure and the man who helped me develop a love of all sports, he'd have been made up to see me succeed for sure, but there's one other thing.

During the Games, there was speculation about whether I might end up with a knighthood in the same way that Sir Chris Hoy did after his great year. People asked me about it, so I did wonder whether I'd accept it if it were to come my way. The point is that I can never see myself being given a title like Sir Bradley Wiggins. I've never considered myself above anybody else. I've always struggled with hierarchy and status. I don't know what it is, maybe just my upbringing, the area I'm from, but I'm quite happy to play second fiddle. I understand my physical capabilities sometimes give me status, but when it's all done and dusted I struggle with that kind of thing. It's not what happens to kids from Kilburn.

I remember saying to my nan, 'So if I get offered a knight-hood or whatever, what do you reckon George would make of it if I turned it down?'

She came back, quick as a flash: 'He would never have spoken to you again.'

So if it comes my way, I just might have to take it.

THAT'S ENTERTAINMENT

November 6, 2012. It had been a really busy day but I was looking forward to getting out on my bike in the evening. There was a group of us planning to go out at 6.30 p.m. just down the road from my home. The aim was to go for a two- or three-hour ride off-road. It wasn't ideal, but at least it would mean I'd been out on my bike that day. So I set off on the mountain bike with the big lights on. I had been going for about a quarter of an hour and was approaching the last few hundred metres before the path drops down below the road to the canal. Before that, though, I had to go past a petrol station at quite a busy junction up by the motorway. There was plenty of rush-hour traffic about.

I was getting close to the exit of the petrol station when I saw this little Ford van coming out. I was thinking, 'She's going to stop, she's going to stop' but before I knew it, the van accelerated out in an effort to get across the road in front of a group of cars. Next thing I knew I was on the ground and in pain. As I lay there I could see the van still moving. I wasn't entirely sure she was going to pull over.

When you crash in a race your initial reaction is to get up as quickly as possible, but when you crash in training you have time to start assessing the damage. You're sitting on the floor hurting, and the first thing that goes through your mind is: how bad is it? You go through the list of the parts that usually get broken: collarbone, wrist, elbow, knee. This time, the first thing I felt was a pain in my back. I was sure I'd done something to my vertebrae, but, as I learnt later, when you damage your ribs, you feel it first in your spine.

There were people coming over, trying to pick me up off the road. I got to my feet and could feel this crackling, rattling feeling in my ribs. It was a bit strange; I could sense things clicking. Something wasn't right. I'd never broken a rib before but that is exactly how it felt to me. I'd hit the front right wing of the van, gone over the windscreen and up over the roof; and, because it continued to accelerate, I kept tumbling across the roof as it moved, then I fell down the back of it. It was as if I was rolling out of a bed, only from a far greater height. I was disorientated from rotating, and I don't know how I landed. What I do know is that I'd broken my helmet, a finger and a rib.

My next thought was: right, I'm hurt. I need an ambulance. I was trying to compose myself, and I was going into a little bit of shock. I knew I had to phone Cath straightaway to say I'd been knocked off and I was all right. I didn't want to get to the hospital and to have someone call her, because then she wouldn't know how bad it was. If she could hear my voice at least she would know I was in one piece. By this time there was a lot of commotion. The van had stopped further down the road and a bloke, who was already in the petrol station, had got me sitting in his car to stay warm while we waited for the ambulance.

After I got to hospital Cath picked up our team doctor Richard Freeman, who was laid up himself as he'd just broken a leg, and drove him to Royal Preston Hospital to assess me. My management company had been trying to get in touch with me, but they had ended up getting hold of Richard instead and the first thing they said to him was 'How long are we looking at?' So, when he got to the hospital and Richard asked me, I said, 'Give me as long as you can.'

'I can give you four weeks.'

So I was lying there thinking, 'Fantastic. I've got a sick note for a month.'

And all of a sudden I had the chance to stop. At last. It felt like I had been on a mad roller-coaster ride since 1 August when I'd won the Olympic time trial. Our lives haven't really been the same since that day. I thought I would be able to see the season out and then have a rest period, but the downtime never arrived. Instead, I was thrust into loads of other work and commitments, so in the end I was just as busy as before. I knew I needed to start riding my bike again, but instead I was wrapped up in all these other distractions. By the time of the crash in November I had already been thinking 'This is bullshit now' but afterwards it was obvious: my life had become unmanageable. I shouldn't have been out training at night. I'd been flat out with work; the next day I was due to do publicity work – for this book, as it happens – a bit of radio, some filming with Graham Norton, and I'd been feeling a bit moody about it. I wanted to get back to riding my bike, feeling healthy again, setting some goals for 2013. I was a bit frustrated. I felt as if I was being pulled left, right and every other way by the demands on my time.

So the crash was a turning point. I was in hospital for a couple of days, spent a week at home recovering and trying to get back on my feet, spent a few days doing rehab with the physio to get my body moving again, then went to Majorca for a couple of weeks. Once there, I started riding up all the climbs where I'd put in the groundwork the winter before the Tour win. I was really unfit. I was struggling because of the broken rib, but it was only then I realised how much I'd missed riding my bike, how much I love it. It was simple, really. I was just enjoying being on two wheels again. In one way, getting knocked off by that van was a blessing in disguise: if it hadn't happened, I might never have got back into a full routine and would have kept on being pulled in so many different directions.

Since the London Olympics, so much had changed for me and my family. The biggest difference in our lives came from how recognisable I was all of a sudden. I never want to make it sound as if I'm complaining about this because I know how much it all means to people – I'm a big fan of sport myself – and I don't for one minute regret anything I've achieved on my bike, but I hadn't realised the impact winning the Tour and the gold medal in the Games would have on people, and how a sort of Wiggomania would take over the country. Once I had completed the Olympic time trial I wanted to go back to normal life, whatever that is, be it going to the supermarket, going out with the children, walking down the street or just going to a pub or restaurant. But all those things will never be how they were before I left home to go to the Tour at the end of June 2012.

We went to our holiday home in Majorca for two weeks of relaxation and fun with the kids. But I couldn't walk through the town or go to our usual restaurant because now I had become a piece of public property. I was adamant that I would go on doing things the way I always have, as far as possible. That stubbornness was probably a mistake but at the same time why should things have to change? It's hard on the children because at the moment everyone wants a piece of me, everyone wants a photo of me with their children and so mine have to move aside while it's going on. My kids don't always understand why, for example, I have to sit with another little girl who wants her photo taken with me when we go to a restaurant. I simply don't know how to deal with things like that. I'm still learning to live with it all.

Now I don't go to the supermarket looking like me any more. The problem was I'd come home and think I could just go out shopping; I expected everything to be how it was. Then the minute I walked in the supermarket with my sideburns, there would be mass hysteria. People couldn't believe I was there. What are you doing in here? What are you doing packing up your shopping? So everyone was looking at me. I became very self-conscious and found it hard to get my head around it. The first few months of that were hard. I can't go into a restaurant and sit down for dinner with Cath because all eyes in the room are on us. There will be whispering, then someone will come over and say, 'Terribly sorry to disturb you, I can see you're having a quiet meal with your wife, but is there any chance of a photo? My brother is a big fan of yours.' So then your meal is taken up with two or three people saying that, and then the restaurant owner wants a photo as well. So I tend not to go out any more. If I go to the supermarket or out with the kids I'll wear a hat or a hood, or a scarf round my neck. I cut my sideburns off a month or two after the Games.

Knowing that Sir Chris Hoy went through a very similar experience after Beijing – Dave Brailsford and Shane Sutton had told me how hard he'd found it – was a bit of a relief to me. You always think people who are famous just take it in their stride and they love it: athletes like Chris and me become famous for our performances, but fame wasn't why I wanted to win the races I did in 2012. I wanted to achieve it all, but you never know the impact it is going to have on other parts of your life.

As I said, I'm not complaining about it, because I understand sport and cycling and I know how much these performances can mean to people, how it can change their lives. That is clear from the amount of letters I've had and the number of people who have come up to me to tell me that they are inspired by what I did and that they've decided to get the bike out of the garage and go out and lose a few stone. Things like that are overwhelming and slightly humbling and it's nice to think of people taking the trouble to write to you. I know it's not going to last for ever; there is no rulebook about how this is going to be.

And being in the public eye has brought opportunities as

well. I've been able to meet some of my greatest heroes, for example. That side of it has been brilliant; I would never have got to do that otherwise. It feels incredibly self-indulgent. Paul Weller was doing a charity gig for Crisis at the Hammersmith Apollo; he got me up on stage for the encores, in front of a packed house, to play The Jam's hit from the 1980s, 'That's Entertainment'. That was incredible, probably the biggest moment of them all. That, or being made a life member of Wigan Rugby League Club.

There were other honours, of course. I didn't expect to win the BBC Sports Personality of the Year. I was very nervous about the whole thing, and incredibly blasé about it. I felt that if I could win it that would be absolutely unbelievable, but I wasn't going to build my hopes up because it's a public vote and you never know which way it will go. People don't realise it, but I'm quite an introverted person so I do struggle with being in public at that kind of occasion; there are 17,000 people there. I struggle to combat it without having a drink to calm myself down. So that's what I did – I went to the pub late in the morning with Cath, her sister, my brother-in-law and some friends, and was in there all day until the ceremony began. When they announced that Andy Murray got third, and Jessica Ennis had come second, my initial thought then was, 'Oh well, Mo Farah's won it, I'm not in the top three.' So when David Beckham opened the envelope and read my name out, my first thought was 'Jesus Christ, Mo's not up there at all.' I'd thought he'd be in the top three, without a doubt.

It's a phenomenal thing to win because it's such an institution in the British sporting world. I've been watching it ever since I was a little kid. Sometimes I look at the trophy in my sitting room and look at the names on it. My two biggest sporting heroes are on there one year after the other: Tommy Simpson and Bobby Moore, 1965 and 1966.

And I did take my nan's advice and accept the knighthood. That was another thing that I didn't expect, even though it had been talked about since August. You have to get the letter first before you even think about whether to accept it. I received the letter quite late and I remember speaking about it to Dave Brailsford, who also received one. It's a phenomenal thing, because if Sports Personality reflects success in a given year, in my case 2012, a knighthood comes because of what you've achieved throughout your entire career. And then it really hit me: 'I'm going to be called Sir Bradley.' That's something I never, ever thought would happen. Whenever I ring up the bank or go to see my lawyer, they will say, 'Do you mind if I call you Sir Bradley?'

'Oh, all right, although I don't insist on it.'

And the Belgian cycling fans have started calling me Sir Bradley too. The French will probably love it as well, given that they already seem to be fascinated by my Britishness. That kind of thing means a lot in Europe. It's a strange feeling, but nice for someone with my upbringing – it's not something that happens to every Tom, Dick or Harry. It's nice to be recognised in that way, and still be active in my sport, because they don't just give it for one-off things. It's about what you've done over the years. And it's going to be nice seeing it on start sheets. There was a funny episode with my racing licence, which came through just before I started my first race of 2013 in Majorca in early

February. The licence had me down as Bradley Wiggins CBE, so I sent it back to British Cycling and asked for a new one with my proper title on it, so that when the *directeur sportif* goes and hands in my licence before a race, it's got Sir Bradley on it.

There were changes at Sky as well as we went into 2013. I'll be going back to the Tour without Sean Yates, who has retired, and Shane Sutton will be less of a presence as well. Sean is a major loss when you think about what his experience of the great races meant to me and the team. If there's one person in the team who was irreplaceable in terms of the time he's spent in the sport, he's the one. You'll have read how close our working relationship was earlier in this book, and I'm going to miss him. He has such a presence at the races; he doesn't always have to say anything, but he is a master of coming out with the one phrase that makes the difference at exactly the right time. It will be really difficult for anyone else to fill his shoes. I'm sad that he's left, but that's the way it is, and all we can do is get on with it and move forward.

With Shane, it's a slightly different story. He wasn't around in 2012 quite as much as he had been in 2010 and 2011 because of his commitments as head coach to the track team, and that's what he's going to be focusing on in the future. The problem with Shane comes when he can't be involved 100 per cent. He works best when he's there day in day out, and when he's not he finds it very frustrating. Because he's got so many other commitments in his life, it becomes too disruptive for me. It took a long time to come to that decision, there were a lot of meetings, but it's for the best. 2012 was a bit of a transitional year for him in any case, in that he was letting Tim Kerrison take the reins more, and Tim has grown into the role to the extent that he can take over completely now, something which has been on the cards for a while as he gained experience in cycling. That change won't be quite as hard to deal with as Shane's absence had already been covered to some extent. And in other ways, Shane will still be there for me, as he's like a father to me. We'll still be talking a lot about what's coming up in 2013.

It was also a shame to lose Mark Cavendish at the end of 2012 when he moved to join Tom Boonen at Omega Pharma-Quickstep. I wish he hadn't left Sky and I would imagine there is a small part of him that probably wishes he was still there. I understand why he had to leave – he needed those opportunities that come up in a team which isn't as focused on the Grand Tours as Sky now is – but, like Sean, he is so good to have around in the big races. I didn't actually spend that much time racing with him in 2012, but he's such a good laugh when he's there. The critical thing with Cav is that if you commit to him, nine times out of ten he will win the bike race for you. That's something you get a lot of pleasure out of as a teammate, or I certainly do. When I start winding down my career and am not going for the big Tours any more, I'd like to see my last couple of years out doing lead-outs for him. It's something I've always enjoyed; helping him to that stage win in Paris in 2012 is an incredible memory.

Helping people out is a good feeling. There's a young bike rider I've been supporting a little bit, a lad called Kieran Friend. I'd given him a bit of moral support, helped him find a team, and then it occurred to me that if I sold off a yellow jersey or something for a couple of grand I could do a bit more. That's when I decided I should do it properly, set up a charity to raise some money, and that's how the Bradley Wiggins Foundation was born. I'd always wanted to have my own sportive, so we ran that in late August. It went well. A lot of people rode it, and it raised a lot of money. We had a dinner later in the autumn, and while the money came out of my own pocket in the first year, now we're at the stage where the fundraising is properly in place, we have someone to run it and it's a matter of sifting through the requests, then trying to help out.

Kieran is our first supported athlete – he's riding with the An Post–Sean Kelly team. And then there's the women's team, where I'm helping the British girls who won gold medals in the London Olympics – Laura Trott, Dani King and Jo Rowsell – with their road-racing careers. We're paying towards their salaries at the Wiggle-Honda team, and with that in place we can start looking at other athletes in other sports. It's not just about cycling, and it's at any level, not just elite sport. One thing we are thinking of doing is getting underprivileged kids onto the velodrome in Manchester. The foundation has grown overnight, but who knows, it might make a difference to a few people somewhere down the line.

There was one other big development over the winter: Lance Armstrong's final confession that he had doped to win his seven Tours. I'd already been shoved up the order to third in the 2009 Tour after he was stripped of the position when the US Anti-Doping Agency report came out, but the interviews he gave to Oprah Winfrey in January brought the whole thing home. It was difficult to watch, seeing him cave in during those first few minutes after so many years of lying so convincingly. It was heartbreaking for the sport, you feel a bit of sadness, a bit emotional, but then the anger kicks in and you think, 'You fucking arsehole', all the natural things that most people must have thought when they were watching it.

Part of me didn't want to have to watch it, to have that perception of him as an amazing athlete broken. One of my favourite races was the world championship he won in 1993 when I was thirteen. I watched him win all those races between 1993 and 1996 – races like Flèche Wallonne and the DuPont Tour in the US. He won the Tour de France for the first time when I was nineteen, riding on the Great Britain track squad, and it was so inspirational seeing what he had come from; I remember all those pictures of him with cancer.

I watched those interviews with my son Ben, who's seven years old – Cath had to leave the room because she couldn't bear to watch. I had to explain to my son what it was all about. I had to tell him: Lance's won the same race that your dad did. But by the end of the hour and a half, I had the best feeling in the world. It was when Lance was welling up about his son, who's thirteen. I'll never have to have the conversation that he had to have with his boy. I know my son's father won the Tour clean. There was an element of feeling a little bit smug. So it was up and down emotionally over the interview, but by the end I thought 'You deserve everything you get.' I feel no sympathy for him whatsoever.

What upset me the most was when he came out and said he

had raced clean in 2009 – the year he finished third ahead of me – and in 2010. I thought 'You lying bastard.' The man I saw on top of Verbier in 2009, where we had a summit finish early in the last week, and the man I saw a week later at the Ventoux, the day before the Tour ended, wasn't the same bike rider. I don't believe anything that comes out of his mouth any more.

Through August and September 2012, I remember thinking that I could retire after the world championship at the end of September if that was what I wanted to do. I was saying that to Cath: I could do it quite comfortably. The thought of training for next year had never entered my head. I felt fine with what I'd achieved in cycling, I was 100 per cent satisfied that I had fulfilled my potential as a bike rider. If I never rode my bike professionally again, I could be happy because I'd won the Tour de France. I'd have stopped with no regrets but while I acknowledged the possibility, I never seriously contemplated retiring. My mind was going that way because I hadn't figured out what to do next, which was largely because I hadn't got off that treadmill of appearances and commitments. From the day I finished the Tour, everyone wanted to know what I was going to be doing next, but it wasn't until 14 December, the day I left Majorca to come back to Britain for the Sports Personality ceremony, that I sat round a table with Dave and Tim to make a decision. It wasn't until then that we actually thought about the next year.

People just assumed I'd want to go back to the Tour and that I'd want to win again the following year, but it's not that simple. I remember when I went to ride my sportive on 19

August, less than a month after the Tour finished, the first question I was asked was, 'When does the training start for next year?' That took me aback a bit. I remember thinking the person who asked me that must be joking, because I hadn't actually got over the first one yet. I think people expected automatically that that was what I was going to do. It was like, 'Brilliant, won that one, let's get Christmas out of the way, then get on to the next.' I felt that people didn't realise just what a big deal it was to win the Tour then add an Olympic gold medal the week after. It didn't occur to them that it might take me a while to get my head around what had happened.

I was frightened of getting to January and to be constantly comparing myself to how I was in 2012. What if I ride Paris–Nice again just to finish third or fourth or something? Will people ask me if I'm on track because I'm not as good as in 2012? Although, of course, before I won it in 2012, they had all said I had peaked too early. I didn't want to pin everything on the Tour and go back and have a disastrous race. I've been through one Tour like that, in 2010, with all the pressure that goes with it, and I don't ever want to have a race like that again. There is one thing that I have always been conscious of: I refuse to go through the motions just because I've won it once.

I wanted to be confident in my goals for 2013, so when we started thinking about the Giro d'Italia I knew it was a race I really wanted to win. It's a new challenge, a completely different goal. I'd love to see that on my palmares; I'd love to be known for winning the Tour de France and the Giro – the only other race I'd place in the same bracket is Paris–Roubaix. All the while that I'd be going to events like the launch for the

2013 Tour de France and so on, it had been going round my mind. But I had to clear it with the team first. Dave thought it was a good idea, a great way to keep my mind fresh the year after winning the Tour, and – given that the Giro is in May – there was no reason why I shouldn't try to back it up with a good Tour in July. In 2010 I had attempted to do just that and it went horribly wrong. So, I was frightened of the thought, but we weren't doing the training then that we are now. There's no reason why we can't do it. A year ago people said: are you jeopardising the Olympics by focusing on the Tour? That worked out, and it's very much the same thing this time around. My focus straight after the Giro finishes will be on recovery – like before the Olympics – go straight into a camp environment and build to the Tour, to be as good as I can be in France. Obviously, however much you plan there is always an element of the unknown in how things will turn out.

So, at the moment it looks like I will be going to the Tour, but the likelihood is that Chris Froome will be the leader of the Sky team there, if the build-up goes to plan for him, and I will be there in a supporting role as he was for me last year. That supporting role does not mean from day one I'll be doing 200km on the front of the peloton every day, swinging off and losing twenty minutes on the run-ins. I'll look to be there as close as I can be through those mountains and if called upon, if there's a moment where we need to ride then that decision comes into play then. Fortunately in 2012 we never got into the position where we had to use all our bodies up and sacrifice Chris's second place. It will work in much the same way going into this year's race.

Taking on the Giro and the Tour is a new challenge, something that no one has done in the recent era and done well, but the guru Tim says it is possible and I take his word for it. Now I've got into it, it feels like a completely different year, working towards a different goal. I'm enjoying my bike riding more than ever. If someone had said to me in August 2012 that I'd be in this position in mid-March 2013, feeling completely re-invigorated about cycling and riding my bike, I wouldn't have believed them.

It's liberating to be able to think about riding the Giro. I don't feel the same burden of pressure as I did last year in the run-up to the Tour. I think I've proved what I'm capable of. The question now is not, 'Can he win the Tour again?' but 'Can he be one of the contenders for the Giro?' Whether I win the Giro or not, I'm up there now, I'm one of the favourites. There shouldn't be any more question marks about my ability to win the Grand Tours. I feel free now.

So has it finally sunk in that I won the Tour de France and an Olympic gold medal? Yes, it has. The smallest things have helped with that process. I think the fame I have in England didn't come because I won the Tour de France. I think it arrived because of what topped it off: the Olympics. It was part of that whole phenomenon of London 2012 – in Britain I seem to be known not so much as the winner of the Tour de France but as our best Olympian ever. But when I'm abroad I notice people see me more as the Tour winner. We've been coming to our training camps in Tenerife for two or three years now and no one's batted an eyelid, but suddenly everyone seems to recognise me more than they did. There are guys working on the roads who call out my name as I go past; I stop in a café and people want to take my photo; I'll be spotted going through airports, or having a weekend away in New York. Getting that recognition when I'm out of the bubble of the UK has helped me to take in what I achieved in 2012.

Every now and then, Cath says to me: you won the Tour, and there is the odd time when I get up in the morning and I go to the bathroom to have a shave, look in the mirror and say: you won the Tour. You wouldn't be human if you didn't do that. It's nice to think it wasn't just a matter of winning it, but *how* I won it has become the biggest source of pride in recent months: yup, I have won the Tour de France – and I won it clean. While I was watching Lance Armstrong's interviews with Oprah Winfrey, hearing him talking about winning at all costs, saying, 'I don't believe I could have won without doing what I did, I was able to sit there and think: I did it differently. That's the pride I have in it, that's a constant source of strength that will always be there.

A few hours before I had that crash in November 2012, when the van came out of that filling station entrance and ploughed into me, I got a new tattoo. It says 'Paris, 22/7/12' – the day I won the Tour de France – and it is on the inside of my arm, near my armpit on the inside of the bicep near the T-shirt line. It's not on my wrist where everyone can see it. It's for my own private viewing, like a tribal thing. I'll never have to get rid of that tattoo. It's a stamp, a permanent mark, and I like that: I won the greatest bike race in the world and no one is ever going to take that away from me.

THE GOLDEN YEAR

A list of my results for the 2012 season.

FEBRUARY 15–19: VOLTA AO ALGARVE, PORTUGAL
Stage one: Dunas Douradas (Almancil) – Albufeira, 151km
Winner, Gianni Meersman (Belgium) Lotto-Belisol in 4hr-02min-17sec; 77th place, B Wiggins at 7sec
Stage two: Faro – Lagoa, 187.5km
Edvald Boasson Hagen (Norway) Team Sky in 4-57-23; 111, Wiggins same time
Stage three: Castro Marim – Malhão (Loulé), 194.6km
Richie Porte (Australia) Team Sky in 4-55-11; 10, Wiggins at 40sec
Stage four: Vilamoura – Tavira, 186.3km
Gerald Ciolek (Austria) Omega Pharma-Quick-Step in 4-35-01; 47, Wiggins st
Stage five: Lagoa – Portimão, 25.8km individual time trial
Bradley Wiggins (GB) Team Sky in 0-32-48; 2, T Martin (Germany) Omega Pharma-Quick-Step st

Overall:

Richie Porte (Australia) Team Sky 19-02-43; 3, Wiggins at 44sec

MARCH 4–11: PARIS–NICE, FRANCE

Stage one: Dampierre-en-Yvelines – Saint-Rémy-lès-Chevreuse, 9.4km individual time trial

Gustav Larsson (Sweden) Vacansoleil-DCM in 0-11-19; 2, Wiggins at 1sec

Stage two: Mantes-la-Jolie – Orléans, 185.5km

Tom Boonen (Belgium) Omega Pharma-Quick-Step in 4-22-15; 11, Wiggins st

Stage three: Vierzon – Lac de Vassivière, 194km

Alejandro Valverde (Spain) Movistar in 4-36-19; 20, Wiggins st

Stage four: Brive-la-Gaillarde – Rodez, 178km

Gianni Meersman (Belgium) Lotto-Belisol in 4-21-01; 10, Wiggins st

Stage five: Onet-le-Château – Mende, 178.5km

Lieuwe Westra (Netherlands) Vacansoleil-DCM in 4-52-46; 3, Wiggins at 6sec

Stage six: Suze-la-Rousse – Sisteron, 178.5km

Luis León Sánchez (Spain) Rabobank in 4-07-58; 41, Wiggins at 14sec

Stage seven: Sisteron – Nice 219.5km

Thomas de Gendt (Belgium) Vacansoleil-DCM in 5-11-48; 31, Wiggins at 9min 24sec

Stage eight: Nice – Col d'Èze 9.6km individual time trial

Bradley Wiggins (GB) Team Sky in 0-19-12; 2, Lieuwe Westra (Netherlands) Vacansoleil-DCM at 2sec

Overall:
Bradley Wiggins (GB) Team Sky in 28-12-16; 2, Lieuwe Westra (Netherlands) Vacansoleil-DCM at 8sec

MARCH 19–25: TOUR OF CATALONIA, SPAIN
Stage one: Calella – Calella 138.9km
Michael Albasini (Switzerland) GreenEDGE in 3-20-04; 165, Wiggins at 1min 32sec
Stage two: Girona – Girona 161 km
Michael Albasini (Switzerland) GreenEDGE in 3-52-07; 16, Wiggins st
Stage three: La Vall d'en Bas (Sant Esteve d'en Bas)– Port-Ainé 210.9km
Janez Brajkovič (Slovenia) Astana, no time given as stage shortened due to snow; Wiggins, did not finish

APRIL 24–29: TOUR OF ROMANDIE, SWITZERLAND
Prologue: Lausanne – Lausanne, 3.34km individual time trial
Geraint Thomas (GB) Team Sky in 0-03-29; 11, Wiggins at 9sec
Stage one: Morges – La Chaux-de-Fonds, 184.5km
Bradley Wiggins (GB) Team Sky in 4-50-23
Stage two: Montbéliard – Moutier, 149.1km
Johnathan Hivert (France) Saur Sojasun in 3-48-11; 42, Wiggins st
Stage three: La Neuveville – Charmey, 157.9km
Luis León Sánchez (Spain) Rabobank in 3-58-29; 22, Wiggins st
Stage four: Bulle – Sion, 184km
Luis León Sánchez (Spain) Rabobank in 4-56-13; 18, Wiggins st
Stage five: Crans-Montana – Crans-Montana, 16.5km individual time trial

Bradley Wiggins (GB) Team Sky in 0-28-56; 2, Andrew Talansky (USA) Garmin-Barracuda at 1sec
Overall:
Bradley Wiggins (GB) Team Sky in 18-05-40; 2 Andrew Talansky (USA) Garmin-Barracuda at 12sec

JUNE 3–10: CRITÉRIUM DU DAUPHINÉ, FRANCE
Prologue: Grenoble – Grenoble, 5.7km individual time trial
Luke Durbridge (Australia) Orica GreenEDGE in 0-06-38; 2, Wiggins at 1sec
Stage one: Seyssins – Saint-Vallier, 187km
Cadel Evans (Australia) BMC in 4-36-21; 61, Wiggins at 4sec
Stage two: Lamastre – Saint-Félicien, 160km
Daniel Moreno (Spain) Katusha in 4-02-38; 9, Wiggins st
Stage three: Givors – La Clayette, 167km
Edvald Boasson Hagen (Norway) Team Sky in 4-22-13; 46, Wiggins st
Stage four: Villié-Morgon – Bourg-en-Bresse, 53.5km individual time trial
Bradley Wiggins (GB) Team Sky in 1-03-12; Tony Martin (Germany) Omega Pharma-Quick-Step at 34sec
Stage five: Saint-Trivier-sur-Moignans – Rumilly, 186.5 km
Arthur Vichot (France) Francais des Jeux-BigMat in 4-42-17; 27, Wiggins at 59sec
Stage six: Saint-Alban-Leysse – Morzine, 167.5km
Nairo Quintana (Columbia) Movistar in 4-46-12; 4, Wiggins at 24sec
Stage seven: Morzine – Châtel, 124.5km
Daniel Moreno (Spain) Katusha in 2-59-37; 19, Wiggins at 10sec

Overall:

Bradley Wiggins (GB) Team Sky in 26-40-46; 2, Michael Rogers (Australia) Team Sky at 1min 17sec

JUNE 30–JULY 22: TOUR DE FRANCE, FRANCE

Prologue: Liège – Liège, 6.4km individual time trial

Fabian Cancellara (Switzerland) RadioShack-Nissan in 0-07-13; 2, Wiggins at 7sec

Stage one: Liège – Seraing, 198km

Peter Sagan (Slovakia) Liquigas-Cannondale in 4-58-19; 16, Wiggins st

Stage two: Visé – Tournai, 207.5km

Mark Cavendish (GB) Team Sky in 4-56-59; 68, Wiggins st

Stage three: Orchies – Boulogne-sur-Mer, 197km

Peter Sagan (Slovakia) Liquigas-Cannondale in 4-42-58; 53, Wiggins at 1sec

Stage four: Abbeville – Rouen, 214.5km

André Greipel (Germany) Lotto-Belisol in 5-18-32; 154, Wiggins st

Stage five: Rouen – Saint-Quentin, 196.5km

André Greipel (Germany) Lotto-Belisol in 4-41-30; 18, Wiggins st

Stage six: Épernay – Metz, 207.5km

Peter Sagan (Slovakia) Liquigas-Cannondale in 4-37-00; 21, Wiggins at 4sec

Stage seven: Tomblaine – La Planche des Belles Filles, 199km

Chris Froome (GB) Team Sky in 4-58-35; 3, Wiggins at 2sec

Stage eight: Belfort – Porrentruy, 157.5km

Thibaut Pinot (France) Francais Des Jeux-BigMat in 3-56-10; 4, Wiggins at 26sec

Stage nine: Arc-et-Senans – Besançon 41.5km individual time trial

Bradley Wiggins (GB) Team Sky in 0-51-24; 2, Chris Froome (GB) Team Sky at 35sec

Stage ten: Mâcon – Bellegarde-sur-Valserine, 194.5km

Thomas Voeckler (France) Europcar in 4-46-26; 13, Wiggins at 3min 16sec

Stage eleven: Albertville – La Toussuire, 148km

Pierre Rolland (France) Europcar in 4-43-54; 6, Wiggins at 57sec

Stage twelve: Saint-Jean-de-Maurienne – Annonay-Davézieux, 226km

David Millar (GB) Garmin-Sharp in 5-42-46; 12, Wiggins at 7min 54sec

Stage thirteen: Saint-Paul-Trois-Châteaux – Cap d'Agde, 217km

André Greipel (Germany) Lotto-Belisol in 4-57-59; 12, Wiggins st

Stage fourteen: Limoux – Foix, 191km

Luis León Sánchez (Spain) Rabobank in 4-50-29; 15, Wiggins at 18min 15sec

Stage fifteen: Samatan – Pau, 158.5km

Pierrick Fédrigo (France) Francais Des Jeux-BigMat in 3-40-15; 22, Wiggins at 11min 50sec

Stage sixteen: Pau – Bagnères-de-Luchon, 197km

Thomas Voeckler (France) Europcar in 5-35-02; 12, Wiggins at 7min 9sec

Stage seventeen: Bagnères-de-Luchon – Peyragudes, 143.5km

Alejandro Valverde (Spain) Movistar in 4-12-11; 3, Wiggins at 19sec

Stage eighteen: Blagnac – Brive-la-Gaillarde, 222.5km

Mark Cavendish (GB) Team Sky in 4-54-12; 19, Wiggins at 4sec

Stage nineteen: Bonneval – Chartres, 53.5km individual time trial

Bradley Wiggins (GB) Team Sky in 1-04-13; 2, Chris Froome at 1min 16sec

Stage twenty: Rambouillet – Paris (Champs-Élysées), 120km
Mark Cavendish (GB) Team Sky in 3-08-07; 54, Wiggins at 9sec
Overall:
Bradley Wiggins (GB) Team Sky in 87-34-47sec; 2, Chris Froome
(GB) Team Sky at 3min 21sec; 3, Vincenzo Nibali (Italy) Liquigas-
Cannondale at 6min 19sec; 4, Jurgen Van Den Broeck (Belgium)
Lotto-Belisol at 10min 15sec; 5, Tejay van Garderen (USA) BMC
at 11min 4sec

JULY 28: OLYMPIC GAMES ROAD RACE, UNITED KINGDOM, 250KM
Gold, Alexander Vinokourov (Kazakhstan) in 5-45-57; Silver,
Rigoberto Urán (Columbia) st; Bronze, Alexander Kristoff
(Norway) at 8sec; 103, Wiggins at 1min 17sec

AUGUST 1: OLYMPIC GAMES INDIVIDUAL TIME TRIAL, UNITED
KINGDOM, 44KM
Gold, Bradley Wiggins (GB) in 0-50-39; Silver, Tony Martin
(Germany) at 42sec; Bronze, Chris Froome (GB) at 1min 8sec

9–16 SEPTEMBER TOUR OF BRITAIN, UNITED KINGDOM
Stage one: Ipswich – Norfolk Showground, 203km
Luke Rowe (GB) Team Sky in 4-51-05; 24, Wiggins st
Stage two: Nottingham – Knowsley, 180.7km
Leigh Howard (Australia) Orica-GreenEDGE in 4-31-09; 34,
Wiggins at 1sec
Stage three: Jedburgh – Dumfries, 152.6km
Mark Cavendish (GB) Team Sky in 3-54-30; 44, Wiggins st
Stage four: Carlisle – Blackpool, 156km
Mark Cavendish (GB) Team Sky in 3-51-33; 21, Wiggins at 9sec

Stage five: Stoke on Trent – Stoke on Trent, 147km
Marc de Maar (Dutch Curaçao) United Healthcare in 3-30-26; 64,
Wiggins at 11min 45sec, and retired

23 SEPTEMBER: UCI WORLD ROAD RACE CHAMPIONSHIPS, NETHERLANDS, 269KM
Gold, Phillippe Gilbert (Belgium) in 6-10-41; Silver, Edvald
Boasson Hagen (Norway) at 4sec; Bronze, Alejandro Valverde
(Spain) at 5sec; Wiggins, DNF

ACKNOWLEDGEMENTS

Without these people none of this would have happened. I am indebted to:

Everyone at Team Sky, but particular thanks to Dave Brailsford, Shane Sutton, Tim Kerrison, Sean Yates, Rod Ellingworth, Dan the physio, Diego, Mario, Gary, Alldis and all the other backroom staff.

The Tour boys: Mick Rogers, Richie Porte, Christian Knees, Chris Froome, Mark Cavendish, Bernhard Eisel, Kosta Siutsou, Edvald Boasson Hagen.

Faces from the peloton: Steve Cummings, Matt Rabin.

Team GB: Matt Parker, Nigel Mitchell, Doug Dailey, Luc de Wilde, Phil Burt, Richard Freeman, Alan Williams, the lads in the stores, all the boys in the workshop.

For help with the book I'd like to thank William Fotheringham, and everybody at Yellow Jersey Press including Matt Phillips, Frances Jessop, James Jones, Bethan Jones, Phil Brown, Penny Liechti, Monique Corless, Justine Taylor,

Alice Brett, Myra Jones, Ben Murphy, Richard Cable, Roger Bratchell and Tom Drake-Lee. My agent Jonathan Marks and his partner in crime Emma Wade and everyone else at MTC.

All the lads at Paul Hewitt Cycles for building wheels for me, Terry Dolan and Steve, Richard and Mick from Sport and Publicity, Mark at Adidas, Scott Mitchell.

I'd like to thank those a little closer to home, too. My mum, my nan, George – who would have loved to have seen everything that's happened this last twelve months – and everyone else who makes up Team Wiggins. My parents-in-law Liz and Dave, Ruth and Neil.

Finally Cath, Ben and Bella. Thank you for giving me the gift of patience and understanding to allow me to follow my dream. And thanks for always reminding me what's most important.

LIST OF ILLUSTRATIONS

INDEX